THE DAILY SHOW AND P

THE BLACKWELL PHILOSOPHY AND POPCULTURE SERIES

Series editor William Irwin

A spoonful of sugar helps the medicine go down, and a healthy helping of popular culture clears the cobwebs from Kant. Philosophy has had a public relations problem for a few centuries now. This series aims to change that, showing that philosophy is relevant to your life – and not just for answering the big questions like "To be or not to be?" but for answering the little questions: "To watch or not to watch *South Park*?" Thinking deeply about TV, movies, and music doesn't make you a "complete idiot." In fact it might make you a philosopher, someone who believes the unexamined life is not worth living and the unexamined cartoon is not worth watching.

South Park and Philosophy
Edited by Robert Arp

Metallica and Philosophy
Edited by William Irwin

Family Guy and Philosophy
Edited by J. Jeremy Wisnewski

The Daily Show and Philosophy
Edited by Jason Holt

Forthcoming

Lost and Philosophy
Edited by Sharon Kaye

24 and Philosophy
Edited by Jennifer Hart Weed, Richard Brian Davis, and Ronald Weed

The Office and Philosophy
Edited by J. Jeremy Wisnewski

THE DAILY SHOW AND PHILOSOPHY

Moments of Zen in the Art of Fake News

Edited by Jason Holt

Blackwell
Publishing

BLACKWELL PUBLISHING

350 Main Street, Malden, MA 02148–5020, USA
9600 Garsington Road, Oxford OX4 2DQ, UK
550 Swanston Street, Carlton, Victoria 3053, Australia

First published 2007 by Blackwell Publishing Ltd

1   2007

Library of Congress Cataloging-in-Publication Data

The Daily show and philosophy : moments of zen in the art of fake news /
edited by Jason Holt.
      p. cm. — (The Blackwell philosophy and popculture series)
   Includes bibliographical references and index.
   ISBN 978–1–4051–6314–9 (pbk. : alk. paper)   1. Daily show (Television program)
I. Holt, Jason, 1971–

   PN1992.77.D28D35 2007
   791.45′72—dc22

                                                                        2007017553

A catalogue record for this title is available from the British Library.

Set in 10.5/13pt Sabon
by Graphicraft Limited, Hong Kong
Printed and bound in the United States of America
by Sheridan Books, Inc.

Blackwell Publishing, visit our website:
www.blackwellpublishing.com

To my parents, Alyce and Larry Holt

CONTENTS

ACKNOWLEDGMENTS

Thanks first to Jeff Dean, Bill Irwin, and everyone else at Blackwell Publishing for making this book possible. Thanks also to the contributors, whose patient hard work made it actual. Thanks to *The Daily Show* (and *The Colbert Report*) for giving us so much to write about, and to those of you fan enough to buy this book.

INTRODUCTION:
GREAT BOOK, OR THE *GREATEST* BOOK?

From Blackwell Publishing's World Philosophy and PopCulture Headquarters in Oxford (and Malden, MA), This Is The Daily Show and Philosophy.

Welcome to *The Daily Show and Philosophy*, my name's Jason Holt, and we have a fine, fine program for you, but first . . . meet me at Camera 3. . . .

Okay, you've made it past the front cover. That's good. Maybe you're considering buying the book. Maybe it's been bought and you're thinking about whether to read it. This might even be a textbook in a course you're taking. Now what?

You already know that *The Daily Show* with Jon Stewart is funny, really funny, and that the performers and writers are pretty smart. You also know that it's not just a run-of-the-mill TV comedy. In its decade-plus run *The Daily Show* has achieved an undeniable, potentially disturbing, cultural significance, as fit for ranting blogs as for academic treatises. This book's Senior Philosophical Correspondents (or *really* stoned slackers, depending on your point of view) are keen to explore what *The Daily Show* has to say about the news media, politics, religion, science, truth, and a host of others topics. Maybe you are too.

But why philosophy? Not only does *The Daily Show* tackle issues that interest philosophers and that matter in many people's daily lives (read "daily" as "four times a week"), it does so in instructive ways that deserve and are well-served by philosophical treatment.

Sometimes philosophers even appear as guests on the show. Each contributor to this book will take the Seat of Heat in showing, each in their own way, why and how *The Daily Show* is philosophically both engaging and significant. If you're hoping that *The Colbert Report* also gets a going-over, you won't be disappointed.

Like the show itself in its usual format, depending on how you count, *The Daily Show and Philosophy* comes in five segments: (1) headlines, (2) correspondent's report, (3) regular feature, (4) interview, and (5) checking in with Stephen Colbert/your moment of Zen. Our first segment looks at fake news, including *The Daily Show*'s critique of the media, how fake news fiction can convey real truth, the political function of fake news, and the potential harm of such programming. Segment 2 casts Jon Stewart as a quasi-philosopher, drawing parallels with public intellectuals such as Socrates, Plato, and the ancient Greek bathtub-living, joke-making cynics. Our third segment addresses critical thinking and bullshit, including Stewart's approach to public debate, *The Daily Show*'s dismantling of political rhetoric, the difference between bullshit and political spin, and whether bullshit might not be so bad in certain rare cases. Segment 4 develops *The Daily Show*'s philosophy of religion, examining religious diversity in "This Week in God," contingency and irony, and the "Evolution, Schmevolution" special. Our fifth segment explores territory beyond the show itself, discussing *America (The Book)* as parody blended with political theory, *Daily Show* and *Colbert Report* neologisms, what truthiness is and what it reveals about irrationality and intuitive knowledge, and the use of irony in Stephen Colbert's *Colbert Report* persona.

On behalf of all the Senior Philosophical Correspondents who contributed to this volume – and it's a cliché, I know, but it's also true – we hope you enjoy reading the book as much as we did writing it.

HEADLINES:
FAUX NEWS IS GOOD NEWS

SEGMENT 1

1
AMUSING OURSELVES TO DEATH WITH TELEVISION NEWS:
JON STEWART, NEIL POSTMAN, AND THE HUXLEYAN WARNING

GERALD J. ERION

While *The Daily Show* is undoubtedly funny, it also provides an intriguing study of our contemporary media environment. Indeed, hidden within many of Jon Stewart's funniest jokes are implicit critiques of the way television tends to report its news and host its public discussions of important issues. For instance, Stewart's opening rundown of the news as television covers it doesn't merely ridicule the day's major players and events, but also makes fun of the way television gathers and presents the news. In this way, over-the-top graphics and music packages, attractive but superficial "Senior Correspondents," and all the other trappings of television newscasts become fodder for *The Daily Show*'s writing staff. More than just a "fake news" program, *The Daily Show* offers a rare brand of humor that requires its audience to recognize a deeper, more philosophical criticism of contemporary television news.

From time to time, Stewart takes these implicit critiques of contemporary media and makes them explicit. Such was the case during his October 2004 appearance on CNN's since-cancelled *Crossfire*, when Stewart begged his hosts to "stop hurting America" with their substitution of entertaining pseudo-journalism for serious reporting and debate. Through this bold, format-breaking effort, Stewart highlighted the difference between thoughtful discussion and the theater of today's vapid television punditry. As we will see, Stewart's analysis of the present state of mass communication echoes that of the celebrated New York University media theorist Neil Postman, whose discerning insights ground some of Stewart's sharpest comic bits.

Amusing Ourselves to Death

Neil Postman's *Amusing Ourselves to Death* is a book about the many forms of human communication and how those forms influence the messages that we communicate to one another. Postman acknowledges a significant intellectual debt here to Marshall McLuhan, and sees his own thesis as something of a revised version of McLuhan's famous pronouncement that "the medium is the message."[1] However, Postman extends McLuhan's ideas in ways that are both distinctive and significant.

For example, consider Postman's discussion of smoke signals. While the medium of smoke might be an effective way to communicate relatively simple messages over intermediate distances, many other types of messages can't be transmitted this way. Philosophical arguments, for instance, would be especially difficult to conduct with smoke signals because, as Postman puts it: "Puffs of smoke are insufficiently complex to express ideas on the nature of existence [or other philosophical concepts], and even if they were not, a Cherokee philosopher would run short of either wood or blankets long before he reached his second axiom. You cannot use smoke to do philosophy. Its form excludes the content."[2] So, the medium of smoke has a significant influence on the kind of content it can be used to communicate. At a minimum, smoke signaling restricts both the complexity and the duration of the messages it carries. Likewise, we shall see that *The Daily Show*'s comedy often reflects the restrictions placed by our contemporary electronic media (including television) upon their content.

The Huxleyan Warning

Now, as Postman sees it, *all* media influence their content, and in a multitude of different ways. He writes: "[Mine] is an argument that fixes its attention on the forms of human conversation, and postulates that how we are obliged to conduct such conversations will have the strongest possible influence on what ideas we can conveniently express" (p. 6). This goes not only for smoke signals, but also for speech and written language, and even for the electronic media that are so important in our contemporary lives.

Of particular interest here is the ubiquitous medium of television, which Postman sees as a historic extension of such earlier media as the telegraph, photography, radio, and film.[3] How does television influence its content, according to Postman? His theory is complex, but in essence it maintains that television's inherent "bias" implies a tendency to render its content – even its most important news reports, political and religious discussions, and educational lessons – more *entertaining* than they would be otherwise, and consequently less serious, less rational, less relevant, and less coherent as well (pp. 67–80, 85–98).

The fact that television provides entertainment isn't, in and of itself, a problem for Postman. He warns, however, that dire consequences can befall a culture in which the most important public discourse, conducted via television, becomes little more than irrational, irrelevant, and incoherent entertainment. Again, we shall see that this is a point often suggested by *The Daily Show*'s biting satire. In a healthy democracy, the open discussion of important issues must be serious, rational, and coherent. But such discussion is often time-consuming and unpleasant, and thus incompatible with television's drive to entertain. So, it's hardly surprising to see television serving up important news analyses in sound bites surrounded by irrelevant graphics and video footage, or substituting half-minute ad spots for substantial political debates. On television, thoughtful conversations about serious issues are reserved for only the lowest-rated niche programs. Just as ventriloquism and mime don't play well on radio, "thinking does not play well on television" (p. 90).[4] Instead, television serves as a hospitable home for the sort of "gut"-based discourse celebrated by Stephen Colbert.[5]

When we grow comfortable with the substitution of televised entertainment for serious public discourse, we begin the process of (to use Postman's words) "amusing ourselves to death." As Postman explains, this form of cultural corrosion is like that described in Aldous Huxley's classic novel *Brave New World*, in which the citizenry is comfortably and willingly distracted by the pleasures of *soma*, Centrifugal Bumble-puppy, and the feelies (pp. vii–viii, 155–6).

Postman and Television News

Postman and the writing staff of *The Daily Show* seem to agree that television's presentation of news tends to degrade its content in significant ways. Consider Postman's explanation of the ironic title of his chapter on television news, "Now . . . This:" "There is no murder so brutal, no earthquake so devastating, no political blunder so costly – for that matter, no ball score so tantalizing or weather report so threatening – that it cannot be erased from our minds by a newscaster saying 'Now . . . this' " (p. 99). Thus, Postman maintains that the use of "Now . . . this" is a tacit admission of the incoherence of television news, and "a compact metaphor for the discontinuities in so much that passes for public discourse in present-day America" (p. 99).

Of course, Postman believes that television does more to the news than disrupt its coherence. Revisiting his general thesis about how television influences its content, Postman also claims that televised news is irrational, irrelevant, and trivial. As he explains, television presents us "not only with fragmented news but news without context, without consequences, without value, and therefore without essential seriousness; that is to say, news as pure entertainment" (p. 100). So, even weighty news subjects can become entertaining under the influence of television, as the typical American newscast showcases a company of attractive reporters skipping from dramatic local stories to dramatic international stories, to celebrity gossip, to weather forecasts, to sports scores, to a closing story about babies or puppies or kittens. Commercials are scattered throughout. Music, graphics, and captivating video footage add touches of theater to the program. Quick transitions from one segment to the next ensure that audience members don't become bored – or troubled – for long.[6] Instead of useful and important information, then, viewers are treated to the impotent but entertaining trivia that Postman calls "disinformation," which isn't necessarily false but *misleading*, creating the *illusion of knowing* and undermining one's motivation to learn more (p. 107). Consequently, Postman writes, "Americans are the best entertained and quite likely the least well-informed people in the Western world" (p. 106).

The Daily Show and Television News

Now, as far as I know, the writing staff of *The Daily Show* doesn't publicly acknowledge Postman's influence. It's even possible that they've never heard of Postman. Nonetheless, it's clear that these general ideas about television news, whatever their sources, can help us to see the significance of some of the program's wittiest and most inspired jokes. *The Daily Show* is often described as a "fake news" program, but in fact, it's more than that. Much of its humor rests on Postman-like insights that highlight the peculiar ways in which the medium of television itself influences the news that it conveys.

For example, most episodes of *The Daily Show* begin with Stewart's rundown of the day's headlines as reported by the major television news programs. A comedy show that only does "fake news" might simply build jokes around the content of these headlines, or perhaps report fictional news stories in a humorous way. On *The Daily Show*, though, the way in which television seems destined to render its news as entertainment often serves as the basis for these opening segments. In recent years Stewart and company have often joked about the major networks' coverage of natural disasters. In many of these cases they simply replay absurd clips of television reporters standing outside during hurricanes, sitting in cars with giant thermometers during heat waves, or paddling canoes through inch-deep "flooded" city streets. Other segments mock the way hordes of television reporters cover celebrity weddings, arrests, and criminal trials. Segments like "International Pamphlet" and "The Less You Know" contain their own jokes but also poke fun at the shallowness of typical television news coverage. Exchanges between Stewart and his Senior Correspondents parody their good-looking but sometimes ill-informed network counterparts.[7] Even *The Daily Show*'s clever graphics packages ("Mess O' Potamia," "Crises in Israfghyianon-anaq," and so on) offer satirical imitations of the logos, diagrams, and pictorial illustrations so essential to today's television newscasts.

Moreover, Stewart himself has attacked the way television is compelled to report "breaking news" with what at times seems to be inadequate or uncorroborated information, mere speculation, and no editing whatsoever; shortly after the Washington, DC-area sniper shootings of 2002, he joked with CNN's Howard Kurtz: "By watching the 24-hour news networks, I learned that the sniper was an olive-skinned, white-black male – men – with ties to Son of Sam, Al Qaeda, and was a military kid, playing video games, white, 17, maybe 40."[8] In these kinds of segments, then, *The Daily Show* is clearly doing more than just "fake news." It's also offering deep satire that relies on its audience's appreciation of the substance of Postman's thesis, that television has a significant and sometimes adverse influence on the news content it reports.

At this point, one might be tempted to suggest that *The Daily Show* simply reproduces the unfortunate transformation of reporting into entertainment, as if *The Daily Show* were itself a source of news for its audience members. For instance, Bill O'Reilly (host of the Fox News program *The O'Reilly Factor*) once famously dubbed viewers of *The Daily Show* "stoned slackers" who "get their news from Jon Stewart."[9] However, at least one prominent study by the Annenberg Public Policy Center found that viewers of *The Daily Show* were *better* informed about the positions and backgrounds of candidates in the 2004 US Presidential campaign than most others. Indeed, it's difficult to see how the deepest *Daily Show* jokes could be appreciated by an audience unaware of the relevant social, political, and other newsworthy issues. As Annenberg analyst Dannagal Goldthwaite Young put it in a press release announcing the Center's Election Survey results, "*The Daily Show* assumes a fairly high level of political knowledge on the part of its audience."[10]

Conversation and *Crossfire*

Postman's ideas about television also illuminate Stewart's infamous October 15, 2004 appearance on CNN's *Crossfire*. First aired in 1982, *Crossfire* was a long-running staple of CNN's lineup that featured curt discussion by hosts and guests supposedly representing both left-wing and right-wing positions on controversial political issues.

Co-hosting for Stewart's visit were the unsuspecting Paul Begala and Tucker Carlson, neither of whom seemed prepared for what would become an extraordinary exchange. Instead of simply participating in a typical *Crossfire*-style debate (described by more than one observer as a "shoutfest"), Stewart quickly launched into a Postman-like criticism of the vapid and partisan punditry that passes for serious discussion on programs like *Crossfire*.

In fact, this theme is one that Stewart had explored before his *Crossfire* appearance. The recurring *Daily Show* segment "Great Moments in Punditry as Read by Children" draws laughs simply by having children read from transcripts of shows like *Crossfire*. Moreover, during an interview with Bill Moyers, Stewart claimed that both *Crossfire* and its MSNBC counterpart *Hardball* were "equally dispiriting" in the way their formats degrade political discourse.[11] And in his interview with CNN's Howard Kurtz, Stewart foreshadowed his *Crossfire* appearance by chiding the news network for offering entertainers instead of "real journalists" and pleaded, "You're the news . . . People need you. Help us. Help us."[12]

On the *Crossfire* set, though, Stewart offered his most sustained attack against the shallow conversational style of television. Before either Begala or Carlson could catch his balance, Stewart was already begging them to "stop, stop, stop, stop hurting America" with their "partisan hackery," which he claimed serves only politicians and corporations and does nothing to help ordinary citizens make informed decisions.[13] "We need help from the media," Stewart said, "and they're hurting us." Carlson tried to counter Stewart's charges with the allegation that Stewart himself had been too lenient during the *Daily Show* appearance of 2004 Presidential candidate John Kerry. Stewart replied that there was a fundamental difference between journalism and comedy, snapping back, "I didn't realize that . . . the news organizations look to Comedy Central for their cues on integrity." And when Begala tried to defend the *Crossfire* format by claiming that it was a "debate show," Stewart pointed to Carlson's trademark bow tie as evidence that *Crossfire* is "doing theater, when you should be doing debate." Finally, Stewart charged, "You have a responsibility to the public discourse, and you fail miserably." Because of such remarks, Stewart's *Crossfire* appearance produced a rare opportunity for reflecting about the effects of television on public discourse. Indeed, the incident sparked much additional discussion in, for example, the *New York Times*, *Newsweek*, and countless electronic media outlets.

Once again, we can see that these are the sorts of criticisms developed by Postman in *Amusing Ourselves to Death*. His deepest discussion of such issues concerns ABC's controversial 1983 broadcast of the film *The Day After*, which depicts the bleak effects of a nuclear strike on the American Midwest. Given the film's grave subject matter, ABC decided to follow it with a roundtable discussion moderated by Ted Koppel and featuring such notable figures as Henry Kissinger, Elie Wiesel, Carl Sagan, and William F. Buckley.[14] With a serious theme and a guest list of unquestionable distinction, Koppel proceeded to march his cast through a fragmented 80 minutes of "conversation" in which the participants rarely engaged one another on points of substance. Instead, they used their camera time to push whatever points they had decided to make beforehand, without regard to the contributions of their fellow participants. Postman writes:

> Each of the six men was given approximately five minutes to say something about the subject. There was, however, no agreement on exactly what the subject was, and no one felt obliged to respond to anything anyone else had said. In fact, it would have been difficult to do so, since the participants were called upon seriatim, as if they were finalists in a beauty contest. (p. 89)

To put it another way, this wasn't a genuine discussion, but a *pseudo-discussion* warped by television's drive to entertain. "There were no arguments or counterarguments, no scrutiny of assumptions, no explanations, no elaborations, no definitions" (p. 90), and yet each of these elements is essential to genuine and thoughtful dialogue.

So, how did ABC go wrong? According to Postman, the root problem remains that thoughtful conversation just isn't entertaining, and thus plays poorly on television. Televised discussions about even the most serious of subjects tend to be rendered in forms that are more amusing or dramatic than reflective. On this both Postman and the writing staff of *The Daily Show* agree.[15] Moreover, CNN President Jonathan Klein cited Stewart's critique when he announced the cancellation of *Crossfire* in January 2005. In an interview with the *Washington Post*, Klein said, "I think [Stewart] made a good point about the noise level of these types of shows, which does nothing to illuminate the issues of the day."[16]

A Huxleyan Moment of Zen?

So, it appears that much of *The Daily Show*'s sharpest comedy requires its audience to grasp a Postmanesque criticism of television news. In addition, Stewart himself seems to offer a more general critique of today's televised public discourse that is reminiscent of Postman's in several significant ways. This isn't to say, however, that Postman and Stewart are in perfect agreement. For one thing, Postman argues that the transformation of serious discussion into entertainment is all but inevitable when this discussion takes place on television. Stewart, on the other hand, seems to believe that television can do better. As we've seen, he has even appeared on CNN and used the news network's own programs to issue his call for reform. Postman and Stewart might also disagree about the suitability of television as a vehicle for sophisticated media criticism. Postman writes, for example, that any televised critique of television would likely be "co-opted" by the medium, and thus rendered in the typical fashion as mere entertainment (pp. 161–2).[17] In his eyes, television is simply incapable of carrying serious public discourse, including serious public discourse about mass communication itself. That Stewart has appeared on *Crossfire* and other such programs to address this issue suggests that he believes otherwise. No doubt this is a question worth further consideration, and through any medium capable of giving it a thoughtful hearing.

Notes

1 Marshall McLuhan, *Understanding Media: The Extensions of Man* (New York: McGraw-Hill, 1964); see especially pp. 7–21.
2 Neil Postman, *Amusing Ourselves to Death: Public Discourse in the Age of Show Business* (New York: Penguin, 1985), p. 7. Subsequent citations will be made parenthetically in-text.
3 Postman develops his sweeping history of American media in chapter 5 of *Amusing Ourselves to Death*, "The Peek-a-Boo World" (pp. 64–80).

4 Postman acknowledges that, in other parts of the world (pp. 85–6) or in non-commercial contexts (pp. 105–6), television may serve different purposes. However, as he sees it, this does nothing to change the way that television most typically functions in contemporary American society.

5 Colbert explained the importance of one's gut in the search for truth during his April 2006 White House Correspondents' Association Dinner performance: "Every night on my show, *The Colbert Report*, I speak straight from the gut, OK? I give people the truth, unfiltered by rational argument." On this point Colbert also compared himself to President George W. Bush, who sat at the head table just a few feet away from Colbert's podium:

> We're not so different, he and I. We both get it. Guys like us, we're not some brainiacs on the nerd patrol. We're not members of the Factinista. We go straight from the gut; right sir? That's where the truth lies, right down here in the gut.
>
> Do you know you have more nerve endings in your gut than you have in your head? You can look it up. Now I know some of you are going to say, "I did look it up, and that's not true." That's because you looked it up in a book. Next time, look it up in your gut. I did. My gut tells me that's how our nervous system works.

6 As Postman writes, "While brevity does not always suggest triviality, in this case it surely does. It is simply not possible to convey a sense of seriousness about any event if its implications are exhausted in less than one minute's time" (p. 103).

7 See also "Stephen Colbert's Guide to Dressing and Expressing Like a TV Journalist" in Jon Stewart, Ben Karlin, and David Javerbaum, *America (The Book): A Citizen's Guide to Democracy Inaction* (New York: Warner Books, 2004), pp. 142–3.

8 *Reliable Sources*, CNN (November 2, 2002).

9 *The O'Reilly Factor*, Fox News (September 17, 2004).

10 "National Annenberg Election Survey" (press release), *Annenberg Public Policy Center* (September 21, 2004), p. 2.

11 *Now*, PBS (July 11, 2003).

12 *Reliable Sources*, CNN (November 2, 2002).

13 *Crossfire*, CNN (October 15, 2004). All quotes below are from CNN's rush transcript of this episode.

14 Postman actually cites Buckley's own legendary program *Firing Line* as a rare example of television as a "carrier of coherent language and thought in process" that "occasionally shows people in the act of thinking but who also happen to have television cameras pointed at them" (p. 91).

Firing Line never received high ratings, though, and spent most of its 33 years on public television.

15 Postman's son Andrew sums all of this up nicely in his "Introduction" to the 20th Anniversary Edition of *Amusing Ourselves to Death*, writing: "When Jon Stewart, host of Comedy Central's *The Daily Show*, went on CNN's *Crossfire* to make this very point – that serious news and show business ought to be distinguishable, for the sake of public discourse and the republic – the hosts seemed incapable of even understanding the words coming out of his mouth" (pp. xiii–xiv).

16 Howard Kurtz, "Carlson & 'Crossfire:' Exit Stage Left & Right," *Washington Post* (January 6, 2005), C1.

17 In the final chapter of *Amusing Ourselves to Death*, Postman describes a then-hypothetical but subversive anti-television television program that's eerily similar to *The Daily Show*. According to Postman, this program would serve an important educational purpose by demonstrating how television recreates and degrades news, political debate, religious thought, and so on. He writes: "I imagine such demonstrations would of necessity take the form of parodies, along the lines of 'Saturday Night Live' and 'Monty Python,' the idea being to induce a national horse laugh over television's control of the public discourse" (pp. 161–2). In the end, Postman rejects the idea of such a show as "nonsense," since he thinks that serious and intelligent televised discussion could never attract an audience large enough to make a difference.

2

THE FAKE, THE FALSE, AND THE FICTIONAL:
THE DAILY SHOW AS NEWS SOURCE

MICHAEL GETTINGS

Welcome to The Daily Show, *your source for news, if you're in a certain demographic.*

Jon Stewart (March 18, 2003)

In a March 2, 2004 story entitled "Young America's News Source: Jon Stewart," CNN reported that a growing number of young people get their news from *The Daily Show*. According to Pew research polls, 21 percent of 18–29 year olds cited *The Daily Show* and *Saturday Night Live* as their regular source for Presidential campaign news in 2004, up from only 9 percent in 2000. The same polls showed that while 39 percent of this group said that they regularly learned about the Presidential campaign in 2000 from traditional network news, this number dropped to only 23 percent in 2004. But *The Daily Show* bills itself as a fake news show, not as a source of "real news." Does this mean that its viewers are misinformed about domestic and international events? Not necessarily. The question of how fake news can inform people about real news touches on a question posed by philosophers: How do we learn truth from a work of fiction, something typically full of falsehoods? After all, a typical work of fiction is about pretend characters in pretend situations doing pretend things. Where's the truth in such a story, where's the reality? If we can classify fake news as fiction, and if we can understand how fiction conveys truth, then we can understand how *The Daily Show* conveys real news to its viewers. Along the way, we'll look at many examples to see just how *The Daily Show* pulls this off.

16

Is *The Daily Show* Fiction?

Our first question should be this: What is a work of fiction? Our first answer may be that fictions simply aren't true, they're false, they're fake instead of real. But this can't be the whole story, since a fake Rolex isn't a work of fiction, nor is a fib a child tells her mother, at least not in the sense that Melville's novel *Billy Budd*, for example, is a work of fiction. The rather obvious problem with calling the fake Rolex a fiction is that it's not a story, it's a watch. So when we're talking about fiction, we should restrict ourselves to stories, or narratives. *Daily Show* news stories are narratives in this sense – they tell stories. Real news reports tell stories as well, it's just that those stories are purportedly true. A child's fib is a kind of narrative too. The reason we don't classify fibs, or lies in general, as fictions in the relevant sense is that fibs and lies are intended to deceive the audience. Most fictions aren't intended to deceive, and this is true of *The Daily Show* just as it is of *Billy Budd*. We might think then that the distinction between fiction and non-fiction is that fictions are false and not intended to deceive while non-fictions are simply true.

This suggestion is still a bit hasty. A poorly researched work of non-fiction isn't intended to deceive and may contain many falsehoods, but that doesn't make it fictional. A simple work of fiction might accidentally contain many truths, but that doesn't make it non-fictional. So the ratio of falsehoods to truths doesn't account for the distinction between fiction and non-fiction. For example, in the television coverage of the 2000 US Presidential election, Fox News, CNN, NBC, CBS, and ABC incorrectly reported that Al Gore was the winner and our next President. While not intended to deceive, and false, the reports weren't works of fiction. Compare this to Stephen Colbert's statement on *The Daily Show* on May 5, 2003: "At 11:09 Eastern Standard Time, *The Daily Show* is projecting that George Walker Bush has won reelection and will remain in office until 2008." While what Colbert said turned out to be true, this doesn't make his report non-fictional. It's still fake news. As Stewart replied: "There's 18 months to go in this campaign, and I think it's a little ridiculous to say that George W. Bush has won anything at this point." One difference between Stephen Colbert and a network news anchor such as Tom Brokaw is that Brokaw has a staff that carefully researches the stories he reads on air. Colbert has a staff of writers who carefully research certain *parts* of his commentary, and then make the rest up. Thorough research, however, is neither necessary nor sufficient to make a work non-fiction. A personal memoir might demand little research, yet it's non-fiction, while some historical fiction demands a great deal of research. A better place to look for the distinction between fiction and non-fiction is in the authors' intentions in writing such narratives.

Hilarious Make-'Em-Ups

In a July 12, 2006 story on Senator Rick Santorum's campaign struggles, Jon Stewart reported that Santorum's campaign had issued a flyer entitled "50 Things You May Not Know About Rick Santorum." Stewart presented the audience with a quiz, asking them to identify which items on a list were included in the flyer and which were not. Some of the items, such as "Rick has been leading the fight against AIDS and world poverty, working closely with U2's Bono" came straight from the campaign literature. Others, including "Rick once compared Democrats fighting to preserve the filibuster to Nazis," which Stewart identified as true, "didn't really make it into the pamphlet." The rest of the quiz, for example "Rick's S&M safe word is 'applesauce,'" was, in Stewart's words, "what we in the business call 'hilarious make-'em-ups.'"

It's this last category that puts *Daily Show* reports into the category of fiction. The writers make up parts of the narrative knowingly and intentionally. Though usually this results in stories that are at least partially false, this isn't essential to the narratives being fictional. If Rick Santorum had a safe word, and if it really were "applesauce," it would turn out that the writers, to their and our surprise, accidentally reported something true. The report would still be a work of fiction, however.

Notice that to make something up in this way, one does so deliberately, but without any intention to deceive the audience. As we saw, this is what distinguishes typical fictions from lies. Writers of fiction don't intend to deceive the audience, and the same goes for the writers of *The Daily Show*.

Although the writers don't intend to deceive the audience, we need to ask: Do they want their audience to believe some of what they write, namely the truths contained in the fictional narratives? And another important question still remains: How does the audience tell truth from falsehood if the news stories on *The Daily Show* are works of fiction? The problem is complicated by the fact that what distinguishes non-fiction from make-'em-ups depends on the intentions of the writers. These intentions aren't always obvious to viewers. In fact, it's part of the show's design that the same deadpan delivery is used when relating both real news and fictional jokes.

Sheer Outrageousness and Surprising Truth

Back in 1729 Jonathan Swift published his controversial pamphlet "A Modest Proposal," in which he apparently advocated breeding human babies as a food source in order to combat famine. That essay is now regarded as a paradigm of satire, though at the time it was met with great outrage and indignation. How was the audience to know that Swift wasn't serious? Swift's earnest tone fooled many readers into thinking he *was* serious, but the content of the essay, namely its promotion of the patently ridiculous measure of cannibalistic infanticide, was a telling clue that he wasn't.

Jon Stewart and his correspondents regularly use an earnest tone when delivering their reports. It's the content of what they say that often tips off viewers that parts of the reports are made up. Sheer outrageousness or hyperbole is one of the clearest indicators that part of a fictional narrative is false or made up. *The Daily Show* uses this technique regularly to indicate to its audience what's true and what's false. For example, on January 23, 2006, Jason Jones discussed questions about the relationship between disgraced former lobbyist Jack Abramoff and President Bush. At issue was a series of pictures of the two men together, suggesting that they might have had a closer relationship than either had admitted. Jones shared a series of ever more ridiculous pictures of the two, starting with a real photo of the two shaking hands in a reception line, moving on to a fake antique photo of Bush and Abramoff in cowboy outfits, then a fake oil painting of the two men with a horse, and ending with an image of Michelangelo's *Pietà* in which Bush's face is superimposed over Mary's and Abramoff's over Jesus'. The combination of deliberately poor image-editing and the increasing outrageousness of images let the audience know that the images were fakes.

Outrageousness or hyperbole is not a foolproof test of the fake, however. As the saying goes, sometimes the truth is stranger than fiction. And when a story is true, but outrageous, Stewart sometimes has to use more direct means to make clear what's real and what's fake. In an August 2, 2006 story on an Arabic language translator discharged from the Army, Stewart reported as follows:

> This week, Bleu Copas became the fifty-fifth Arabic translator discharged under the Army's "Don't Ask, Don't Tell" policy. How did they know Copas was gay? After being tipped off by anonymous emails, investigators asked him if he had any gay friends, and – this is true – if he was involved in community theater.

The onscreen graphic contained the quotation "if he was involved in community theater," taken straight from a CNN.com story, and backing up Stewart's assertion "This is true." Without Stewart's assurance of its truth and the graphic displaying the quotation, viewers might easily assume that the community theater question was made up by the *Daily Show* writers, which otherwise would be an understandable mistake, given the writers' sense of humor.

The Role of "Senior" Correspondents

Examples such as the Bush/Abramoff story above illustrate a second feature of *The Daily Show* that helps the audience distinguish the fake from the real. When Stewart talks with his correspondents and commentators, he almost always plays the straight man, stating the truth about the topic under discussion, while the correspondent or commentator often makes the jokes, albeit with a straight face. The images presented by Jason Jones in the Bush/Abramoff report are fake, but Stewart's questions about the relationship between Bush and Abramoff were real questions in the news.

In another Stewart-correspondent exchange, Samantha Bee reported on Porter Goss's resignation from the CIA (May 18, 2006). Stewart spoke to her about why Goss left:

> *Stewart:* So I'm watching, Sam, the speculation on why Porter Goss left. I understand the turf war aspect, the bureaucratic reshuffling. What's all this about prostitutes and limousines?
>
> *Bee:* Yes, Jon, apparently Goss may be caught up with the infamous Duke Cunningham, who organized poker and hooker parties at the Watergate hotel. So basically the departure is due to either longstanding clashes between the CIA and the NSA, or Goss has been buying and selling underage Thai hookers who sexually service him while injecting heroin into the tip of his penis. 50/50.
>
> *Stewart:* Sam, even in the news reports I hadn't heard anything quite that specific.
>
> *Bee:* Well, I'm assuming. It's a party at the Dukester's – someone's getting their penis injected with something.

Here the sheer outrageousness of Samantha Bee's suggestion "tips" us off that she's making it up. As the earnest straight man, Stewart provides us with something closer to the facts, namely that though Goss's resignation is most likely the result of bureaucratic reshuffling or a turf war, speculation about limos and prostitutes is also being circulated. When Stewart questions Bee's speculations about sex acts, she responds with "I'm assuming," letting the audience know that this part of the story is made up. She even goes so far as to say that the chances of the prostitute story being correct are 50/50, as if the mere possibility of a story being true is sufficient to make it as likely as not. Bee's part of the story is ridiculous, while Stewart sticks closer to the plausible part.

The audience quickly understands the roles of Stewart and his correspondents. After you've seen *The Daily Show* a few times, it's clear that he's more likely to speak the truth while they're more likely to make things up. Genre fiction often works in a similar way. For example, take typical first-person detective fiction. When one reads a detective story told in the first person, the narrator tends to be reliable. What we know as fact, at least within the story, is what the detective/narrator relates to us. But other characters in the story, particularly those who are potential suspects, aren't reliable; what another character says might be false, and as readers we understand this because of our familiarity with the genre. One way *The Daily Show* helps us distinguish the real from the fake comes from the implicit conventions of complementary anchor/correspondent roles to which we quickly become accustomed.

Playing Dumb

Regular viewers are also familiar with another common practice, that of correspondents being surprisingly ignorant of the stories they cover, often discussing some topic other than the story they're supposed to be covering. This allows Stewart to ask leading questions or make comments about the real story, while the seeming ineptitude of the correspondents provides laughs. On July 20, 2005, Stewart and Ed Helms discussed President Bush's nomination of John Roberts to the Supreme Court:

> *Helms:* The left wishes the President picked someone they wanted, not someone he wanted. I mean, who gave him the authority? It's an abuse of power.
>
> *Stewart:* I think it's in the Constitution.

Any eighth grade civics student knows that the Constitution grants the President the power to make Supreme Court nominations, but Helms' apparent ignorance gives Stewart the opportunity to remind the audience, in case they've forgotten. Works of fiction frequently use this device. Insert an ignorant character into a situation so that relevant information has to be explained to that character, and you thereby inform the audience.

So in Stewart's interaction with correspondents we see that correspondents are often the ones who make things up, and they often play ignorant, leaving Stewart as the reliable source of real news. Of course, when Stewart delivers news stories on his own, not everything he says is reliable. For one thing, *The Daily Show* is comedy, and viewers understand that every fake news story has a punch line, if not several. Since *The Daily Show* makes fun of real news, usually the structure of a fake news story is to begin with facts and end in farce. This means that the beginning of Stewart's report is mostly real, while the ending tends to be fake. Visual cues, such as photographs and graphics, help indicate to the viewer when the story has turned fake, a device used frequently by both Stewart and the correspondents. On February 1, 2006, Jason Jones reported on President Bush's promotion of alternative fuels, including switchgrass. Jones explained what he called a simple switchgrass engine. The onscreen graphic showed detailed parts of the "engine" until, at the end of his explanation, an overview schematic showed it to be nothing other than a bong. At times like this the visuals are essential to revealing the joke to the audience, who glean that the so-called "engine" is fake.

So we have seen that there are at least three general means for the audience to determine what is real and what is fake when they watch *The Daily Show*: hyperbole or outrageousness, the complementary host/correspondent roles, and the use of graphics and photos. In our examples so far the truths conveyed by the show have been particular facts, such as "The Constitution grants the President the power to make Supreme Court nominations" and "The likely reasons Porter Goss left the CIA are turf war issues and bureaucratic reshuffling." But the scope of truths conveyed by the show isn't limited to particular facts.

The Daily Show, the Bush Team, and Other News Outlets

Philosophers often distinguish at least two kinds of truths expressed in fiction. The first kind consists of particular truths, as we've seen in examples from the show. But the second category of truths – general truths – is no less, and perhaps more, important. For example, Jane Austen's *Pride and Prejudice* begins with this general observation: "It is a truth universally acknowledged, that a single man in possession of a good fortune, must be in want of a wife."[1] Such general claims in fiction often serve as commentaries on the human condition or the state of the world, and help explain the action to follow. *The Daily Show* tends to focus its general commentaries on two topics: the government and the news media, particularly the cable TV news channels.

The Daily Show repeatedly touches on certain themes concerning the Bush administration: the secrecy among Bush and his advisors, the misplaced confidence Bush has in his decisions, the administration's mismanagement of foreign policy, and the divide between Bush's concerns and the concerns of ordinary Americans, to name a few. Rather than taking great care to avoid editorializing, *The Daily Show*, and Stewart in particular, use editorial commentaries as running jokes. Unlike the "hilarious make-'em-ups" mentioned above, however, these running jokes aren't simple falsehoods, they express what Stewart and the *Daily Show* writers see as truths. The focus on criticism of the Bush administration results, at least in part, from the fact that they're the people in power, as the Clinton administration was during the show's early years. *The Daily Show* casts general criticisms at present-day Democrats too, typically by depicting them as clueless and powerless in the current political climate (although after the midterm 2006 elections, the political landscape has changed significantly).

The second topic of general commentary is the news media itself, particularly 24 hour television news such as CNN, MSNBC, and Fox News Channel. *The Daily Show* considers these news outlets sensationalistic, inclined to copy each other, prone to overexposing news stories, and desperate to manufacture news in order to fill airtime. In an August 3, 2006 commentary on 24 hour news channel coverage of the Israel/Lebanon conflict and general strife in the Middle East, Stewart discussed footage from CNN, MSNBC, *Good Morning America*, and Fox News Channel. Each of these news sources discussed whether the crisis in the Middle East was a sign of Armageddon. MSNBC's graphic read "The End of Days?" *Good Morning America*'s read "Apocalypse Now: Is the End Near?" and CNN used both "Armageddon" and "Apocalypse Now?" – revealing common sensationalistic trends in the news media. Paula Zahn of CNN referred to a certain website which assigns a numerical value to the likelihood of Armageddon, the so-called "Rapture Index," which on that day was 156, a number Stewart jokingly referred to as "arbitrarily terrifying." In his comments, Stewart sarcastically called Zahn's approach "scientific," revealing the evident lack of investigative standards in such reporting.

Fox News Channel interviewed a priest for part of its "Armageddon" coverage, and the Fox News correspondent was more concerned with *when* the world will end than *whether* it will: "I get so many conversations, on the street too, that say this is imminent. When people say this is imminent, what are we talking about, a year? Six months? Nostradamus says August of 2006. But is it 18 years from now? What is it, Father?" Again, the lack of journalistic integrity is obvious. Robin Roberts of *Good Morning America* went even further. In one interview, an evangelical Christian guest advised: "There's no alternative, you either accept Jesus or you're going to go through terrible times." Roberts replied, "That's why mom always says you'd better get right. You'd better get right in these times we're living in." Stewart responded to this footage by commenting: "This is Robin Roberts saying Jesus is the way and the light." In other words, some news personalities aren't nearly as unbiased as they'd like us to think.

Stewart finished his summary of the news channels' "Armageddon" coverage by asking whether, just possibly, we're living in such dark times that this coverage is somehow justified. He answered this question by airing footage of Jane Pauley from November 14, 1999. She spoke about the coming dawn of the new millennium, and was followed by this voicecover: "The threat of Y2K, AIDS, and the recent earthquakes in nearby Turkey and Greece are all part of the prophesied tribulations before Christ's return." Stewart commented: "Now *that* was an end of the world." The clear message is that news organizations sometimes sensationalize a story that really isn't news in the first place.

In a similar vein, Stewart and Rob Corddry offered a combined commentary on both the news media and the Bush administration on October 31, 2005. Stewart asked Corddry about the timing of the White House news of the nomination of Samuel Alito to the Supreme Court. The White House announcement came at a time when the media had been reporting on the indictment of Scooter Libby, the Vice President's Chief of Staff, and on suspicions that Dick Cheney and Bush's Deputy Chief of Staff Karl Rove were involved in leaking the identity of former CIA agent Valerie Plame:

Stewart: Do you think the White House announced this nomination this morning because they thought it would distract the media?

Corddry: Jon, the White House just put this giant ball of tin foil out on the lawn and . . . it's so shiny. . . . I'm sorry, you were talking.

Stewart:	I was asking about the timing of the Alito nomination with respect to the Scooter Libby indictment.
Corddry:	Right Jon, now the Scooter Libb-what-indict-what? Oh, oh, oh, no, I know what you're talking about, the Friday thing. Jon, that was practically last month, man. Get with the times. There's been a change of topic.
Stewart:	But doesn't the media itself have some power over what the important story is?
Corddry:	No, Jon, no. We have no ability to decide what's important. Look, I'm a reporter. I'd love to stick with the Libby case. We're talking about corruption in the Vice President's office. *Huge* story, but something new happened. If the Alito nomination weren't more important, it wouldn't have happened more recently. Its "nowness" trumps the less "recentitude" of that thing with Liddy [*sic*].

In this exchange, Stewart and Corddry hit on three general criticisms: (1) the White House manipulates the news media for its own political ends; (2) the news media is unable or unwilling to resist this manipulation; and (3) the news media puts such a premium on new stories that sometimes more important stories are ignored. Criticisms like these are at the core of general truths communicated by *The Daily Show*. As fake news, it satirizes traditional news by reporting in a style similar to network and cable TV news, but it amplifies their biases, mistakes, and deficiencies to ensure that viewers hear them loud and clear.

Fake News, Real Messages

At the end of the day, *The Daily Show* informs as well as entertains. *Daily Show* news stories are works of fiction, in that they consist partly of made-up material that isn't intended to deceive. As with most works of fiction, the fake is mixed in with the real, and the audience can usually tell the difference. As televised media, *The Daily Show* makes use of not only verbal language, but body language, vocal delivery, and visual imagery. Various cues let the audience draw the line pretty clearly between the fake and the real, and the moderately attentive viewer leaves the show better informed about the world, especially the political climate and current state of the media. It's fake news conveying real messages, and great entertainment to boot.

Note

1 Jane Austen, *Pride and Prejudice* (New York: Bantam Books, 1981), p. 1. We might debate whether Austen's statement is actually true. Rather than worry about the actual truth of what Austen, or *The Daily Show* for that matter, says, for convenience I will continue to call these "general truths." More accurately, they're general assertions the writer or speaker makes, that is, they're asserted as truths believed by the speaker or writer.

3

THE FAKE NEWS AS THE FIFTH ESTATE

RACHAEL SOTOS

America (The Book) begins with a foreword by Thomas Jefferson.[1] That's right, Jon Stewart and the *Daily Show* folks are so bold as to use the name of America's third president to set the stage for their mock high school textbook. *America*'s Jefferson comments (in remarkably current vernacular) that it seems somewhat preposterous that "Irv over at Warner Books" could convince him, *a Founding Father*, to pen the foreword for a book connected to a show that's "not even network." Jefferson explains, however, that he agreed because the book is actually "funny," and because he wants to use the opportunity "to dispel some of the mythology" about him and his fellow Founders (p. x). Jefferson says he's tired of all this "worshipping at the altar" of the Founders. Sure, they were "awesome" and "accomplished," but they were also, without a doubt, *imperfect*: "Adams was an unbearable prick and squealed girlishly whenever he saw a bug. And Ben Franklin? . . . a boozed-up snuff machine." Moreover, *America*'s Jefferson continues, way back at the time of the Founding, the Founders themselves were certainly aware of their fallibility, and they likewise knew that the US Constitution was imperfect. It was for this reason that they allowed for amendments: "because they *amend*!" With righteous indignation, Jefferson concludes as follows:

> My point is composing the Declaration of Independence and Constitution was hard work. God didn't dictate it for us to transcribe from some sort of dictation-transcribing machine. . . . Our purpose was to create a living document based on principles that transcended the

times we lived in, and I think we did that. We created a blueprint for a system that would endure, which means your lazy asses shouldn't be coasting on our accomplishments. We were imperfect. It was imperfect. And we expect our descendents to work as hard as we did on keeping what we think is a profoundly excellent form of government supple, evolving and relevant. After reading this book, you should be better prepared to do just that. (p. x)

When Jefferson insists that we should get off our bums and work hard to perfect the work of the Founders, he affirms an expansive sense of democratic freedom and political participation. He exhorts us to carry forth the creative, revolutionary spirit ourselves.[2] Unfortunately, not everyone is as optimistic as Jefferson about our capacity for independent thinking and creative self-determination. Indeed, there are many who continue to "worship at the altar" of the Founders, believing that citizens should have *an obedient and unquestioning attitude toward authority* (whether it's the authority of the law, the current government, the *first* government, or God – all alleged to be, in some sense, infallible).[3]

Now, I don't mean to argue here that there's no legitimate place for conservative views in American politics, for certainly there is. But a strong case can be made that the *Daily Show* folks are on the right track when they attribute an open and expansive sense of freedom to the Founders. An obedient and unquestioning attitude toward authority doesn't really fit the profile of the Founders, who were, let's recall, *revolutionaries*. Let's also remember that when George Washington refused to be king, then also refused a third term of office, *he made space for our freedom*. Jefferson, the real Jefferson, was so intent to extend the creative, revolutionary spirit to posterity that he suggested it would be good, despite the impracticality, for *every generation* to experience founding a new political system, to have its own Constitutional Convention.[4]

But of course, just as there are many who prefer regimented hierarchy to an expansive sense of freedom and participation, so many would balk at the idea that the fake news, Comedy Central style, is politically relevant. Certainly many would reject the claim that *The Daily Show* carries forth the creative, revolutionary spirit of the American Founders. Bill O'Reilly, for instance, told Barbara Walters in a *20/20* interview that *The Daily Show* is "just for laughs," its audience a bunch of "stoned teenagers" (September 22, 2006). In an appearance on *The O'Reilly Factor*, Geraldo Rivera was even more disparaging, charging Stewart and Stephen Colbert with "making a living putting on videos of old ladies slipping on ice and people laughing." The remarkable fact ignored by O'Reilly and Rivera is, of course, that the fake news, Comedy Central style, has a real voice in American politics. *The Daily Show* and *The Colbert Report* are constantly referred to in other media, quoted in op-ed pieces in major newspapers, featured on political talk shows, and of course, faithfully itemized, organized, and documented in the blogosphere. In an age when CNN boasts that it's "the most trusted name in news" and Fox News promises to be "fair and balanced," Jon Stewart is, in the eyes of many – precisely *because* of his irreverent patriotism – a legitimate news authority, "today's Walter Cronkite."[5]

The Fake News and the Revolutionary Spirit

Although the textbooks we read in school don't typically present it this way, Jefferson and the other Founders enjoyed humor and believed it had great political importance. According to the American historian and literary theorist Colin Wells, during the Revolutionary period satire was arguably "the most popular and politically important literary form in American political life."[6] The revolutionaries used literature as well as muskets; satirical works were "weapons in a literary and ideological war to decide the future of the new Republic" (p. 159). Sometimes this meant depicting King George III and the Loyalists simply as buffoons, but early American satire often involved much subtler methods, including – fascinatingly – an early form of fake news:

> American satirists were especially drawn, for instance, to writing verse parodies of other printed texts such as newspaper articles or official government documents. During the war, broadsides proclaiming martial law or demanding the arrest of rebels were frequently answered by anonymous verse parodies . . . ridiculing not only the colonial official who issued the proclamation but the language of political authority itself. (p. 159)

Obviously the assertion of infallible authority makes an easy target for ridicule, but it's important to underscore the fact that satire generally, and parodies of the news more specifically, aren't inherently revolutionary, progressive, or liberal. Satire wouldn't be amusing for very long if it were nothing more than political propaganda. It's really, lastingly funny because it engages free thought and imagination. In this respect, we might say that satire is best understood as a playful way of addressing reality, one which necessarily assumes that there's more than one plausible way to interpret things. Just as now one can read political parodies from all points of view on the internet, so too during the American Revolution a variety of satire was available, including Loyalist satire that ridiculed the rebels.

To locate *The Daily Show* in the tradition of American satire more precisely, it will help to consider the genre of the fake news a bit more carefully. In his recent book, *Infamous Scribblers*, journalist and historian Eric Burns draws a vivid parallel between early and present-day America.[7] Fascinatingly, then as now, there was a spectrum of more and less reputable characters. Samuel Adams, it turns out, wasn't just a "brewer and a patriot," but a muckraking journalist, so committed to the American Revolution that his journalism turned yellow fighting for the red, white, and blue. According to Burns, Adams literally fabricated stories to turn the tide of public opinion, accusing the British soldiers of "beating children, forcing their attention on young ladies [and] violating the Sabbath by getting drunk and racing horses through the streets of Boston" (p. 148). But inflammatory fabrication, intended to inspire the ire of fellow colonists, is far removed from the sophisticated satire his more literary compatriots composed. Indeed, fabrication isn't satire at all, but simply fake news as straight propaganda. Unfortunately, such propaganda is familiar in our world as some elements of the media consciously distort and omit in order to promote a specific political agenda (even as they claim to be "fair and balanced").[8]

At the other end of the spectrum of the fake news is *The Daily Show* and, interestingly, the American Founder and elder statesman Benjamin Franklin. As Burns reminds us, Franklin wasn't only a man of many inventions, but also "the first American humorist" and "as ethical a journalist as America produced in the eighteenth century" (p. 91). As many did in his time, Franklin often wrote pseudonymously, in the voice of fictional characters he created: Silence Dogood (a middle-aged widow and severe critic of society), Polly Baker (a prostitute who protests the sexual double-standard), and Poor Richard Saunders (a henpecked farmer with folksy wisdom, not necessarily Franklin's own). Writing the fake news under these pseudonyms, Franklin respected his readers, thinking them "sophisticated enough to know the ruse" (p. 91).

In the nineteenth century, the most famous, and infamous, practitioner of the fake news was Samuel Clemens, writing of course as Mark Twain. As it turns out, in the new age of mass journalism, his audience didn't always prove of subtle enough mind, and Clemens got into some trouble, losing two jobs because of his satirical news pieces.[9] Once more clearly separated from journalism proper, the fake news enjoyed a vibrant existence in the twentieth century: *Mad Magazine*, *Saturday Night Live*, *The Onion*, and of course, *The Daily Show*. At their best, satirists in the fake news tradition carry on Franklin's spirit of "constructive irony," irony that respects its audience and is intended to inspire critical reflection.

The fake news, Comedy Central style, certainly is true to Franklin's blend of journalism and comedy. And while I can't predict the future, I wouldn't be at all surprised if we soon see doctoral dissertations and books comparing the "journalists" of *The Daily Show* with Franklin's pseudonymous characters. Samantha Bee is perhaps today's Silence Dogood and Polly Baker, Stephen Colbert our Poor Richard. For unlike most of the talking heads of real television journalism, but like the literary characters of Franklin's imagination, the fake news "journalists" bring a depth of humanity to our perception as they simultaneously inspire critical reflection.

Jon Stewart, who's less "persona-fied" than the other "journalists" on *The Daily Show*, is faithful to Benjamin's constructive irony in a more nuanced, and perhaps more philosophical, way. At the risk of pressing a comparison a bit too far, we can compare Stewart's comic manner of reporting, often with gasps of exasperation and bewilderment, to Socrates, the first great ironist in history. As we learn in the dialogues of Plato (which are a good bit comedy), Socrates practiced philosophy *ironically*, talking with anyone who claimed to know, while proclaiming himself to be ignorant. And brilliantly, it's precisely Socrates' ironic claims to ignorance that make him so effective. Because he isn't trying to press his own position, he's able to expose the ignorance of his interlocutors. In parallel, Stewart's comic reading of the news is *a kind of dialogue* with contemporary newsmakers and reporters. Through his ironic reports, he presses the *logic* of his interlocutors to their *illogical* extremes. Like Socrates, Stewart often reveals the gap between a reasonable view of things and the quite dangerous assumptions of those in power and pompously claiming to be experts.

The Colbert Report's regular "The Word" segment offers us another example of thought-provoking "constructive irony." It certainly undermines any claim that the fake news, Comedy Central style, is "just for laughs." Matching Colbert's every mindless slogan and banal cliché, the sidebar provides an ongoing commentary. The result is not only biting parody but often political wisdom in the form of an elegant literary vignette. "The Word" proves that at least some Americans have kept faith with their literate and politically conscious forbears.

The Fake News and the Separation of Powers

With his delightful "apple-pie authoritarianism" Stephen Colbert continually claims that he believes *only* in the presidency, the executive branch of government. He cheerfully insists that we might as well do away with the legislative branch (Congress), and that we certainly can do without an independent judiciary (Supreme Court). As he puts it in "The Word": "It's a lot easier to run a government with a separation of powers when nobody's checking the powers" (September 25, 2006). This, of course, is constructive irony at its finest. As we rightly learned in school, for all their optimism about the possibilities of freedom, the Founders were deeply skeptical about human nature and profoundly worried about centralized power. It was for these reasons that they created a political system that not only promised to protect individual rights, but divided power between the states and the federal government, and, of course, among the three branches of government. While it wouldn't be wise to confuse our present political situation with tyranny, Colbert deserves kudos for repeatedly raising the issue. Citizens should be, as the Founders were, on guard against the illegitimate centralization of power.

Although not ensconced in the Constitution as an official part of government, the press is often referred to as the "Fourth Branch of Government," or "Fourth Estate." As the Founders surely understood when they provided the extensive protections of the First Amendment, the press plays an essential role in a free society. At their best, newspapers and other news media impartially report events, and in doing so they necessarily help to shape public opinion and, ideally at least, keep an eye on the rich and powerful. It's only in this way that the press can serve as "the voice of the people" and offer another check on the other three branches of government.

If we think in institutional terms, we are grateful to the fake news for guarding the separation of powers, and this extends far beyond our ironic delight in Colbert's simpleminded affirmation of fascist efficiency. In today's homogenized corporate media world, the fake news in fact serves an essential function, operating as a kind of "Fifth Estate," the watchdog of the Fourth. Today, there's widespread concern that our news organizations are failing to serve their institutional function. Recent deregulation has permitted great centralization of media power: currently six mega-corporations – Disney, Viacom, Time Warner, News Corp, Bertelsmann, and General Electric – own more than 90 percent of the newspaper, magazine, internet, film, radio, television, and cable media. Critics charge that journalistic independence and integrity are threatened when news organizations are subsumed by entertainment groups and ever-increasing emphasis is put on the bottom line. Moreover, close alliances between ideologically driven media moguls and specific political parties are an obviously troubling phenomenon.[10] If the press takes its talking points from the powers that be, what happens to the "voice of the people?" But this is just where the fake news comes in, serving as the Fifth Estate when the Fourth Branch fails.

We can track the institutional function of the fake news, Comedy Central style, in various ways. Sometimes the fake news actually fills in for the Fourth Branch, taking up the slack when the "free press" fails. Of course it isn't *The Daily Show*'s professed ambition to be "hard news," but research indicates that *Daily Show* viewers prove to be more informed than consumers of mainstream news. According to the Annenberg Public Policy Institute, *Daily Show* viewers come out on top "even when education, party identification, following politics, watching cable news, receiving campaign information online, age and gender are taken into consideration."[11]

In other cases the fake news serves an institutional function, not by filling gaps, but by serving as a "constitutional check" on the mainstream press. In recent years this has entailed, not quite a "constitutional crisis," but definite *events of historic proportions*. In Stewart's live appearance on CNN's *Crossfire* (October 15, 2004), he shocked Paul Begala and Tucker Carlson, boldly chastising them for their "partisan hackery." Stewart took *Crossfire* and all the info-tainment cable shows to task for their failure to use an important public forum for civilized debate. Here Stewart really did speak in the legitimate voice of the press, and by extension the people, when he said, "Stop, stop, stop, stop hurting America."[12]

Stephen Colbert's hosting of the White House Correspondents' Dinner was another event of historic significance (April 29, 2006). Colbert's entire speech is worth extended analysis, but the following segment nicely captures the fake news's critique of mainstream media:

As excited as I am to be here with the President, I am appalled to be surrounded by the liberal media that is destroying America, with the exception of Fox News. Fox News gives you sides of every story, the President's side and the Vice President's side. But the rest of you, what are you thinking? Reporting on NSA wiretapping or secret prisons in Eastern Europe? Those things are secret for a very important reason, they're super depressing. And if that's your goal, well, misery accomplished. Over the last five years you people were so good over tax cuts, WMD intelligence, the effect of global warming. We Americans didn't want to know, and you had the courtesy not to try to find out. Those were good times, as far as we knew.

But, listen, let's review the rules. Here's how it works. The President makes decisions, he's the decider. The press secretary announces those decisions, and you people of the press type those decisions down. Make, announce, type. Put them through a spell check and go home. Get to know your family again. Make love to your wife. Write that novel you got kicking around in your head. You know the one about the intrepid Washington reporter with the courage to stand up to the administration. You know, fiction.

Famously, Colbert's roast not only burst Bush's bubble,[13] it sent the media into a tizzy. Nearly everyone who's anyone commented, some with delight, but many with offense, complaining that Colbert was "rude" or simply "not funny."[14] He struck a nerve, to be sure, and if he didn't tickle everyone's funny bone, it was because the fake news was speaking truth to power, not only to the President but also to the media elite.

In a less monumental but no less important sense, the fake news serves as the Fifth Branch of government in the *way* it covers the daily news. Recall that the fake news covers the news by *covering the news media covering the news*. So operating, the fake news serves a *philosophical* function by offering a "metaview" of the Fourth Estate. Consider it this way: while it would be impossible for a single individual to pay attention to all of the media all of the time, the fake news does us a great service by *continually monitoring* CNN, Fox, ABC, CBS, NBC, MSNBC, and so on. *The Daily Show* usually begins with a video montage that gives critical commentary on the day's media coverage. Instead of just watching the news, we're invited to reflect on how it's being covered. By encouraging this reflection, the fake news provides a philosophical inoculation against the mindless onslaught of sound bites and pandering infotainment; we become critical consumers, if not more responsible citizens.

Strikingly, the role the fake news plays supervising the Fourth Estate can be understood in light of a traditional role that philosophy plays countering *mere rhetoric*. Since the very beginning of Western philosophy in ancient Greece, philosophers have criticized politicians and rhetoricians for their irresponsible manipulation of emotions at the expense of reason. As viewers know, such criticism is often the substance of *The Daily Show*'s comedy. Here Samantha Bee is a heroine of the fake news, having perfected saucy parody of such sensationalist fluff. But Colbert, with his ironic affirmation of "the gut" over book-learning and the "factinistas," is clearly the comic master of this traditional form of philosophical critique.

This isn't to say that fake news, Comedy Central style, always endorses reason over emotion. *The Daily Show*'s critique of media rhetoric also encourages awareness of the way our emotions are manipulated and distorted. A memorable example comes from the beginning of the war between Israel and Lebanon. On July 16, 2006, *The Daily Show* reported how the major television news broadcasts hemmed and hawed for days, refusing to name the conflict a "war."

But it was even more disturbing that Fox, ABC, and CNN all ran nearly identical commentaries on the "relevant" effect in the United States. As Stewart devastatingly set it up, "How is all the carnage in a region we perhaps helped destabilize affecting us? Is there a place where we can quantify our feelings regarding the devastation being wrought? Perhaps in our hearts or minds?" No such luck with the Fourth Branch. As *The Daily Show* revealed, Fox, ABC, and CNN all cynically echoed each other in their so-called analysis: "We will feel it at the pump"; "feel it at the pump"; "feel it at the pump."

If we have any doubt that the fake news operates in this *philosophical* fashion, inoculating us against the cynical onslaught of pandering infotainment, we should recall the "Moment of Zen" clips that conclude every episode of *The Daily Show*. These clips are often silly, occasionally sublimely absurd. Above all, in their sheer ridiculousness, they're our nightly "transcendent reference point," reminding us – through comedy – of the abyss between the world as it is and the world as it ought to be.

Truthiness and the New Media

Let's conclude this investigation of the fake news's philosophical function by considering where critical consciousness really counts today: in the politics of the "new media." On the debut broadcast of *The Colbert Report* (October 17, 2005), Colbert made "truthiness" the subject of "The Word." A flurry of commentary followed, in the *New York Times* and *Newsweek*, and on ABC and CNN. Less than three months later, the American Dialect Society voted "truthiness" the Word of the Year for 2005. It was another historic moment for the fake news!

According to Frank Rich, op-ed columnist for the *New York Times*, Colbert's neologism "truthiness" captures "the politics of spin" spun out of control. It captures a time when high-level politicians admit that it is no longer a matter of spinning facts, but *ignoring* facts altogether, of bypassing "the reality-based community."[15] In this respect, Colbert's "truthiness" is first and foremost a damning indictment of the spin doctors and of the mainstream media for failing to keep them in check. But the denunciation is just the starting point, for the fake news, Comedy Central style, is all about *constructive irony*. As Colbert explains in an out-of-character interview in *The Onion*, his ironic intervention has an ethical dimension:

> It used to be, everyone was entitled to their own opinion, but not their own facts. But that's not the case anymore. Facts matter not at all. Perception is everything. . . . Truthiness is "What I say is right, and [nothing] anyone else says could possibly be true." It's not only that I *feel* it to be true, but that *I* feel it to be true. There's not only an emotional quality, but there's a selfish quality.[16]

When Colbert identifies the selfishness underlying the politics of truthiness, he indicates that our attention to the facts which compose *our shared reality* is a *moral* issue. Colbert's truthiness intervention is thus an exhortation to pay attention, to do justice to reality itself. Accordingly, Colbert doesn't rest content with indictment; he also calls us to action, to do "good works." He continually encourages us, his audience, "the heroes," to intervene in the new media. Of course, Colbert doesn't explicitly advocate direct political action: entering a homemade video in the "Green Screen Challenge" and sending emails to have a Hungarian bridge named "Colbert" are far from serious political acts (they're rather opportunities to playfully promote his megalomaniacal cult of personality). Still, however silly, these interventions are politically significant; they signify the possibility of collective action in an interconnected world.

No doubt the internet, where people have hundreds of intangible friends and live "second lives," isn't the same as a traditional political forum, where – as in a town hall meeting or political protest – people meet face to face. But now young people – who've been notoriously apathetic for decades – are empowered by technology in ever-new ways; they register to vote on Facebook. In many respects the new political environment is dangerous, but this is precisely the backdrop against which we can understand why *The Daily Show* is so loved and revered, and why Jon Stewart is "today's Walter Cronkite." The fake news is not only – in its own way – more true to the facts, it's closer to the cutting edge of new possibilities for political participation. We might say that the fake news keeps faith with the Founders, reminding us that as citizens we have power. When, on August 1, 2006, Colbert asked his "heroes" to add comments to Wikipedia, the free online encyclopedia, stating that the population of African elephants has tripled in the last decade, he claimed that we could thus "create a reality we can all agree on." The message, though ironic, is clear: it's up to us, now more than ever, to preserve our world and our relationship to it: with "truthiness" comes responsibility.

Notes

1 Jon Stewart, Ben Karlin, and David Javerbaum, *America (The Book): A Citizen's Guide to Democracy Inaction* (New York: Warner Books, 2004). Subsequent references will be made parenthetically in-text.
2 For further guidance consult the "Classroom Activities" at the end of *America (The Book)*, chapter 2: "1. Found a country" (p. 33).
3 In law, such a "conservative" attitude has been associated with the so-called "strict constructionist" theory of constitutional interpretation, which *America* discusses in a "casually oversimplified" fashion: "A strict constructionist interprets the Constitution according to the language and original intent of the text at the time of its writing, in much the same way as a fundamentalist views the Bible. Fortunately for strict constructionists, they have been endowed by God with the superhuman gift of being able to read the minds of people who died 200 years ago. Naturally, they use this power only for good" (p. 87).
4 Jefferson's letter to Samuel Kercheval, July 12, 1816, quoted in Hannah Arendt, *On Revolution* (New York: Penguin, 2006), p. 226.
5 Steve Young, "The 1974 Cronkite," *LA Daily News* (September 20, 2004), N11.
6 Colin Wells, "Satire," *The Encyclopedia of the New American Nation*, ed. Paul Finkelman (New York: Charles Scribners' Sons, 2006), p. 158. Subsequent references will be made parenthetically in-text.
7 Eric Burns, *Infamous Scribblers: The Founding Fathers and the Rowdy Beginnings of American Journalism* (New York: Public Affairs, 2006). Subsequent references will be made parenthetically in-text.
8 It's certainly no accident that Burns, a journalist for Fox News, found himself inspired to explore the wide spectrum of more and less reputable fake news in the American tradition.
9 Another example of failed fake news – where the audience missed the point, and with unfortunate consequences – is Orson Welles' legendary radio adaptation of *War of the Worlds*.
10 See Jeff Cohen, *Cable News Confidential: My Misadventure in Corporate Media* (Sausalito: Poli Point Press, 2006). Discerning citizens with free

time and sufficient curiosity are able to inform themselves, but even so, mainstream media largely sets the agenda and determines the parameters of public debate.

11 "National Annenberg Election Survey" (press release), *Annenberg Public Policy Center* (September 21, 2004), p. 1.

12 As a CNN executive later said, Stewart's appearance was key in the decision to cancel the show. Perhaps it was also a cause of Tucker Carlson giving up his silly bow tie.

13 Signs of the popped bubble include Bush's pained reaction to Colbert's performance, the fact that Bush himself mentioned it in a press conference months later (August, 2006), and that shortly after the speech an effort was made to present Bush in the press as "a reader," allegedly reading Camus' *The Stranger* and Shakespeare during the summer of 2006.

14 For a good summary of the coverage, see Dan Froomkin, "Why So Defensive?" in the op-ed special to the washingtonpost.com (May 4, 2006): www.washingtonpost.com/wpyn/content/blog/2006/05/04/BL2006050400967.html.

15 Ronald Suskind famously reports a conversation in 2002 with a Bush administration official who joked about the difference between the administration and the "reality-based community," in "Without a Doubt," *New York Times Magazine* (October 17, 2004), Section 6, p. 51. See also Frank Rich's op-ed article, "Truthiness 101: From Frey to Alito," *New York Times* (January 22, 2006), Section 4, p. 16 for a biting analysis of the politics of "truthiness" in our time. Rich's recent book, *The Greatest Story Ever Sold: The Decline and Fall of Truth from 9/11 to Katrina* (New York: Penguin, 2006) is itself an elaborate Colbertian critique of the Bush administration and the contemporary media environment.

16 Interview with Nathan Rabin in "The A.V. Club," *The Onion* (January 25, 2006), 42 (3), p. 23.

4

THE GOOD, THE BAD, AND *THE DAILY SHOW*

In recent years an increasing number of Americans have turned away from mainstream media sources and tuned in to alternative, fake news programs such as *The Daily Show* with Jon Stewart. By cleverly blending comedy with coverage of newsworthy events, these programs create a hybrid form of entertainment-news. However, this new form of "infotainment" raises a number of unique ethical questions. Is it good to have large numbers of people getting their news from a comedian? What kind of information – or misinformation – do fake news programs impart to their audience? Might fake news like *The Daily Show* have a negative effect on the media and the culture at large?

Like most things, *The Daily Show* isn't all good or all bad. The question isn't whether Jon Stewart or the show's producers and writers are morally corrupt people, but whether or not fake news is, on the whole, beneficial or damaging to society. What questions should we be asking about this apparent shift in journalism? What should we expect from the media? We wouldn't have to worry about such questions if fake news programs weren't influential, but their popularity requires us to examine them critically. As I will argue, *The Daily Show* exhibits both virtues and vices. The real challenge will be to assess the overall impact of fake news.

Before we can assess the news value of *The Daily Show*, we must first ask why we should care about where people get their news and whether it's important for them to be informed. The dissemination of news is extremely important in a democratic state. Just think of the damaging effects state-controlled media have on North Korea, Iran, or Iraq under Hussein's regime. An informed public is the grease that keeps democracy running properly. Although foreign and domestic issues aren't settled by popular vote, an informed public wields great democratic power. An indirect test of this is the emphasis that politicians place on packaging their partisan messages, often in the form of a coordinated attack on the hearts and minds of the public. If our opinion didn't really matter, why would politicians go to such lengths? If our opinion does matter, then it seems we should be concerned with having the proper institutions in place to ensure that we're being properly informed.

Journalists like Tom Fenton have blamed the media for failing to anticipate the pre-9/11 threat posed by terrorism.[1] By reducing the number of foreign correspondents and cutting down on hard news stories, real foreign policy issues had been more or less remaindered to the periphery of the news. Threats like Al Qaeda were able to fly under the media's radar, even after the first World Trade Center bombing in 1993. Having a population concerned and informed about relevant facts and issues helps guide the future course of the country. Although the media is supposed to report stories "in the public interest," Fenton complained: "The networks are obsessed with the ratings race. Politicians and statesmen line up to appear on the ersatz news *Daily Show*, and bloggers seem to be breaking the real news. Even as the urgent problems of Iraq, Iran, North Korea, and a resurgent Russia compete for our attention, the news media fiddle while Rome burns" (p. x). Do fake news programs merely reflect this shift in media and culture, do they themselves change the journalistic landscape, or does the influence run both ways?

The Vices of Fake News

Ted Koppel, former host of ABC's *Nightline*, commented, "a lot of television viewers – more, quite frankly, than I'm comfortable with – get their news from the Comedy Channel on a program called *The Daily Show*."[2] What's the cause of Koppel's discomfort? I see two potential problems with so-called fake news programs: *deception* and *dilution*. Unlike dramatizations such as *The West Wing*, *The Daily Show* uses real events as a vehicle for comedy. Furthermore, the program's guest list would turn the head of any network news exec. Calling

The Daily Show fake news is somewhat misleading (so we'll put the term in scare quotes – "fake" – from here on). At the same time, *The Daily Show* bills itself as "a nightly half-hour series unburdened by objectivity, journalistic integrity, or even accuracy." This leaves us with a tension: the show is "unburdened by objectivity," and yet "informs" large swaths of America about foreign and national news events. I'll call this the problem of deception – cloaking (even if it is unintentional) a real news program as entertainment. The second concern I'll call the problem of dilution. The success of *The Daily Show*, which attracts over 1.4 million for their daily dose,[3] may prompt traditional journalistic venues, such as nightly news programs on major broadcast networks, to infuse hard news with entertainment, which might dilute the news media at large. Each of these criticisms will be dealt with in turn.

The popularity of *The Daily Show* reflects its entertainment and comedic value. People tune in to watch Jon Stewart and his onscreen staff because they're funny. But laughs aren't the only thing viewers take away. The jokes and skits are based on, and peppered with, real news items and real stories. Whether people tune in to be entertained, to be informed, or both, the fact is that *The Daily Show* shapes people's perspective on the world. Once we realize this, we can and should question the quality of the information viewers are receiving.

Although the incidental imparting of news might be seen as a benefit (as I will discuss later), one could raise the complaint that, because of its use, because of how it functions, or is taken to function, *The Daily Show* should, but doesn't, hold itself to the same journalistic standards traditional news agencies do. Can a show "unburdened by objectivity" be expected to communicate news to the public accurately and responsibly? Can a program concerned with getting ratings through comedy be expected to provide objective and responsible coverage of world events? Of course "deception" means "the intentional imparting of false information to another," and it doesn't seem that *The Daily Show* fits this definition. For one thing, it's probably not meant to deceive anyone, and for another, it claims to be something other than a legitimate news source. However, is this claim fair? As already mentioned, the show's content and guest list suggest otherwise. Of course there are many purely entertaining, merely funny segments, but most of the show is centered on the news and newsworthy events. Furthermore, I'm not suggesting that viewers can't distinguish between the pure entertainment and the news-driven stories. I'm assuming that the audience is intelligent enough to thresh the wheat from the chaff. Even so, people might well think they're being fully or sufficiently informed when they watch *Daily Show* news segments. Can one be expected to get quality reporting from a comedy show? Does a comedian have the expertise or rigorous standards to communicate newsworthy events reliably?

Analogous arguments are often levied against violent video games and sexist music videos. Invariably, the creators of these perceived violent or offensive media claim that their products are fictional and not intended to be taken literally. Intentionally or not, if negative but predictable consequences result from particular media, the creators should, in some sense, be held accountable. Likewise, if people watch *The Daily Show* to become informed, either explicitly or implicitly, then the show may have obligations to provide a responsible product.[4]

A more pernicious form of deception occurs when entertainment is presented under the guise of unbiased, objective reporting. There are clear examples of this form of media deception emanating from both political parties and a variety of special interests. Anecdotally, I viewed Michael Moore's notorious film, *Fahrenheit 9/11*, at a university screening. While I cringed at many points during the screening, the undergraduate crowd erupted in cheers. My discomfort had little to do with my political leanings, and more to do with Moore's fallacious and rhetorical style, which is dangerous because many students likely took the film to be an unbiased retelling of events surrounding 9/11. The reasoning that leads to a conclusion is often as important as, if not in some ways more important than, the conclusion itself. There are a lot of unsound or invalid arguments that have true conclusions. You want an argument to yield a true conclusion, yes, but only when it has proper premises and strong reasoning to take you to that conclusion. Whatever the take-home message of *Fahrenheit 9/11* was, however justified it may be otherwise, it wasn't well argued for.

Although, unlike Moore's movie, which claimed to be a documentary, *The Daily Show* doesn't claim to be a news show, it may fall prey to similar criticism. While I find myself agreeing with many of the points made on the show, the path taken to these points is often short, even slight. Rather than prolonged discussion or detailed analysis of a particular topic, *Daily Show* news is, and must be, molded into joke form. The journey to a conclusion is often too quick, the answers too pat. When journalism is done well, it gives people enough information to make up their own minds. But substandard media tends to be pandering, not informing, often to the lowest common denominator, as Jon Stewart himself self-effacingly admits. Where *The Daily Show* falls on the continuum between substandard news media and good hard news remains an open question.

Another potential problem with "fake" news is the threat of dilution, undermining the integrity and substance of hard news. There are two ways that *The Daily Show* may be contributing to such dilution of the mass media. The first is that "fake" news, along with blogs and other alternative forms of media, fragments the face of journalism, making it difficult to decide which news sources to trust, perhaps unduly undermining audience confidence in news agencies. As such, *The Daily Show* may simply be part of a greater problem. For example, the internet has transformed research in a variety of ways, often for the worse. At my fingertips are staggering numbers of resources, an overwhelming amount of information. However, while the quantity and immediacy of access to information has certainly increased, it's not clear that the quality has. Practically anyone can put practically anything online whenever they want. Similarly, some have argued that the ever-increasing quantity of academic journals has reduced the quality of many of these journals. Not all sources or resources are created equal. If *The Daily Show* increases this dilution by adding another alternative to hard news, so much the worse.

A second form of dilution may be a result of the show's influence on the media at large. Make no mistake, like *The Daily Show*, mainstream media is part of the profit-driven corporate world. The pattern of mixing entertainment with news, mastered if not created by *The Daily Show*, might and perhaps already has spilled over into hard news, although whether *The Daily Show* is really to blame for this is another matter. Some see the hiring of Katie Couric as lead anchor of the *CBS Nightly News* as a nod to style over substance. Critics have noted that Couric clearly isn't being cast as a Walter Cronkite or Edward R. Murrow, but rather as an entertaining, engaging personality that can attract more viewers. The more popular "fake" news programs become, the more likely traditional media will continue to follow suit, softening hard news with mere and mixed entertainment. To echo Fenton, the fiddling becomes louder.

The Virtues of "Fake" News

Not all the news on "fake" news is bad. The criticisms raised in the previous section focused on the negative but unintended effects of "fake" news. If we can criticize *The Daily Show* for such consequences, then we should also be able to praise it for any unintentional, not to mention intentional, benefits. Matthew Baum argues that "fake" news imparts knowledge of certain issues (especially foreign policy) to an otherwise inattentive portion of the population.[5] Backed by extensive empirical data, Baum argues that regular viewers of "fake" news programming are more aware of foreign affairs than those who don't watch such programming. Like sneaking vegetables onto a pizza, *The Daily Show* delivers the news in a way better suited to our ever-shrinking attention spans. From this perspective, the show isn't "converting" viewers from traditional media venues, but rather informing an untapped segment of the population which would be uninformed otherwise. If true, this seemingly would be a genuine benefit, even if unintentional. In some ways Baum's view has been confirmed by a 2004 National Annenberg Election Study which found that *Daily Show* viewers could correctly answer *more* questions about the Presidential candidates than viewers of national television news or newspaper readers.[6] Unlike Baum, the authors of the Annenberg study were quick to point out that *The Daily Show* itself might not be responsible for raising the knowledge level of its viewers. Perhaps the show is simply more appealing to those who *already* happen to be informed.

Let's assume at least that Baum is correct in that *The Daily Show* attracts and informs an otherwise inattentive and uninformed segment of the public. Is this enough? Not necessarily. More than the content itself, the quality of the news is important. If *The Daily Show* simply informs viewers enough to be able to identify certain people, places, and events, to know that certain things are going on in the world, it's not clear that the show provides a valuable public service.

It isn't enough to simply report the facts or certain interpretations of them; news should be balanced and comprehensive, informing the audience in a useful, robust way. If viewers simply parrot what they happen to hear on *The Daily Show*, how can they be expected to make informed decisions about public policy? As the saying goes, "a little knowledge can be dangerous." To show that *The Daily Show*'s imparting of minimal knowledge to an otherwise inattentive audience is really beneficial, something more is needed than what "fake" news usually provides. What's needed is for "fake" news to provide depth and insight, and not just make viewers aware, say, of where to locate Venezuela on a map. (This in itself would be no small feat, given Americans' poor knowledge of geography. But the news is supposed to do more than this.)

It would be truly beneficial to have *The Daily Show* impart a kind of knowledge that traditional news can't. Surprisingly, this might be the show's greatest virtue, and perhaps also a significant reason for its success. Being "unburdened by objectivity," *The Daily Show* is unfettered by the typical constraints of traditional news. It has more freedom to comment on, and to counteract, the spin that so often accompanies news stories of the day. Through sarcasm, cynicism, parody, and irony, the show can impart a kind of information inappropriate and unavailable to conventional news outlets. Furthermore, *The Daily Show* isn't afraid to offend political parties, business concerns, religious (and other) groups, or individual people. To this extent, the news presented by *The Daily Show* is often more honest in certain respects than hard news is. Jon Stewart has the freedom to say the things that most anchors can only say off camera.

It's important to note that political and social changes are often initiated by a variety of means. Three stories come to mind. One fateful night at a campaign rally in Iowa, Howard Dean, in a moment of hyper-excitation, screamed into the microphone. This embarrassing moment was caught by, and caught on in, the media, especially "fake" news. Shortly afterward, Dean's campaign ran out of steam – many think because of the "yawp heard round the world." It wouldn't be the first time that a Presidential candidate fell due to an unfortunate turn of events. During his bid for the presidency, Bob Dole fell off a stage during a campaign stop in Chico, California. Most commentary on the evening news concerned how many points Dole's fall would cost him in the polls, not whether such a cost would be in any way justified. What on earth could falling off a poorly constructed stage reveal about the quality of a Presidential candidate?

In contrast to these cases, consider the origin of the modern environmental movement in America. Rachel Carson's famous book, *Silent Spring*, brought to light the dangers of pesticides and their destructive effects on ecosystems. Consequently, DDT was banned and the environmental movement was born. Dean's scream and Dole's fall, although embarrassing, seem irrelevant to the qualifications of either as Presidential candidates. Carson, on the other hand, not a scientist but a nature writer, brought about significant change by raising relevant concerns in an innovative way. She didn't merely tell us that pesticides harm the environment, she made a strong case for why we should *care* about the environment.

The lesson here is that non-traditional news stories and non-traditional news outlets can be catalysts for political and social change, bad or good, the means relevant or irrelevant. As an unconventional outlet with a wide audience, *The Daily Show* is just the kind of vehicle that can, and often does, make a difference. Through amusing presentation of serious stories, *The Daily Show* humanizes them, imparting more than just facts, providing some perspective on them, reflecting and informing our concerns – exactly what good reporting ought to accomplish.

Teaching to the Top of the Class

To review, the potential hazards of "fake" news include deception and dilution, while the potential benefits include informing an otherwise inattentive audience and providing informed individuals with a different kind of information than that of traditional hard news. For these reasons, *The Daily Show* was both condemned and praised for being "unburdened by objectivity." Critically speaking, the lack of traditional journalistic standards doesn't require "fake" news to be especially thorough or impartial. Important but uninteresting news events may not be covered unless they can be made funny somehow. At the same time, the lack of journalistic standards allows "fake" news the liberty and the tools to inform the audience in ways unavailable to mainstream media. Can both of these be true? Yes. Although *The Daily Show* may be limited in the scope of events it covers, it often says insightful things about the stories it does cover. This is true not only of *The Daily Show*, but of a variety of "fake" news shows and other types of new media: blogs, quasi-documentaries, and cable news programming.

One important difference between *The Daily Show* and traditional media sources is that "fake" news typically doesn't gather the news, but rather comments on stories first reported by traditional news. As Aaron McKain puts it, traditional media acts as a "gatekeeper" for "fake" news.[7] So even when *The Daily Show* criticizes the traditional media they may provide a different perspective on news content, but they don't provide a true *alternative* to it. McKain illustrates this problem by pointing to a particular episode (April 18, 2004). That day, mainstream media was focused on Michael Jackson's indictment, not on more newsworthy events like the Presidential election or the war in Iraq. "All the while, this episode of *The Daily Show* similarly focuses all of its news segment on Jackson because, formally, it cannot do otherwise. It doth protest too much" (p. 418). Similarly, when Jon Stewart is confronted by mainstream media criticism, his tactic is to claim that *The Daily Show* is comedy, not a news show. This seems at best rather convenient and at worst perhaps a bit hypocritical, and reinforces the charge of deception aired earlier. Nonetheless, the show can still be a useful foil to mainstream media. Even if *The Daily Show* is a little hypocritical in criticizing the media without offering a real alternative, it doesn't follow that the show is unreliable, or that its content is false. If a smoker tells his children not to smoke because it's bad for their health, he may be a hypocrite, but it doesn't follow that smoking isn't bad for one's health. To argue that because someone is a hypocrite, what they say is false, is an informal fallacy called *ad hominem*. To reject the advice simply because the advisor doesn't follow it is called *tu quoque*.[8]

The final verdict on *The Daily Show* seems to depend on its overall effects. How, for instance, would the mainstream media deal with the diluting effect of "fake" news? Reacting to "fake" news, conventional news could "harden," focusing more on breaking real news stories and less on sensationalism. That would be good. An unfortunate reaction would be for conventional news to follow *The Daily*

Show's lead and become even more entertainment orientated. Mainstream media could drift more towards MTV than PBS, although certainly this might happen without "fake" news entering into the picture. Mainstream media could instead be unaffected by "fake" news programming. The thinking here would be exactly what was argued for by Baum, namely that people who watch *The Daily Show* aren't consumers of mainstream news to begin with, or they have their views reinforced rather than changed by "fake" news programming.

Assessing the overall impact of *The Daily Show* depends, then, not only on media reaction, but also on the net effect on the viewing audience. Here too there are several possibilities: good, bad, and indifferent. First, the show might provide, as said before, additional insight for already-informed individuals. Again, *The Daily Show*'s fresh perspective on stories attacks them from angles unavailable to mainstream media. Another possibility is that *The Daily Show* draws viewers who would typically go elsewhere, even though it's not a true alternative to conventional news and would, in that case, perform a public *disservice*. Finally, the show might minimally inform viewers who otherwise would be ignorant about newsworthy events. Although the information isn't up to hard news standards, it's perhaps better than nothing. Here, the benefit would be marginal, with some low-grade information getting through in *The Daily Show*'s less-than-comprehensive coverage.

Of course, these phenomena might well occur in combination. The empirical investigations discussed earlier seem to reflect both the good and the relatively indifferent scenarios. Baum's study suggests that "fake" news informs people who are previously uninformed, while the Annenberg study found that *Daily Show* viewers are well informed, thus supporting the "good" scenario. It's important to note that while Baum's study focused on "fake" news in general, including segments of shows such as *Late Night* with David Letterman and the *Tonight Show* with Jay Leno, the Annenberg study focused specifically on *Daily Show* viewers compared with control groups. Thus the Annenberg study seems to more accurately reflect the relationship between watching *The Daily Show* in particular and audience awareness, supporting the "good" scenario. Taken together, the studies suggest that we shouldn't treat all "fake" news the same way.

Again, due to *The Daily Show*'s emphasis on humor and constraints such as the gatekeeping function of mainstream media, it's not a true alternative to mainstream news. The position of *Daily Show* writers, producers, and performers is in a way analogous to the situation that often occurs for teachers, who frequently have to choose who to teach to. Do you try to get a majority of students in a class involved? Do you teach only to the bright kids? Or do you make sure that even the slower students make some progress? This choice is realized in the battle between classroom content and students' interests and attention spans. The more difficult the material, the drier and the less relevant it seems, the more students become uninterested. Some teachers believe it's not their job to be entertaining, seeing themselves as professionals employed to impart knowledge, and students as responsible to motivate themselves. Others think that a good teacher does both – grabbing students' attention, often in entertaining ways, as a means of imparting information.

A few questions can be teased apart here. Is there a necessary connection between entertainment value and informational content? Is there necessarily a trade-off when one teaches to the majority, or when one focuses instead on the gifted or the more challenged minority? What exactly is the educator's responsibility? It's not obvious that there are clear, much less known, answers to these questions. On a practical level, it's often a matter of the educator's choice and personal teaching style. Although the best teachers seem to strike an appropriate balance between information and entertainment, it's tough to say anything useful about how to find this balance.

Some might argue that because *The Daily Show* is entertainment, it's a paradigm case of teaching to the *bottom* of the class, or at the very best, to the middle of the class. However, this judgment would be hasty. If the Annenberg study is correct, it seems that the show's audience is composed of reasonably well-informed individuals, whether already informed or informed to some extent by the show. As I argued earlier, there's a unique and valuable kind of information that the show conveys to its audience. This means that *The Daily Show* actually teaches to the *top* of the class, imparting a higher form of information to those "in the know." Many of the jokes and skits on *The Daily Show* rely on sophisticated forms of humor and a sophisticated understanding of world events. There are, of course, gag skits which are simply entertaining. Perhaps *The Daily Show* teaches to the top of the class while providing entertainment for the rest.

Ultimately, it's each individual's responsibility to be informed. This only works when there are legitimate news sources available to choose from. It seems that as many legitimate media choices exist right now as existed before *The Daily Show* became a major cultural force, although sifting for these resources might be much harder now than it used to be. Who do you listen to? How can you distinguish between spin and fact? This is where *The Daily Show* can help. Rather than substituting for mainstream news, the show can *enhance* our understanding of mainstream media. To return to the teaching example, students must take an active role in their education. As the old saw goes, "you get out of it what you put into it." If you want to be an informed citizen, you must take some responsibility for seeking the truth in our increasingly foggy media landscape.

The Great Switcharoo

A solution to the problems described above is one which is wholly unlikely to occur. I believe that it would be best for *The Daily Show* and Rush Limbaugh to swap their respective audiences. Limbaugh fans should curl up on their couch and flip on Comedy Central every evening and *Daily Show* fans should listen to a portion of Limbaugh's radio broadcast (listening to the full three-hour broadcast would be beyond the pale). I advise this because both broadcasts are playing to the home crowd. *The Daily Show*, with its left slant, may just reinforce the views of its decidedly left-leaning audience, thus leaving them feeling superior and smug without really having engaged the other side on many issues. The same goes for "the right" and Rush. Listening to the opposition, instead of being continually congratulated for holding on to preexisting views, would press individuals to actively debate the arguments in question, even if it's within one's own mind. Too often in the great debates of our time (for example, abortion, euthanasia, the war in Iraq, and stem cell research, to name a few) each side envisions a particular characterization of the opposition. In reality, the positions on either side of these debates are often well argued. The debates exist because the issues in question are complex. To ignore this complexity is to become a characterization yourself.[9]

Notes

1 Tom Fenton, *Bad News: The Decline of Reporting, the Business of News, and the Danger to Us All* (New York: Harper Collins, 2005). Subsequent references will be made parenthetically in-text.
2 Lisa de Moraes, "Seriously: Kerry on Comedy Central," *Washington Post* (August 24, 2004), C1.
3 Thomas Goetz, "Reinventing Television," *Wired* 13 (09) (2005): www.wired.com/wired/archive/13.09/stewart.html.
4 Considering how, or if, we should hold them accountable would take us too far from the focus of this chapter.
5 Matthew Baum, "Sex, Lies, and War: How Soft News Brings Foreign Policy to the Inattentive Public," *American Political Science Review* 96 (1) (2002), pp. 91–109.
6 "National Annenberg Election Survey" (press release), *Annenberg Public Policy Center* (September 21, 2004).
7 Aaron McKain, "Not Necessarily Not the News: Gatekeeping, Remediation, and *The Daily Show*," *Journal of American Culture* 28 (4) (2005), pp. 415–30. Subsequent references will be made parenthetically in-text.
8 For more on fallacies, see Liam Dempsey, "*The Daily Show*'s Exposé of Political Rhetoric," chapter 10 in this volume.
9 Thanks to Jason Holt and Bill Irwin for helpful suggestions.

CORRESPONDENT'S REPORT:
JON STEWART (NOT MILL) AS PHILOSOPHER, SORT OF

SEGMENT 2

5

JON STEWART AND THE NEW PUBLIC INTELLECTUAL

TERRANCE MACMULLAN

No one ever went broke underestimating the intelligence of the American people.

H. L. Mencken

Buy my album Paris; *it's hot.*

Paris Hilton

This chapter is about why intellectuals, especially philosophers, should study and emulate Jon Stewart if they want to be relevant to the public. Stewart's increasing intellectual clout is surely a bit odd since he's not an academic, but rather host of the fake news program *The Daily Show* and the lead author of *America (The Book)*. Anyone who's watched his show or read the book knows that he's both very funny and exceptionally intelligent. However, a careful look at his work reveals more – a public intellectual who fosters critical thinking across an enormous audience and who defends democratic principles from erosion by partisan punditry and the government's apparent disregard for genuine debate.

Stewart is a living testament to the obvious yet easily forgotten truth that in order to be a public intellectual, the public first needs to hear you. He illustrates how a well-crafted presentation style is essential for cutting through the din of proliferating media voices to reach an audience. Stewart doesn't expect people to listen to him simply because he offers a cogent critique of the government and the media. Instead, he uses a wide range of tools, especially irony, to make his audience think while they laugh. Though he certainly sacrifices a lot of intellectual street-cred for doing things like putting on a Geraldo mustache or showing clips of a monkey washing a cat, such bits let him educate an audience many times larger than that of any conventional intellectual.

America desperately needs this sort of popular intellectual criticism, since we live in an age when honest debate is giving way to invective and spin. Indeed, Stewart's fake news is an example of the engaged political philosophy originally cultivated and still practiced by American philosophers. But before we look more closely at Stewart, let's consider why Americans hate intellectuals.

Why Americans Hate Intellectuals

We Americans distrust smart people. Decent Americans know, deep in their guts, that in order to be tricky, you must first be smart. For example, we love to trick our dogs with that fake throw-the-ball thing. We say to our pet, "You are *so* stupid, you stupid dog! I only *pretended* to throw the ball, but I really held it in my hand, stupid!" While we trick our dogs, our dogs never trick us. They might chew our shoes or poop on our couches, but those aren't tricks; those are just gross, stupid things our dogs do while we're out doing things that they couldn't even *comprehend*, like googling our names at work. Americans don't like smart people because we suspect they might trick us like we trick our dogs.

Being a philosopher, I will use a very old tool of philosophy, called a syllogism, to examine the sort of reasoning that leads many Americans to distrust smart people:

(1) All tricky people are smart.
(2) No tricky people should be trusted.
Therefore,
(3) No smart people should be trusted.

As a philosopher, I have to point out that this is actually an example of a fallacy, an error in reasoning. Even if all tricky people are both smart and untrustworthy, it doesn't follow that all smart people are tricky. Someone might be smart *and* honest (like Yoda or Jesus).

But there I go, trying to be smart! "*Ooh*, look at how smart I am," I'm saying. "I studied Aristotle, so I know what a syllogism is, while you went to business school for three years just to learn 'Buy low, sell high.'" Now you hate me. Worse yet, I'm a *long-winded* philosopher who's gone on for nearly a page without mentioning *The Daily Show* or Jon Stewart, which is what this chapter is about. Sorry.

In addition to making the mistake of thinking that all smart people are tricky, Americans also make the opposite mistake of thinking that dumb people are honest. This is likely why George W. Bush won the presidency – *twice*. Or he won once and tied once. Whatever. We think he must be honest since he's no elitist egghead from New England. We think this even though he was born a millionaire in New Haven, Connecticut and has two Ivy League degrees. Whatever. Eggheads poke fun at him for saying stuff like, "You teach a child to read, and he or her will be able to pass a literacy test," or "We need an energy bill that encourages consumption," and of course, "My answer is: Bring them on."[1] But eggheads don't seem to understand that these statements *prove* his honesty for many Americans! They show he's the opposite of Bill Clinton, who's very smart and therefore very tricky, so tricky, in fact, that he tried to trick us about simple words like "is" and "sex."

The fact that most Americans think that smart people are tricky and dumb people are honest makes it difficult to be a public intellectual in America. Luckily, Americans also enjoy a good laugh, which is why people who want to be public intellectuals need to learn from Jon Stewart.

You Know It's Hard Out There for a Public Intellectual

It's hard to say exactly what a public intellectual is. Perhaps they're a bit like what Justice Potter Stewart said about pornography: you can't define them, but you know them when you see them. Prominent legal scholar Richard Posner wrote a book titled *Public Intellectuals: A Study of Decline*, which gives a pretty straightforward analysis of how the once proud office of public intellectual has degenerated into schlocky punditry. Posner describes a public intellectual as "a person who, drawing on his intellectual resources, addresses a broad though educated public on issues with political or ideological dimensions."[2] Despite his protestations to the contrary, this description fits Jon Stewart to a T.

As a wannabe intellectual myself, I've read many books, some of which indicate that Americans didn't always hate intellectuals. Apparently at one time we actually respected them for dedicating their lives to the cultivation of an informed democratic citizenry.[3] Americans used to listen to them, and even weirder, *read* their work! Another big difference between then and now is that intellectuals used to speak to the entire public, instead of just to each other, which is what they mostly do these days. Public intellectuals of yore – people like Ralph Waldo Emerson (1803–82), William James (1842–1910), Jane Addams (1860–1935), John Dewey (1859–1952), and W. E. B. Du Bois (1868–1963) – knew how to connect with a very broad audience without dumbing down their message.

Furthermore, public intellectuals played a special role in the unique philosophical tradition of the United States. Cornel West – public intellectual, superstar academic, rapper, bit player in the *Matrix* sequels, and all around cool guy – argued in his classic book, *The American Evasion of Philosophy*, that the only school of philosophy indigenous to the United States – pragmatism – distinguishes itself from other philosophical traditions by urging philosophers to be less academic and more publicly engaged.

> [Pragmatism is] a form of cultural criticism in which the meaning of America is put forward by intellectuals in response to distinct social and cultural crises. In this sense, American pragmatism is less a philosophical tradition putting forward solutions to perennial problems in the Western philosophical conversation initiated by Plato and more a continuous cultural commentary or set of interpretations that attempt to explain America to itself at a particular historical moment.[4]

This ideal of the articulate thinker whose voice encourages debate and fosters democracy is still cherished by many philosophers who think that philosophy should matter to all people.[5] They try to make philosophy relevant by recovering it in each new age. As John

Dewey, the most renowned American public philosopher, wrote: "Philosophy recovers itself when it ceases to be a device for dealing with the problems of philosophers and becomes a method, cultivated by philosophers, for dealing with the problems of men."[6]

Unfortunately, this connection between philosophy and the public has largely broken down. One reason for this is that we have shorter attention spans than we used to.[7] Whether we rank them by media mentions (which according to Posner makes Henry Kissinger, Patrick Moynihan, and George Will the top three [p. 209]) or scholarly citations (which yields Michel Foucault, Pierre Bourdieu, and Jürgen Habermas as the top three [p. 212]), these public intellectuals, sadly, have only a tiny fraction of the influence wielded by people like Ann Coulter and Oprah.

Another reason for this phenomenon is that most intellectuals simply don't bother trying to engage the public. This started in large part with the radicalization of American universities in the 1960s, which led many intellectuals to write off non-intellectuals as dupes, and many non-intellectuals to dismiss academia as a hotbed of leftist propaganda. This disdain for university intellectuals was perhaps best expressed by the lion of American conservatism, William F. Buckley, when he famously said in the 1960s, "I would rather be governed by the first 2,000 names in the Boston phone book than by the faculty of Harvard University."[8] The isolation of intellectuals became more extreme when they started emulating European theorists, such as Jacques Derrida (1930–2004), who used extremely dense and jargon-laden language. Perhaps academics speak mostly to each other because they think other academics are the only people who can keep up with them intellectually. I suspect, however, that this isolation is largely self-imposed, for the sake of convenience, since it's much easier and more comfortable to speak to someone who shares your assumptions and uses your terms than someone who might challenge your assumptions in unexpected ways or ask you to explain what you mean. Richard Rorty, perhaps the most famous living American philosopher, understands this well. Left-leaning thinkers in the humanities are derided because the left "is extraordinarily self-obsessed and ingrown."[9]

The sad result of these two factors – the public's short attention span and intellectuals' unwillingness to address a public audience – is that the place of the public intellectual has become occupied by media pundits who are usually neither smart nor committed to the common good. I imagine most intellectuals would be horrified at the idea of calling people like Paul Begala or Rush Limbaugh intellectuals, since such figures play on the fears and desires of their audiences, substituting rhetoric for reason and corroding genuine debate. While intellectuals bemoan this state of affairs, they often fail to accept their share of responsibility for it. Because of the disdain most intellectuals have for engaging the public, they've left a cultural void that's easily filled by pseudo-intellectuals eager to command large audiences. If intellectuals are ever going to connect with the public again and improve the quality of crucial public debates, they need to step down from the Ivory Tower and step up to communicating with the general public.

Stewart's Ironic Blah, Blah, Blah

The example of Jon Stewart offers valuable insights for how we might make intellectuals more public and the public more intellectual. Stewart's brand of public intellectual work involves extensive use of irony, a very hot topic nowadays.[10] Much ink has been spilt about this word, but irony in this sense simply occurs when there is a gap between what is *literally said* and what is *actually meant* or understood. Just about every aspect of *The Daily Show* mines irony for laughter: the graphics that look just like the ones from real news shows, the headline segments (like the story on Hezbollah's reconstruction efforts in Lebanon, accompanied by the title "Hez Dispensers"), and the "serious" field reports from "senior correspondents."

The Daily Show isn't *just* funny and ironic, however. If that were all it had to offer, *The Daily Show* wouldn't be an Emmy and Peabody winning hit with 1.6 million viewers, and Stewart wouldn't have been named the fifth most powerful person in television news.[11] *The Daily Show* satisfies a desire among Americans (who might not be that daft after all) for critical commentary. The greatest irony of the show is that even though Stewart isn't a news anchor and his writers couldn't get jobs on *Family Guy*, they're still able to exceed, in many respects and for a fraction of the cost, the quality of news shows produced by real journalists. As fake reporters, the staff of

The Daily Show is able to one-up the real journalists by speaking the truth about our society, government, and media that conventional news usually either can't or won't. The program actually fits West's definition of pragmatist philosophy, by "explaining America to itself at a particular historical moment" (p. 5). Along with making us laugh, I think the *Daily Show* writers and producers are trying to explain why we should be skeptical about our government, which often seems dangerously disconnected from reality.

Many Americans (and most Canadians) have suspected for some time that the Bush administration has raised the bar on lying, spin, and bullshit.[12] One particularly chilling indicator of its tenuous relationship to reality was the now famous story in the *New York Times* by Ron Suskind called "Without a Doubt," where he presents a portrait of the last superpower nominally headed by a man with no intellectual curiosity and who steers the ship of state by the compass of instinct and faith. Suskind describes the most disturbing element of this faith-based presidency: "open dialogue, based on facts, is not seen as something of inherent value."[13] Even more disturbing was the conversation with an unnamed senior advisor who chided Suskind for failing to understand how the world now works:

> The aide said that guys like me were "in what we call the reality-based community," which he defined as people who "believe that solutions emerge from your judicious study of discernible reality." I nodded and murmured something about enlightenment principles and empiricism. He cut me off. "That's not the way the world really works anymore," he continued. "We're an empire now, and when we act, we create our own reality. And while you're studying that reality . . . we'll act again, creating other new realities, which you can study too, and that's how things will sort out." (p. 51)

This really scared a lot of people across the political spectrum. People who base their beliefs on experiences of discernible reality and open debate used to be called "sane," while people who create private realities in this way were deemed "crazy." Now we're just two different "communities," like cat-owners and dog-owners. What's even scarier is that after this piece Bush *won re-election*! There was clear evidence that world-changing decisions were being made by someone who didn't know the difference between Switzerland and Sweden, while television news outlets were more interested in John

Kerry's Vietnam War record. It was only in August 2005, when the grotesque devastation of hurricane Katrina served as the backdrop for Bush's "Heckuva job!" congratulation of FEMA Director Mike Brown, that the mainstream media finally caught on that the emperor had no clothes (or emergency preparedness plans).

The Daily Show explains our political landscape to us by poking fun at both the government's casual disregard for facts and the media's apparent willingness to play along. Take, for example, this exchange from July 12, 2005 between Stewart and his "Senior Journalistologist" Stephen Colbert (back when he was just Stephen Colbert, "*Daily Show* stooge," and not "Stephen Colbert of *The Colbert Report*") about reports that Karl Rove, despite his denials, was involved in leaking former CIA agent Valerie Plame's identity:

> *Stewart:* What are the ramifications of this now that Rove's involvement is known?
>
> *Colbert:* Well, Bush has a real problem on his hands here, Jon. What honor should he bestow on Karl Rove?
>
> *Stewart:* Did you say "what honor"?
>
> *Colbert:* Yes Jon. George "Slam-dunk" Tenent got us into Iraq on mistaken intel. He got the Medal of Freedom. Condi Rice sees a memo warning "Bin-Laden Determined to Strike the United States," ignores it. Boom! Gets kicked upstairs to the Secretary of State. For a bungle this bad, I think we might be looking at Chief Justice Karl Rove.

This exchange is a perfect example of pragmatist philosophy *à la* Cornel West, showing Americans that their government's disregard for reality is a serious political crisis. By lampooning the way government tries to spin every mistake as a triumph, *The Daily Show* spurs the sort of debate and critical thinking that are central to healthy democracies and yet are under assault in our "either you're with us or you're with the terrorists" political climate.

We see another instance of critical intellectual work dolled up as yuks in the story "Forced Perspective" (August 22, 2006), where Jon Stewart asks Aasif Mandvi about claims by President Bush and Secretary of State Rice that Iraq isn't in the midst of a brutal civil war, but is merely experiencing a "moment of opportunity" or undergoing "the birth pangs of a new Middle East." Mandvi, pretending to report from Iraq, assures Stewart that he, like everyone in the Middle East, shares this optimistic view, saying, "Every day the cafés and outdoor markets of the Middle East explode with anticipation." When Stewart cites the angry protests against America in Iraq, Mandvi reassures him:

> Well, what did you expect? I mean, as Secretary Rice said, we are going through some birth-pangs here. And you know how people tend to scream and say things they don't mean when they are in labor. Nonsense like, "How could you do this to me?" and "Death to America!" And then, the baby arrives, and all is forgiven. What we are going through is exactly like that. I mean, we all understand it in exactly those terms.

At that moment, we hear an explosion, and Mandvi turns around but is otherwise unfazed. Stewart asks, "Are you OK?" and Mandvi breezily waves his hand saying, "Oh yeah, I'm fine. That was just an improvised explosive opportunity. I believe it was filled with the flying shards of a better tomorrow." At the end of the segment, Stewart comments on Mandvi's optimism, calling it "an incredible way to look at a terrible situation." Mandvi looks quizzically at Stewart saying, "Well, I'm sure it's no different from the way your nation views the events of 9/11 – tough day, great opportunity." This sort of irony forces the viewer to reflect on the disparity between how our government asks us – rightly – to remember and mourn the deaths of innocents on 9/11 even as it criticizes – wrongly – the media for even mentioning the far greater number of dead innocents in Iraq.

Many peddlers of the truth-like-substance Stephen Colbert dubbed "truthiness" fear Stewart's ability to use irony to call us on our stupidity and the administration on its lies.[14] They often don't know what to do with him, since his use of irony is very funny (which makes people watch the show) but also smart (which makes people think and therefore not watch Fox News or MSNBC). Sometimes they make very sad and unfunny attempts to make him look bad, as when Geraldo toadied up to Bill O'Reilly by accusing Stewart and Colbert of "existing in a small, little place, where they account for nothing." Yes, that's right: *Geraldo* actually called *someone else* meaningless. Another example is when Joe Scarborough complained in his blog "Regular Joe" about the popularity of Stewart's show, saying: "It is all the rage with the kids, after all. How they get their news. The next generation of information. An ironic look at blah, blah, blah."[15] You see, since he's a self proclaimed "Regular Joe" he has to try to make fun of the word "ironic" by going "blah, blah, blah." Remember that Americans generally hate the smart and trust the dumb? He's trying to make you hate Stewart by calling him smart. Get it? Unfortunately, he shows only that he envies Stewart's popularity, and maybe doesn't know what "ironic" means.

The Master Debater

Stewart's greatest quality as a public intellectual is his commitment to democracy as an evolving, experimental process that needs debate in order to survive and thrive. Note Thomas Jefferson's fake foreword to *America (The Book)*, where Stewart lampoons American idolatry of the Constitution:

> I was . . . looking forward to this opportunity to dispel some of the mythology surrounding myself and my fellow Founders – particularly the myth of our infallibility. You moderns have a tendency to worship at the altar of the Fathers. "The First Amendment is sacrosanct!" "We will die to protect the Second Amendment!" So dramatic. Do you know why we called them amendments? Because they *amend*! They fix mistakes or correct omissions and they themselves can be changed. If we had meant for the Constitution to be written in stone we would have written it in stone. Most things were written in stone back then, you know. I'm not trying to be difficult but it's bothersome when you blame your own inflexibility and extremism on us.[16]

Behind all the jokes, both witty and sophomoric, is an unalloyed faith in the power of the American political project to improve people's lives. Stewart's critique in clown-paint reflects John Dewey's statement that democracy should be understood as "a way of life . . . controlled by personal faith in personal day-by-day working together with others."[17] *The Daily Show* and *America (The Book)* offer us alternatives to the invective that threatens to overwhelm legitimate debate in America.

Stewart is most effective as a public intellectual when he invites conservatives onto his show, like former Senator Rick Santorum and

Bernard Goldblum, whom he engages in honest and pointed debate. This inclusiveness is an antidote to the divisiveness spewed by those who've hijacked American conservatism and liberalism alike. Stewart's willingness to engage in vigorous but amicable debate is perhaps his greatest contribution to our democracy, renewing our faith in the power of dialogue to bridge even the widest of political divides.

Notes

1 www.politicalhumor.about.com/library/blbushdumbquotes2.htm, accessed 08/28/06.
2 Richard Posner, *Public Intellectuals: A Study of Decline* (Cambridge, MA: Harvard University Press, 2003), p. 170. Subsequent references will be made parenthetically in-text.
3 For a good history of intellectuals in America, see Russel Jacoby, *The Last Intellectuals: American Culture of Academe* (New York: Basic Books, 1987) and the classic by Richard Hofstadter, *Anti-Intellectualism in American Life* (New York: Knopf, 1963).
4 Cornel West, *The American Evasion of Philosophy* (Madison: University of Wisconsin Press, 1989), p. 5. Subsequent reference will be made parenthetically in-text.
5 One group that I think is doing great work toward this end is the Society for the Advancement of American Philosophy.
6 John Dewey, "The Need for a Recovery of Philosophy" [1917], in *The Middle Works*, Vol. 10, ed. Jo Ann Boydston (Carbondale: Southern Illinois University Press, 1980), p. 46.
7 Oh! Remember we're talking about Jon Stewart and *The Daily Show*, and how he's the new public intellectual?
8 www.en.wikipedia.org/wiki/William_F._Buckley,_Jr.#Quotations, accessed August 30, 2006.
9 Richard Rorty, "The Humanistic Intellectual," in *Philosophy and Social Hope* (New York: Penguin, 1999), p. 129.
10 For more on irony, see Kevin Decker, "Stephen Colbert, Irony, and Speaking Truthiness to Power," chapter 19 in this volume.
11 Michele Greppi, "10 Most Powerful People in TV News," *Television Week* 25 (17) (2006), p. 59.
12 For a great study of the Bush administration's Orwellian manipulation of language, see Henry Giroux, "The Politics of Lying," *Tikkun* 21 (2) (2006), pp. 36–40.

13 Ron Suskind, "Without a Doubt," *New York Times: Sunday Magazine* (October 17, 2004), p. 47.

14 "Truthiness" is a word coined by Colbert on October 17, 2005 in the premiere episode of *The Colbert Report*. The term refers to "what you know with your heart," instead of "what you think with your head."

15 Joe Scarborough, "Only Jon Stewart can have it both ways," *Regular Joe* (August 22, 2006), www.msnbc.com/id/6330851, accessed August 28, 2006.

16 Jon Stewart, Ben Karlin, and David Javerbaum, *America (The Book): A Citizen's Guide to Democracy Inaction* (New York: Warner Books, 2004), p. x.

17 John Dewey, "Creative Democracy – The Task Before Us," in *The Later Works*, Vol. 14, ed. Jo Ann Boydston (Carbondale: Southern Illinois University Press, 1988), p. 228.

6

STEWART AND SOCRATES:
SPEAKING TRUTH TO POWER

JUDITH BARAD

Consider this description of a society:

- People pride themselves on their democratic form of government and constitution.
- There are great differences in wealth and social status; many of the poor join the military.
- People are very materialistic and concerned with "getting ahead."
- The arts flourish and people love entertainment.
- There are two political factions, often at odds with each other.
- It's a great manufacturing power, supplying other nations with industrial products.
- It's a great military power, which belongs to a coalition of other nations.
- There is a problem with immigrants crossing its borders.
- The political climate is tense.
- Although in principle religion and state are separate, in practice they overlap.

Now the question: Which society is being described? Twenty-first-century America? Or fifth-century BCE Athens? Without any further details, the description could apply just as well to either. And the two societies have one other thing in common. They both have controversial reformers who use similar methods to urge people to *think*. However unlikely it may sound, John Stewart plays the role of reformer in America today much as Socrates did in Athens long ago.

Here Come the Sophists!

As in America, most Athenian citizens received a basic education that made them literate and gave them simple skills. But if Athenian families wanted their children to be successful, more was needed. This concern with success led to the birth of sophism in the second half of the fifth century BCE. Traveling from one city to another and charging *very* hefty fees, the sophists claimed that their students would become admired, competent, and, above all, rich. For those able to afford their teaching, the sophists emphasized rhetoric, the art of persuasion. More specifically, they taught their students to persuasively argue both sides of any case. And from teaching people how to make the weaker argument appear to be the stronger, it was just a short step to questioning whether there even *is* such a thing as true or false, right or wrong. Unfortunately, the sophists didn't care *what* their students were trying to persuade others to do or believe. And so, in effect, the sophists helped people to promote their own interests, even if it meant sacrificing the interests of their community.

Although the roots of sophistry lie in ancient Greece, the practice has never gone out of style. After all, isn't the primary goal of advertisers and salespeople to persuade a consumer to purchase a product regardless of whether the product is good for her or not? Don't public relations specialists manipulate the uninformed public? Don't defense attorneys try to persuade juries that their guilty-as-hell clients are innocent? Thankfully, *The Daily Show* commonly takes on such sophists in its satirical news segments. It's surprisingly easy to do. A reporter simply asks audacious questions of people so blinded by their pursuits that they don't even realize they're being mocked.

To Scoff at the Sophist in Office

Stewart's primary objects of derision, though, are sophists in politics and the mainstream media. Political sophists do their best to persuade their constituencies to vote for them, but their deceptive rhetoric wouldn't be so successful without the media sophists. So Stewart regularly attacks media sophists for their complicity with political sophists by delivering verbal jabs at both. During the 2004 Presidential election, Stewart asked "reporter" Ed Helms if he knew what was going to happen at the Presidential debates the next day. Helms read him the report he was going to file. Stewart responded that Helms had written the report as if the debates had already happened. Helms admitted that he wrote the report the day before the event. Incredulous, Stewart asked him, "You write your stories in advance and then put it in the past tense?" Admitting "all the reporters do that," Helms explained: "we write stories in advance based on conventional wisdom and then whatever happens, we make it fit that storyline." When Stewart asked why they do that, Helms answered, "We're lazy? Lazy thinkers?"

Opposing the way the traditional media has stayed clear of confrontations with the Bush administration since 9/11, *The Daily Show* is unrelenting in its ironic assaults, highlighting how media sophists sacrifice the investigation of newsworthy stories for ratings and access to the White House. Stewart called *Crossfire* hosts Tucker Carlson and Paul Begala "partisan hacks" and berated them for not raising the level of talk on their show beyond sloganeering. At a time when the mainstream media was focused on Vice President Cheney's daughter, Stewart continued to hammer the media for its coverage of the Presidential debates. He said: "The things is, we need your help. Right now, you're helping the politicians and the corporations and we're left out there to mow our lawns." In contrast to such self-interested agendas, Stewart uses the following criteria in deciding to put something on *The Daily Show*: "Is that funny? Is that smart? Is that good?"[1] As a matter of moral principle, Stewart has said that there are some guests he simply wouldn't invite on his show, such as Mike Tyson and Bob Novak.[2] Indeed, Stewart has called Novak, who revealed the identity of a CIA agent, a "douchebag for liberty" and awarded him, in absentia, the "Congressional Medal of Douchebaggery."

The moral question is something sophists simply don't consider. Instead of asking whether an action is right or just, the sophist asks, "Will reporting this story or supporting this policy advance my career?"

Media sophists, like Ann Coulter, encourage conformity with the tacit message that what most people think is how everyone should think. When people buy this message, the sophists simply have to announce what most people think. The unfortunate outcome is that the general public become disinclined to think for themselves. Instead, they uncritically accept the ideas or values of a larger group, such as their church or their political party or Fox News host Bill O'Reilly's audience. Blindly conforming to majority opinion, they don't consider that most people once believed that the Earth is flat, that slavery is natural, and that women belong in the home.

Men with a Mission

Newsweek's description of Stewart as offering "fearless social satire" while "battling pomposity and misinformation"[3] fits Socrates like a glove. And just as Stewart is now being taken seriously as a politico-societal force, Socrates was a politico-societal force in his day.

In ancient Athens, people wanted the same thing most contemporary Americans want – pleasure and material success. These desires, however, were in conflict with their traditional moral and religious values, including patriotism and regular temple (church) attendance. The Athenian government, desiring stability and cohesiveness, saw these values as a means to their end. Just as in twenty-first-century America, the government of ancient Athens tried to preserve traditional religious beliefs and values as much as possible. If anyone questioned these beliefs and values, the government interpreted this as an attack on the state.

Enter Socrates, who encouraged people to raise questions about accepted customs in ethical and religious behavior. The philosopher who asked "Is something pious because the gods love it? Or do the Gods love it because it is pious?" would certainly applaud "This Week in God." But in societies that are so absorbed with getting ahead and so preoccupied with being entertained, *how* can anyone motivate others to raise questions about traditional values and beliefs? It ain't easy, so our boys better have a method for their mission.

Socrates' mission was "to persuade each one of you not to think more of practical advantages than of his mental and moral wellbeing, or . . . to think more of advantage than of wellbeing in the case of the state or of anything else."[4] He was sure that for individuals wisdom and virtue are far more important than money and power.

So too the good of the state lies first and foremost in its wisdom and virtue rather than in profit or political might.

Like Socrates, Stewart knows that the ethical and political well-being of any society depends of the ethical and political wellbeing of each of its citizens.[5] But people sometimes need prompting to put important issues in the right perspective. As Stewart put it, describing The Daily Show in Newsweek, "This is a show grounded in passion, not cynicism" (p. 71). People sometimes experience the passion of Socrates and Stewart as unsettling, since their questions raise serious doubts about some aspects of socially accepted values.

Ignorance often gets in the way of pursuing the truth. To fulfill their mission, Socrates and Stewart are driven to tear off the masks of arrogance and self-deception, which allow ignorance to masquerade as wisdom and knowledge. For instance, to show that anyone can be called an "expert," correspondents on The Daily Show are always labeled as "Senior Correspondents" in whatever area they are reporting on, usually for the first time. The show has featured, among others, a "Senior Futlbologist," a "Senior Terrorist Analyst," and a "Chief International Finance Correspondent."

The process of unmasking "experts" and exposing ignorance has had an effect on The Daily Show's audience. According to one study, viewers of The Daily Show had a more accurate understanding of the facts behind the 2004 Presidential election than people who primarily read newspapers and watched major network newscasts.[6] Socrates and Stewart know that ignorance isn't dependent on one's formal education or status in society. To discover the truth all that's needed is the spirit of inquiry and an open mind.

Although viewing others as ignorant may seem arrogant, neither Socrates nor Stewart are elitist. Knowing they're fallible, they regularly confess their own ignorance. Frequently, they insist that they're exploring territory that's as uncharted to them as it is to the person each man talks with. This insistence is part of their method.

A Method to Their Madness

Socrates' method of fulfilling his mission was so unique it became known as the "Socratic method." The method, which is now one of the classic question-and-answer techniques of education, is distinctive in its reliance on one-on-one encounters. Socrates was convinced that the only way to reach people is to treat them as individuals capable of independent judgment.

Here's how his method works. First, Socrates approaches someone who claims to know something about a subject like justice, courage, or politics. He flatters the guy and thanks his lucky stars that he's found someone who really knows something that he, Socrates, has been searching for all his life. He then humbly entreats the "expert" to impart his wisdom. The man, at this point, is confident he knows the answer and condescendingly "teaches" Socrates, who seems very impressed by the response. I imagine Socrates may even have made one of those awestruck faces Jon Stewart is famous for.

At this point, the expert gets a swelled head. Yet, in the expert's self-confident response, Socrates finds one or two little difficulties, which provide material for another question, a deeper one. The man offers what he thinks is a quick fix, by providing some conventional "wisdom." After Socrates asks him to draw out the consequences of the quick fix, the man realizes that he's trapped in a position he can't reasonably hold, often a contradiction. Peeling away layer after layer of shallow beliefs, Socrates exposes not only the bruised fruit of false opinions, but also the ripe core of truth.

The method Stewart and *The Daily Show*'s correspondents use in questioning their guests has an uncanny resemblance to Socrates' method. Approaching someone who claims to know a lot about a subject, the correspondents proceed to flatter them. Then they entreat the expert to impart his or her wisdom. At first, the "expert" confidently proceeds to produce his case until the correspondent picks out one or two minor problems, which provide material for another question, a deeper one. The expert offers what he thinks is a quick fix, by providing some conventional "wisdom." After the correspondents ask him to draw out the consequences of the quick fix, the person realizes that he's trapped in a position he can't reasonably hold, often a contradiction. In these interactions, the correspondents follow the practice of Socrates, who, peeling away layer after layer of shallow beliefs, exposes not only the bruised fruit of false opinion, but the ripe core of truth.

Like Socrates, Stewart usually refrains from lengthy speeches that might simply overwhelm his listeners. He shares Socrates' appreciation of one-on-one encounters, and he resembles the ancient sage when he pretends to be confused and requests explanations that underscore how ridiculous someone else sounds. Neither Socrates nor Stewart merely presents and dissects ideas, remaining detached from the focus of the discussion. Instead, they enter the stage and become the actors and the focal points of action, the watching audience and the watched performers. Neither wants people to agree with them for reasons they don't understand. So they ask questions. While asking these questions, Stewart, like Socrates, actually listens to the people he's conversing with, attempting to understand what they're saying.

Since many of us prefer to hear our own voices, we don't often really listen to other people. We often see disagreement as a competition where the object is simply to win. With this attitude, so very characteristic of sophists, people become angry with one another and raise their voices to drown out or continually interrupt other people. (For an abundance of examples, just tune in to *The O'Reilly Factor* any night of the week.) Listening indicates that you're secure enough in your position that you're not threatened by someone's differing viewpoint. When you calmly listen to someone else, you drop your defenses and it's more likely the other person will respond in kind.

The Audience: Questioning Youths or Stoned Slackers?

By exposing the ignorance of politicians and other know-it-alls, Socrates taught people to look at their cultural traditions and laws in a new light. His unsparing criticisms of the politicians' incompetence and narrow-minded patriotism fostered a critical attitude towards the government and its laws among the younger generation. Socrates showed them that people may have high positions and power, yet at the same time be irrational and deeply confused. He revealed politicians' irrationality and confusion by continually cross-examining them with questions they should have been able to answer, such as: Since you're a leader of the state, where exactly are you leading the state? Since you're in a position of authority, what are your credentials for that authority? What does justice really mean?

Although Socrates turned the conversation to intellectual subjects, he didn't put on intellectual airs. Like Stewart, he was a man of the people and spoke only the vernacular of his friends. Like Stewart, he saw himself as short, amusing, and unimportant. A group of appreciative young men began to follow Socrates. When they saw that the politicians couldn't support their answers to Socrates' questions, not only were the young men entertained, they learned a valuable lesson: don't simply assume those in authority possess knowledge and wisdom. They adored Socrates for his efforts, the ultimate in questioning authority. And having witnessed Socrates' cross-examinations, his followers started questioning authority themselves.

Like Socrates, Stewart is aware that democracy is only effective to the extent that the public are well informed about issues and can think independently and critically about those issues. Stewart, too, has a large group of young people who follow him on a regular basis. The median age of *The Daily Show* audience is 33, which is relatively young compared to that of traditional news shows. Most viewers (73 percent) fall in the 18–49 age range, a demographic that sophists in the advertising industry and the political arena are eager to cultivate.

The Daily Show is particularly popular among college students. As Katherine Bullen, a University of Iowa sophomore, explained in *Newsweek*, "He's one of the few 'adults' that mocks the things we mock, and he can do that without talking down to us" (p. 71). More specifically, the 2004 Class Day speaker of Yale University said that students don't have "a spectrum of critical analyses represented in the mainstream media" and this is why *The Daily Show* has substituted for the traditional news. "Stewart's combination of irony and satire, of facts and jokes, his willingness to lay bare the process of 'news' fabrication, has endeared his brand of humor to so many of us, and won him the kind of critical acclaim that indicates just how influential his show is."[7]

Not everyone, however, sees the attraction of youth to *The Daily Show* as something positive. Bill O'Reilly, for instance, disparages Stewart's hold on what he calls the "stoned slacker" crowd,[8] claiming that "dopey college kids" like Bullen must be "stoned" to watch *The Daily Show*.[9] Had he been there, O'Reilly might well have made similar comments about the youthful crowd that gathered around Socrates. But of course this crowd would have included one very famous slacker – Plato! Time will tell who will emerge from Stewart's crowd.

The Irony of It All

As the Yale student observed, the way that Stewart accomplishes his mission relies heavily on ironic humor. Socrates was also well known for using ironic humor to achieve his mission. "Socratic irony," as it came to be called, involves pretending to be ignorant, to know less than you really know. Not simply a verbal disclaimer of knowledge, Socratic irony involves a way of behaving. As Socrates' reputation grew, it became difficult to convince other people to converse with him. So he behaved as a humble inquirer claiming to need instruction from an expert. Stewart, of course, adopts a similar pose on *The Daily Show*.

Disarming as the unassuming façade of both men may be, lurking beneath it lies a sharp-witted intelligence, which quickly perceives the paradoxical and the ironic. But what is irony? Irony can take many shapes, such as understating or overstating the point. Stewart used understatement to emphasize the audacity of then-Defense Secretary Rumsfeld's comment (issued during the Senate hearings on the torture of Iraqi prisoners at Abu Ghraib), "They are human beings." Stewart quipped, "It may not seem like much, but for this administration it's a huge policy shift." Irony can also take the form of saying the exact opposite of what you mean or using an ambiguous expression deliberately. Generally, irony is a method of communication in which someone intends to get across one meaning while saying something that seems to have another meaning. The real meaning, which isn't obvious, is detected by certain hints, such as the context in which the words are used or the tone of voice expressing the words. Think, for instance, of billing *The Daily Show* as "The most mistrusted name in fake news!"

Another kind of irony comes from the background knowledge shared by the ironist and the audience who appreciates the real meaning of the words. When irony depends on the mutual background, it's like a private joke between the ironist and the audience to whom the real meaning is directed. For instance, *Newsweek* reported that prior to taping one episode, Stewart announced excitedly, "We've got us a Democratic general!" Then he quipped, "That's like a gay black Republican. It's a rare beast" (p. 71). Understanding the private joke, the audience cracked up.

Irony can also be similar to a riddle intended to amuse people who are sufficiently perceptive to recognize the difference between the real meaning and the sham one. Frequently, Stewart shows a brief clip of President Bush speaking and then, without a word, looks quite confused, dumbfounded, or horrified. The camera just shows his facial expressions and mute astonishment, which says all that needs to be said. Of course, even if the irony is obvious, some people are such idiots they won't "get it." Yet if they do get it, the irony's effect can be thought-provoking. In suddenly perceiving the irony of a statement, a person can achieve a depth of insight into its truth that can't usually be matched by a more explicit, straightforward method.

"Monkey" Idol or Thoughtful Partisan Satirist?

Stewart's use of irony has raised some serious questions. Ken Tucker, writing in *New York Magazine*, asks, "Is [Stewart] the Emmy-winning 'monkey,' idol to millions of young couch-skeptics, or the thoughtful partisan satirist who'd like to be a player in the national discourse?"[10] Tucker suggests that if Stewart were *really* a political critic, he would concentrate on getting results and downplay his use of irony. Is there a tension between Stewart the entertainer, who aims at provoking laughter, and Stewart the political critic, who has some responsibility to the truth?

The question Tucker raises was highlighted when Stewart appeared on CNN's *Crossfire* in October 2004. Stewart derided the two hosts for their dishonest "partisan hackery," rather than holding themselves to journalistic integrity. Tucker Carlson, a Republican commentator, said, "I thought you were going to be funny. Come on. Be funny." Stewart fired back, "No. No. I'm not going to be your monkey." Earnestly stating his purpose in attending the show, Stewart said, "I'm here to confront you, because we need help from the media and they're hurting us." Stewart was suggesting that the media is hurting Americans by keeping them ignorant of important information. So, he charged, although *The Daily Show* bills itself as doing fake news, it was actually *Crossfire* that was hurting the public through its incessant spin and fake debates. As a result of this confrontation, Stewart received wide public support, and in January 2005, *Crossfire* was taken off the air.

Given all the commonalities between Stewart and Socrates, we could also ask the same question of his ancient Greek counterpart: "Hey, Socrates! Are you merely trying to entertain people or are you a serious critic who is trying to bring out the truth?" Now the fact that Socrates aims at truth is hardly to be doubted. Looking back at Socrates, we get a broader perspective on him than we'd be able to get if he were around today. It's easy to see that he used irony as a *means* to getting at the truth. Can we say the same thing about Stewart? We can, since not only are laughter and truth compatible, the one can be a particularly useful means of arriving at the other. Messages about serious, important issues are more digestible if delivered with a smile, not a scream.

The ironic element in Socrates' and Stewart's method should not be denigrated or underestimated, for it's what helps both of them to attract such large audiences. By having more than a superficial meaning, irony keeps listeners on their toes. For Socrates and Stewart, the most important point of communicating with others is to engage them in an issue. Irony helps to keep their audiences alert, actively listening, and critically thinking. It also keeps people aware that things may not always be what they seem. For instance, when the Republicans kept referring to a Democrat-proposed Iraq exit strategy as "cut and run," Stewart asked us to reflect on whether exit strategies can be broken down to just two verbs and a conjunction. People appreciate the use of ironic humor to make such a point. Why? It's simply more enjoyable to use the mind in an active way rather than passively absorb information. Irony requires the mind to be active since it makes us "read between the lines." Enjoyment also makes the message more likely to stick. When people catch on, they're entertained. Yet, at the same time, irony helps people to establish a network of likeminded individuals. Based on a shared understanding of the deeper underlying meaning of an ironic exchange, people bond, and bond more closely. In their way, both Socrates and Stewart seek to create a dialogue among people who use their minds in an active way. Just as Socrates was the inspiration for a network of change in his time, Stewart may provide the same inspiration in ours. Socrates was, of course, ultimately convicted of impiety and corrupting the youth, and he was executed. Thankfully, no matter how much Stewart may rub some people the wrong way, he's safe from sharing Socrates' fate – I think.

Notes

1 Gary Younge, "Such a Tease," *Guardian* (October 1, 2005); www.arts.guardian.co.uk/features/story/0,11710,1582009,00.html.
2 "Speech for Newhouse School," *American Perspectives*, C-SPAN (October 14, 2004).
3 Marc Peyser, "Who's Next 2004: Red, White & Funny," *Newsweek* 143 (December 29, 2003), p. 71. Subsequent references will be made parenthetically in-text.
4 Plato, *Apology*, trans. Hugh Tredennick, in *The Collected Dialogues of Plato*, ed. Edith Hamilton and Huntington Cairns (Princeton: Princeton University Press, 1978), p. 21.
5 On *Larry King Live* (February 27, 2006) Stewart said that there's no such thing as "*the* American people. . . . I mean the whole thing is a melting pot, a collective of individuals."
6 "National Annenberg Election Survey" (press release), *Annenberg Public Policy Center* (September 21, 2004). The survey was conducted at the University of Pennsylvania; www.annenbergpublicpolicycenter. org/naes/2004_03_late-night-knowledge-2_9-21_pr.pdf.
7 "2004 Class day speaker needs irony, wit," *Yale Daily News* (January 12, 2004).
8 *The O'Reilly Factor*, Fox News (September 17, 2004).
9 O'Reilly made this comment about college kids who watch *The Daily Show* on the June 14, 2006 edition of his nationally syndicated radio show.
10 Ken Tucker, "You Can't Be Serious!" *New York Magazine* 37 (November 1, 2004), p. 63.

7

CAN *THE DAILY SHOW* SAVE DEMOCRACY?
JON STEWART AS THE GADFLY OF GOTHAM

STEVEN MICHELS AND MICHAEL VENTIMIGLIA

Most people are surprised to discover that philosophers have traditionally been ambivalent about the wisdom and stability of popular government. Plato, most famously, feared that democracy would lead to tyranny. Perhaps he would have been somewhat less concerned about the future of democracy had he ponied up for cable.

While it's increasingly obvious to many Americans that democracies are difficult to create, Plato understood that democracies are difficult to sustain. Democracy, Plato thought, was among the least stable forms of government, by its very nature vulnerable to a charismatic leader – a man of the people – who would be willing to use fear, misinformation, and brute force to consolidate power. As the masses pursued material goods and physical pleasures, an individual elected to maintain order and serve the many would eventually become a tyrant. While Plato's low opinion of democracy may not resonate with most twenty-first-century Westerners, his analysis of the vulnerability of democracy is a reminder that its emergence and continued existence – at home or abroad – is not a given.

Enter *The Daily Show*, a not-quite-daily Comedy Central program that awakens the masses to the sheer absurdity of how political discourse and power are exercised in our democracy. In a political system threatened by leaders centralizing power and news outlets peddling infotainment, *The Daily Show* – ostensibly presented for entertainment rather than news – awakens us to our democracy's fragility, uncovering the disingenuous, the contradictory, and the just plain ridiculous in the rhetoric of our leaders and the media. Jon Stewart does this, incidentally, in a way surprisingly similar to Plato's own mentor, Socrates – a man who stirred the pot in ancient Athens for long enough to wind up as the founding member of the Hemlock Society. Like Socrates, the original Gadfly of Athens, Jon Stewart – the Gadfly of Gotham, if you will – undermines the authority of those in power simply by allowing them to embarrass themselves, letting them fall on their own swords. Stewart confronts politicians and media personalities by turning their own words against them, drawing out the absurd and comic implications of their statements and ideas. In this sense, *The Daily Show*'s method is nothing if not Socratic. It proceeds by asking revealing if not tough questions of those making claims to truth or wisdom, speaks in terms easily accessible to most people, and presents its message through accounts and anecdotes rooted in the realities of political and social life. And, also like Socrates, Stewart has assembled a group of young, eager admirers who are increasingly suspicious about the veracity of the words, images, and ideas employed by those who have power and manipulate information. In short, Stewart illuminates the cave by shining a light on the shadow makers.

A Tale of Two Republics

Ancient Athens wasn't what modern Americans would consider free and democratic. In addition to having institutionalized slavery, both citizenship and voting rights were reserved only for the few, and even the most privileged had nothing close to what we enjoy as liberties today. Nevertheless, the comparison between Athens then and America now, particularly as pertains to popular government, is similar enough to be helpful. Specifically, both democracies fall far short of what Plato considered the best form of government. Plato's ideal republic was not what we could consider a republic at all. It was not a democracy, but, rather, an aristocracy in which philosophers ruled as kings. In Book VIII of *The Republic*, he ranks democracy *fourth* among various kinds of government, preferable only to the tyranny of a single individual.[1] Stewart certainly has a higher estimation of democracy than Plato, but he also treats it far more critically than many of our officeholders or media personalities. This is most evident in *The Daily Show*'s grand treatise, *America (The Book)*, a *New York Times* bestseller.[2] The book places democracy front-and-center, at the heart of the program's mission. The first chapter opens with a quote from Pericles describing how Athens is a proper democracy, ruled by the many rather than the few. Also included is a fictitious reply from Socrates: "Yes, Pericles, but have you gotten a load of the many?" (p. xii). In the section "Your Unelectable Founders," the book claims John Adams was unelectable because he "actually made principled, unpopular decisions" (p. 21). As these cases illustrate, *The Daily Show* is remarkable in its willingness to consider democracy a less than perfect form of government.

This isn't to say that Stewart and company are mere nay-sayers, barbecuing sacred cows for the sake of delicious comedy. In the chapter "The Future of Democracy," they claim that "democracy will continue to exist in that delicate balance between lofty ideals and human fallibility" (p. 117). More to the point, the book ranks democracy as the best available form of government. (Of course who wouldn't prefer democracy to "Totalitarian Regime," "Third-World Resort Island," or "Constitutional Robocracy.")

It's not a stretch to suggest that the perspective offered by *The Daily Show* is more sophisticated than the one offered by the current administration. Consider President Bush's repeated claims that democracy and freedom are God's gifts to mankind. By contrast, *America (The Book)* lists six stages of democracy: infancy, childhood, adolescence, adulthood, middle age, and old age. Its humorous take on democracy and democratization exhibits an understanding of the difficulties involved in forging and maintaining a democracy. If only those attuned to the shortcomings of democracy are in a position to heal it, we can easily see how *The Daily Show* might be just the right medicine. We might assume, conversely, there's nothing to be gained by interfering with the supposed will of God.

The first paragraph of *America (The Book)* also pokes fun at the notion that America invented or perfected democracy, but the thesis of the chapter, and perhaps even *The Daily Show* itself, is revealed in the next paragraph: "As heirs to a legacy more than two centuries old, it is understandable why present-day Americans would take their own democracy for granted" (p. 1). This isn't to say that a lack of participation is the only thing wrong with American democracy. In addition to made-up excuses – "Too tired," "Had a thing" – *America (The Book)* points to systemic causes of why Americans go to the polls in such low numbers:

> A president freely chosen from a wide-open field of two men every four years; a Congress with a 99% incumbency rate; a Supreme Court comprised of nine politically appointed judges whose only oversight is the icy scythe of Death – all these reveal a system fully capable of maintaining itself. (p. 1)

To the extent that our democracy is broken, it's clear that *The Daily Show* does not see the general public as the root cause. We should focus our attention, then, primarily on its officeholders and, its lifeblood, the media.

Stewart and the Elites

You don't seem to know jack shit about holiness, Euthyphro.
Socrates

In a July 2003 interview with Bill Moyers, Stewart pointed out that the United States is not just a democracy but a republic – not the ideal city of Plato's *Republic* or even the direct democracy of Plato's Athens – but a representative democracy. It is not surprising, therefore, that Stewart is focused on and most effective in his treatment of democracy's powerbrokers.

Not bound by the norms of mainstream media, Stewart is free to approach issues in ways which are less orthodox but often more effective. In a taped segment, "Pump My Ride," Ed Helms took on Bill Dressler, an oil industry lobbyist who opposed a bill allowing New Jersey residents to pump their own gas. It featured Helms not-so-accidentally dousing himself with what appeared to be gasoline. Of course it was Dressler himself who had already done the most damage to his credibility by suggesting that people need a lifetime of training in order to fill their tanks. Socrates would be proud.

In addition to regularly attacking officeholders for their arrogance, Stewart also delights in pointing out their ignorance. A recent segment's target was Senator Ted Stevens (R-AK), the Chairman of the Senate committee in charge of overseeing the Web. Stewart showed a clip of Stevens giving a speech on the Senate floor in favor of the Net Neutrality Act. Stevens showed himself to be amazingly unaware of how the internet works. Afterwards, Stewart pounced: "You don't seem to know jack shit about computers or the internet. But hey, that's OK; you're just the guy in charge of regulating it, so what difference does it make?" Substitute the words "piety" and "holiness" for "computers" and "internet" and you've got the essence of what Socrates said to Euthyphro, a man who prosecuted his own father for impiety.

Perhaps the most visited theme in *The Daily Show* is politicians' self-interest and lack of ethics. Discussing John McCain and other politicians, Stewart remarked, "When it ultimately comes down to it, it appears to be that their self-preservation instinct is stronger than their governing or country instinct." Rarely is the nightly news so honest and direct. Simply put, the public's lack of interest in politics is not unrelated to the integrity of our leaders. Consequently, our elected officials have a special responsibility that Stewart takes seriously, even if they don't.

Stewart and the Media

I'm not going to be your monkey.

Jon Stewart on *Crossfire*

It's not surprising that some journalists have taken issue with the scope and style of *The Daily Show*. Introducing Stewart on a *Nightline* telecast from the 2004 Democratic National Convention, Ted Koppel said, "A lot of television viewers – more, quite frankly, than I'm comfortable with – get their news from the Comedy Channel [*sic*] on a program called *The Daily Show*." Responding to Stewart's claim that viewers watch for a "comedic interpretation" of the news,

Koppel claimed that viewers watch to be informed; they "actually think they're coming closer to the truth with your show."

Although it has been deemed a "fake news" program, *The Daily Show*'s reports and commentaries are factually based, and they provide an incisive and not untruthful take on current events. The show is informed by a playful philosophy – what Friedrich Nietzsche called a "gay science" – and its value lies precisely in its unwillingness to take itself too seriously. Although there has been little research in this area, it wouldn't be surprising to discover that *The Daily Show* provides, in its way, a perspective more realistic than that of other news programs, programs where – although the expectations for accuracy are higher – the spin is more subtle and hence more pernicious.

Stewart has also been criticized by Tucker Carlson for not asking tough questions of his guests. There is some truth to this claim. When Michael Continetti appeared on *The Daily Show* in support of his book *K-Street Gang*, a study of Republican ethics, Stewart asked him, "How far do you think this integrity thing you're doing is going to get you in this Washington game?" Stewart obviously supported Continetti, which gave the interview a degree of levity absent from other interviews. The program is certainly not unique in this regard, but it's possible for humorous questions to be tough. Consider what Stewart asked of Democratic Party Chairman Howard Dean in response to President Bush's wave of unpopularity: "How are the Democrats going to screw this up?" Stewart could have asked the question in any number of ways, but in addition to getting to the point, it also reminded viewers, and Dean, of the Democrats' long history of disorganization and political ineptitude.

Nevertheless, Stewart isn't content to sit idly by while he and the show are attacked. However negatively politicians are portrayed, *The Daily Show*'s true vitriol is reserved for the media. In his October 2004 appearance on CNN's now-defunct *Crossfire*, Stewart accused the show of "partisan hackery," and not-so-subtly reminded the hosts of their "responsibility to the public discourse." Similarly, after acknowledging the importance of a "free and independent press," *America (The Book)* refers to members of the media as "spineless cowards" and "indecent piles of shit."

Perhaps *The Daily Show* and its spin-off, *The Colbert Report*, will be taken more seriously in light of Colbert's now-infamous attack on Bush at the 2006 White House Correspondents' Association Dinner, which quickly became one of the most-watched items on the Web. Among Colbert's many zingers was his illustration of Bush's alleged preference for style over substance:

> I stand by this man. I stand by this man because he stands for things. Not only *for* things, he stands *on* things. Things like aircraft carriers and rubble and recently flooded city squares. And that sends a strong message: that no matter what happens to America, she will always rebound – with the most powerfully staged photo ops in the world.

Ouch. The reaction afterwards was as interesting as the speech itself. The debate concerned not only the propriety of the material, but also whether Colbert was even funny.

The Daily Show's method has significant advantages over more traditional news formats. While the mainstream media is driven, in part, by a profit motive tied to supporting the status quo, the success of *The Daily Show* is determined by the extent to which it challenges the authority and prudence of elevated individuals and existing institutions. Although it too is a money-making enterprise, *The Daily Show*, in effect, serves as a loyal opposition to the party in power, exploring waters uncharted by those more concerned with the next election or the bottom line. As Bill Moyers remarked to Stewart, "I do not know whether you are practicing an old form of parody and satire or a new form of journalism."

Research has shown considerable differences, in substance and impact, among nightly comedy shows. Some scholars, Matt Baum most prominently, have incorrectly placed *The Daily Show* in a category of "soft news," along with other late night comedy shows.[3] But more recently, the National Annenberg Election Survey used content-analysis of monologues during the 2004 Presidential election and discovered considerable differences between *The Daily Show* and other major late night programs, *The Tonight Show* and *The Late Show*. The segments on *The Daily Show* "are less likely than a Leno or Letterman joke to use a quick punch-line to make fun of a candidate," Dannagal Goldthwaite Young, a senior research analyst, wrote of the study's findings. "Instead, Stewart's lengthier segments employ irony to explore policy issues, news events, and even the media's coverage of the campaign."[4]

The criticism of *The Daily Show* by the mainstream media appears to be driven, at least in part, by professional jealousy. The show's popularity and impact on political discourse is rivaled by only a handful of other individuals and programs. Appearing on Fox News' *The O'Reilly Factor*, an incensed Geraldo Rivera argued that Jon Stewart and Stephen Colbert "make a living putting on video of old ladies slipping on ice and people laughing," that they "exist in a small little place where they count for nothing." Meanwhile, viewers of Carlson's show on MSNBC might notice that the now-tanned and bowtieless host – perhaps in between his *Dancing with the Stars* performances – concludes every program with an appearance by senior producer Willie Geist for his comic take on the news.

More to the point, however, is that the critiques offered by Koppel and Carlson are inspired by an idealistic if not naïve view of the media. Although punctuated briefly with a post-World War II emphasis on professionalism and objectivity, partisanship and bias is, for all intents and purposes, the norm. The outcry for a return to "the good old days" should be replaced by an optimism provided by the growing number of media outlets and the increasingly egalitarian nature of information sharing. In that respect, *The Daily Show* is just another voice in the wilderness, and a much-needed one at that.

In addition to its awards for comedy and variety, the show has won two Peabody Awards for its election coverage, "Indecision 2000" and "Indecision 2004," and in 2004 it was the first comedy show to win Outstanding Achievement in News and Information from the Television Critics Association. During his recent appearance on *The Daily Show*, actor Kevin Spacey called the program "The best damn news show in America." It's a sad commentary on the media that this remark can't be considered wholly in jest.

Let's Not Forget the *Hoi Polloi*

The seven marvels that best represent man's achievements over the last 2,000 years will be determined by Internet vote, so look for Howard Stern's Private Parts *to come in No. 1.*

Jon Stewart

It's easy to forget that Socrates, the man who spent his life unmasking the ignorance of the powerful and supposedly wise, was less than impressed with those who possessed no power and had no pretension to wisdom. As Socrates recounts his life's work during his trial in the *Apology*, he points out that it's not just the elite who lack knowledge; it's also the masses, the ordinary people who think that because they know how to make a shoe or train a horse they know what's best for the polity.

Although elites are its favorite target, *The Daily Show* regularly and mercilessly lambastes middle-class America for its strange habits, interests, and preoccupations. In "There Goes the Gayborhood," for example, Ed Helms profiled Jeremy Paul, a man who moved to the Castro, the gay district in San Francisco, and proceeded to complain about the overt displays of homosexuality. During its 2006 "Midwestern Midterm Midtacular" the show had a series of correspondents in front of various Applebee's restaurants portraying the locals as thoroughly uninterested in politics, caring only about local sports teams. Elites might be the main target, but no one is safe; *The Daily Show* is an equal opportunity offender. *The Daily Show* disregards majorities – and minorities, too, for that matter – of all kinds, therefore strengthening the kind of pluralism through dissent that classic liberals such as James Madison and John Stuart Mill so deliberately encouraged.

Democracy in Action

While Plato's focus was on the ignorance and influence of the masses, Alexis de Tocqueville feared that democracy would lead to excessive individualism and a decline of civic virtue and participation. Stewart seems to share these more recent concerns as well.

Jody Baumgartner and Jonathan Morris recently studied the impact of regular *Daily Show* watching on the political attitudes of its audience during the 2004 election. After viewing clips of the program, participants in the study were found to be less trustful of the political system and to have a more negative view of the media. The authors concluded that "exposure to *The Daily Show* brand of political humor influenced young Americans by lowering supports for both presidential candidates and increasing cynicism."[5] Noticeably lacking in this study is any consideration of whether negative views of politicians are justified. The suggestion that American democracy and the media ought to be viewed uncritically, without any consideration of whether such treatment is deserved, is a peculiar one, particularly coming from people who should be more thoughtful about such things.

Stewart's perspective on politics might foster skepticism and doubt, but it can just as easily lead to action as apathy. Although the authors didn't question the character of those who would eschew their civic duty because of a television show, they did acknowledge that such exposure could actually lead to greater democratic participation by people seeking to make a difference. To the extent that comedy educates, the show fosters an individual's "internal efficacy" – that is, the sense of knowing enough to make informed decisions during elections and about public policy. Although viewers were more likely to be more cynical about the political system, Baumgartner and Morris also found that "viewers of *The Daily Show* reported increased confidence in their ability to understand the complicated world of politics" (p. 341). Moreover, as psychologists Eron Berg and Louis Lippman have demonstrated, comedy is a powerful tool for reinforcing memory.[6]

In addition to educating and entertaining, comedy can address sensitive issues and bring the country together in difficult times. The best example may be from *The Onion*, a newspaper in the spirit of *The Daily Show*, former home of head writer/supervising producer David Javerbaum and Ben Karlin, the show's recently departed executive producer. The paper used the headline "Holy Fucking Shit" on September 26 in response to the attacks of 9/11. Contrast this with the muted and uncertain reaction of *Saturday Night Live*, which walked the line more gingerly. Their first post-9/11 show opened with then-New York Mayor Rudy Giuliani and members of the city's police and fire departments singing a song in tribute to their fallen colleagues. Producer Lorne Michaels asked Giuliani, "Can we be funny?" Actor-comedian Ben Stiller was scheduled to host the following weekend, but canceled, saying it was "impossible to be funny at times like this." We can only hope that the country is never again in such a quandary over the need for comic relief.

To the extent that it provides a public square for debate and consideration of important issues, watching *The Daily Show*, and discussing it at home, at work, or on campus, fosters the kind of free and open dialogue required for a thriving democracy. In many respects, it's the twenty-first-century equivalent of a New England town meeting.

Lord of the Gadflies?

Socrates was found guilty of corrupting the youth. One of these corrupted youths turned out to be Plato, arguably the most influential thinker in Western history. Although Stewart maintains that his goal is to be funny, public opinion data reveal that regular viewers of *The Daily Show* are more educated and more informed about current events than the average citizen. Consequently, the popularity of the show is hardly a sign of democracy in decay. If anything, it suggests that all hope for an engaged citizenship and a vibrant democracy is not lost. Perhaps our real concern should be with those who don't get the joke.

Can *The Daily Show* save democracy? Probably not. *The Daily Show* alone can't provide the antidote for all of democracy's ills. But the analytic and rhetorical skills of our modern day gadfly counteract the tendency of the public to acquiesce to the will of the image-makers. If a lack of education or sense of civic duty is the problem, *The Daily Show* does its part in correcting that as well. Though the show may not be able to save democracy single-handedly, democracy would be in even more peril without it. And it certainly wouldn't be as funny.

Notes

1 Plato, *The Republic*, trans. Allan Bloom (New York: Basic Books, 1991), 564a.
2 Jon Stewart, Ben Karlin, and David Javerbaum, *America (The Book): A Citizen's Guide to Democracy Inaction* (New York: Warner Books, 2004). Subsequent references will be made parenthetically in-text.

3 Matthew A. Baum, "Soft News and Political Knowledge: Evidence of Absence or Absence of Evidence?" *Political Communication* 20 (2003), pp. 73–190.

4 "National Annenberg Election Survey" (press release), *Annenberg Public Policy Center* (September 21, 2004), p. 3.

5 Jody Baumgartner and Jonathan S. Morris, "The *Daily Show* Effect: Candidate Evaluations, Efficacy, and the American Youth," *American Politics Research* 34 (3) (2006), p. 361.

6 Eron Berg and Louis Lippman, "Does Humor in Radio Advertising Affect Recognition of Novel Product Brand Names?" *Journal of General Psychology* 128 (2) (2001), pp. 194–205. See also Jim Lyttle, "The Effectiveness of Humor in Persuasion: The Case of Business Ethics Training," *Journal of General Psychology* 128 (2001), 206–16.

8

JON THE CYNIC:
DOG PHILOSOPHY 101

ALEJANDRO BÁRCENAS

I know my role, I'm the dancing monkey.
Jon Stewart on *Nightline* (July, 2004)

Jon Stewart, a cynic? Perhaps not, according to some diehard fans. But it's not difficult to imagine that for many viewers of *The Daily Show*, even those who enjoy watching the host "speak truth to power," Stewart is no more than a neatly dressed cynic. Critical articles in newspapers, magazines, and scholarly journals reveal growing concern about how *The Daily Show* might be affecting its viewers, perhaps instilling disillusionment and apathy in young people. These concerns have been reinforced by a survey-based study published in 2006 on this so-called *"Daily Show* Effect." After exposing a group of college students to clips taken from *The Daily Show*'s coverage of the 2004 Presidential campaign, the researchers concluded that "increased exposure to TDS is significantly related to cynicism for young adults."[1] Their conclusion seems to confirm what many had already suspected: lampooning politicians and other public figures – showing clips of George W. Bush mispronouncing words, for instance – might, despite the humor, have a down side. Perhaps the laughs come at the high price of generating a jaded audience, decreased trust in politicians, the media, and even democracy itself.

Even if *The Daily Show* has this effect, of course, the key question is whether or not such cynicism is warranted. So before we start a campaign to cancel the show, let's consider some historical and philosophical facts concerning the word "cynic." Nowadays we generally think of a cynic as someone with a very low opinion of humanity. Stewart's popularity rests in part on his irreverent and amusing news reports, where no topic is sacred, no institution off limits, no person beyond criticism, and this seems to fit the mold of a modern cynic. But calling him a cynic in this sense might be, to a certain extent, misleading. Stewart seems much more negative about institutions, conventions, and *certain* people than he is about humanity as a whole, which means that he might be a cynic in a different, much older, and much richer sense.

Cynicism originated in ancient Greece, and it's important to realize that the label initially had very different connotations from what our current term would suggest. The ancient cynics were a ragtag bunch of philosophers who were seen – really – as dog-like (*kynikos* or "cynic" in Greek). Why dog-like? What do dogs have to do with philosophy? We tend to think of dogs as loyal, devoted, and obedient creatures, but the Greeks saw them very differently, as indecent, corrupt, and disobedient animals. Dogs symbolized shamelessness, audacity, and a kind of immoral independence, because even though they lived among people and shared their homes, they didn't follow human customs, but only their own true nature (*physis*). For those who wanted to bark at, or take a bite out of, the prevailing social norms, an association with the canine species wasn't at all inappropriate or displeasing. In turn, the cynics came to embrace this popular characterization of their actions, in particular the most notorious "dog philosopher" of all, Diogenes of Sinope (ca. 412–324 BCE) – later we'll see how Diogenes earned this notoriety.

Provoking outrage was the cynics' calling card. The cynics lived in the heart of ancient democracies, confronting accepted habits, unchallenged assumptions, and above all institutional corruption. They confronted those who abused their power in the manner they knew best: by being outrageous (*anaideia*). Their aim wasn't just to avoid what they considered to be harmful pursuits and practices, but to expose and ridicule those traditions that most people unreflectively considered moral and proper. If we look at Stewart in the context of this "dog philosophy," we'll shed light on the meaning of his role in contemporary culture. We might find that he not only bears similarities to, but also at heart is a modern version of, these ancient dog philosophers.

Rebel with a Cause

We have precious little from the early cynics themselves. For the most part, we must rely on a few scattered fragments and the biographies by third-century CE Greek historian Diogenes Laertius.[2] We have, however, a very accurate picture of the politics of ancient Greece, which bears surprising resemblance to ours.[3] The cynics lived in Athens during turbulent times (fourth and third centuries BCE), when the political system of the city-state was the precarious first democracy the world had ever seen.

Ancient democracy didn't function the way ours does today.[4] Theirs involved direct participation in government. Any free male citizen native to the city could potentially lead the administration if he was able to convince the assembly (*ekklesia*) to vote in favor of his proposals. But the most radical aspect of the Athenian practice of direct democracy was that holding some special offices, such as being a member of the *boule* – a 500-member council – was decided, believe it or not, by lottery. In contrast, modern democracies are representative; citizens aren't assembled to cast votes on every single issue. And, of course, no lottery system is in effect; rather, people are elected to represent various constituencies. The Founding Fathers, in fact, intentionally avoided, or to be more accurate, feared the Athenian model of "pure" democracy because of its tendency to move back and forth between tyranny and anarchy.

Putting aside some of the organizational differences between the two democracies, there are, owing to human frailty, many commonalities as well. One characteristic of all democracies deserves special attention, namely that becoming a leader depends on the abilities of the individual candidate. In contrast to other, non-democratic systems of government, individuals aren't born into positions of power, nor do they depend on a king or religious leader to entitle them to power. They must rather obtain positions of power by winning the approval of ordinary citizens.

Citizens needed certain skills, rhetoric in particular, to participate effectively in politics. Consequently, public speaking teachers, such as Gorgias, Prodicus, Hippias, and other sophists, roamed the streets of the city-states seeking students who aspired to rule. One such student was the notorious Alcibiades, who came to represent the ugly side of the participatory system for being able to seduce crowds into voting for his own ultimately selfish schemes. Alcibiades, however, wasn't an isolated case; many of the initiatives brought up in the assembly were motivated by personal agendas. Eloquent speakers could persuade others to accept measures of benefit to the speakers and their families, without any concern for what would benefit society as a whole. Such trends in contemporary politics are, of course, common targets of *Daily Show* humor. A persuasive politician in Athens could convince the assembly to vote for an ill-considered war (the expedition to Syracuse in 414 BCE, for instance). Witnesses to turbulent times, the cynics – just like Stewart in airing regular installments of "Mess O' Potamia" – decided that the best response wasn't to stay quiet, but to speak out against what they saw as bad policy. Their irreverent, non-conformist responses to self-destructive, unreasonable behavior continued the tradition, started by Socrates (470–399 BCE), of exposing and ridiculing those who were responsible for such social unrest and political debacles. In their time, they too "spoke truth to power."

The cynics were relentless in their denunciation of the moral corruption of those in power, despite the perils in which such opposition placed them. Even the Macedonian kings Philip II and Alexander the Great, who conquered Greece and temporarily suspended Athenian democracy, were confronted by the daring cynics. It's said that Diogenes, after being captured in Chaeronea (338 BCE), the key battle for the control of Greece, was violently brought to King Philip II. Fighting on the losing side of the Athenians, he was very likely to end up as a slave or even be executed right on the spot. But after Diogenes told the king that he was a longtime observer of the ruler's "insatiable greed," Philip set him free in admiration (p. 44). Diogenes knew that kings, and others enamored with their own status and power, tend to crave praise, and they often don't realize the dangerous consequences of their usually blind ambition. Since Diogenes was released, the point of the story might be that the king sought, but seldom got, honesty from people. Perhaps Philip realized the truth of the cynic's daring words, and so respected Diogenes for being something other than a timid "yes man," whose words are nothing but empty flattery, even in the face of death. Later on, we'll see what happened when Diogenes met Alexander the Great.

In less harsh circumstances, Stewart regularly voices his discontent with the current political climate, showing the harmful side of common practices, attitudes, and assumptions. For instance, he playfully took President Bush's self-labeling as "the decider," the one who makes the decisions, and made him into the hero of an imaginary comic book, *The Decider* (April 18, 2006). This showed what might have seemed to be a display of vigorous and assertive leadership to be, on the contrary, an impetuous declaration that his decisions ought to be treated as *beyond* criticism or rational discussion. Stewart has also regularly exhibited his concerns about the way discussions take place in Congress, when, despite their apparent seriousness, in most cases important issues and debates are either diffused by irrelevant considerations, or reduced to a battle of slogans and superficial metaphors.

Stewart also uses the "fake news" format to express his profound disapproval of contemporary journalism. The media's general lack of depth and too-common appeal to what sells over what really matters is a recurring theme of *The Daily Show*. The defunct *Daily Show* segment "Even Stevphen," with alumni Steve Carell and Stephen Colbert, highlighted how what many media outlets present as legitimate debate, as two opposing sides defending their respective positions, is indeed what, on *Crossfire*, Stewart called "partisan hackery" (October 15, 2004). Only the day before the now infamous *Crossfire* appearance, Stewart had announced publicly, "I'm advocating that the media come back to work for us. . . . Their job can't be: 'What do you think Donna Brazile? OK. What do you think Bay Buchanan? We'll be right back.' "[5]

The ancient cynics and the contemporary Jon Stewart share and express a pervasive sense of discontent with the dangerous, uncritically accepted aspects of their cultures. This discontent unfolds, deliberately or not, into a search for the truth that lies behind the façade of common practice and public perception.

Humor Leads to Truth

As we've seen, ancient cynicism emerged during a period of unrest and discontent in Athens, and it became the leading subversive response to the culture of the time. The rebellious manner of the cynics was intended to overcome ignorance and passive consent by denouncing, in unusual ways, the breakdown of society. Often this criticism took the form of odd behavior, in direct opposition to accepted customs, in extreme, ridiculous ways, with the intention of poking fun at things generally considered serious, important, and not inherently funny. Stewart's scribbling and doodling at the start of each episode ironically undermines the seriousness of taking crucial, last-minute notes on headline news segments. Similarly, but more extremely, Diogenes lived in a bathtub to show that the pursuit of wealth and comfort was taken much too seriously in his time, that it's not wealth or comfort that makes us human, or morally good, for that matter. Such actions characterize the rebellious side of philosophical cynicism. But their playfulness can be deceiving. Both Stewart's and the cynics' attitudes are well considered and their actions carefully orchestrated. The purpose of their comedic, often outrageous acts isn't simply entertainment; the means are entertaining, but the objective is very serious.

On the other hand, Stewart was criticized on CNN's *Crossfire* for not living up to the standards that he asks others, particularly journalists, to follow. However, his role as a comedian, as important as it might be, shouldn't be confused with journalism, as Stewart continually points out. For instance, it would be unreasonable to expect that *The Daily Show* should, or could, assume the same responsibility for reporting as is supposed to be assumed by news agencies. As Stewart told Paul Begala and Tucker Carlson, "I didn't realize that – and maybe this explains quite a bit – that the news organizations look to Comedy Central for their cues on integrity. After all," he continued, "you're on CNN. The show that leads into me is puppets making crank phone calls."[6] Needless to say, nobody really believed that Stewart's credibility was somehow undermined by *Crank Yankers*, the preceding show on Comedy Central at the time. When he's sitting behind that desk, Stewart means serious business. What he says carries a lot of weight even if, and especially because, his methods are entertaining.

Stewart confronted the hosts of *Crossfire* face to face, with the gravitas of a cynic, but Begala and Carlson weren't the first ones to recognize the potentially powerful influence of the seemingly innocent comedy of the "dog philosophers." The cynics were a force to be reckoned with right from the start. The Roman Emperor Julian (332–363 CE) acknowledged them as his "most estimable rivals," and even Alexander the Great realized how formidable they really were in his famous encounter with Diogenes. Alexander supposedly told Diogenes to ask for anything that he wished, to which Diogenes replied, "Do not shade me; stand out of my light" (p. 40). Obviously there's more to the story than Diogenes' desire to mock the great ruler. The cynic's intention was to show that Alexander's display of power was not only, in effect, insignificant but also ultimately irrelevant, a mere hindrance, to the search for wisdom. By blocking from Diogenes' view a traditional symbol of truth, the sun, the Macedonian ruler was seen to represent the corrupt nature of politics. As a philosopher, Diogenes, not Alexander, however great, is the one in direct contact with the truth, and his aim was to teach people the path to discovering and fulfilling their nature as rational beings. It was those who were true to their nature – to themselves – that Diogenes famously sought – but didn't find – when he walked about in broad daylight with his lamp (p. 42).

The cynics offered an unorthodox method, disguised in the comedic style, to get out of the "deception lane" created by the demagogues. Although counter-conventional, their methods weren't intended to deviate from, but rather to help in reaching, the highest and noblest philosophical end, namely wisdom. This alternative method of instilling or "awakening" knowledge, by example and through humor, is importantly distinct from more traditional methods of argumentation and debate. Since they were clearly among the best-educated people in Athens, the cynics weren't opposed to culture or education (*paideia*) generally, but only to culture that hindered the natural, rational development of human beings. In fact, another influential cynic, a student of Diogenes, Crates of Thebes (ca. 368–288 BCE), said, "One should study philosophy until seeing in generals nothing but donkey drivers" (p. 94), a statement that the *Daily Show* writers would no doubt happily approve.

The use of humor as a guide in the discovery of wisdom was aimed to generate in the public the kind of "awakening" described by Aristotle (384–322 BCE) in his *Poetics*, a transformation caused by the sudden recognition of truth (*anagnorisis*).[7] Comedy helps the observer to become aware of deception and to understand how common conceptions and opinions (*doxa*) that "look like" (*pseudos*) the real thing, pretend to stand in for truth and knowledge. Coming to a recognition (*anagnorisis*) of reality *as it truly is* is perhaps one of the best expressions of the ancient Greek idea of truth as arriving at the unhidden (*aletheia*).

Despite the many similarities between ancient cynicism and *The Daily Show*, the program has no explicit pretensions of having such a philosophical agenda. Still, it's not hard to see how Stewart's reporting, in particular during the opening headlines segment, doesn't indulge in merely provoking empty laughs, but presents issues from a delightful and instructive perspective, helping to reinforce an awareness of things *as they are*, in contrast to how they're often presented by politicians and the media at large.

A Healthy Dose of Cynicism

Although the early cynic movement originated in antiquity during a time of democratic crisis, it didn't disappear completely after the crisis. Some forms of philosophical cynicism survived beyond the Hellenistic era and into the Roman Republic. The cynic's attitude thrived wherever discussion and argumentation were valued in a culture. Philosophical cynicism flourished in its most refined form in this more open-minded historical context, and I'd like to think, and there's reason to suppose, that it's a key distinguishing feature of democracy. With our political system comparable, in many ways, to that of ancient Athens, it might be more useful than ever to reflect on the role played by cynicism in ancient Greece, particularly when today there are signs of comparable attitudes among influential people, like Stewart.

First, let's see how political influence is achieved in a democracy. Generally speaking, in ancient and modern democracies, those who receive the approval of the majority are rewarded with prestige and authority. High popular recognition (*eudoxia*) can be considered "virtuous" in a democratic system because it gives a person power. According to the cynics, though, pursuing this kind of success promotes mostly demagogy and deception, and so turns politics into a struggle for mere popularity and not for what's truly virtuous (*arete*). The cynic, intending to oppose and denounce the moral and ethical shortcomings of those who corrupt the system and abuse their power for mere personal gain, naturally becomes the target of the offended parties. Because of distorted public perceptions, the cynics actually considered unpopularity (*adoxia*) to be a good thing (*agathon*), a sign that they were getting at the truth, that their opposition was on-track (p. 12). In Stewart's case, too, it's perfectly fitting, even necessary, for him to have, and to have *earned*, a "bad reputation" (*adoxia*), because his way of thinking diverges from that of the majority. In this respect Stewart, in true cynic fashion, understands and accepts his lot: "As someone who is held in contempt by much of the country," he said at the Newhouse School Press Breakfast, "it's really not that bad. You will get some stares at the mall, every now and again an email referring to your heritage . . . but other than that, being held in contempt is quite comfortable."

The role that the "dog philosophers" took on, regardless of public perception, was to embrace certain essential elements of democracy to help turn the system away from its vicious and corrupt ways. For example, access to public spaces allowed the cynics to speak freely (*parrhesia*). Not surprisingly, Athenians often abused free speech, using rhetoric to placate crowds by appealing to the lowest common denominator, furthering their own interests in the process. The cynics, however, transformed *parrhesia* from a servant of decadence into an instrument of democratic shock therapy.

When Diogenes was asked "what's the most beautiful thing in the world? his answer was *parrhesia* (p. 70). *Parrhesia* became the key instrument for "defacing the currency" of tradition, a cynic's metaphor for the conflict between philosophy (which does the defacing) and common opinion (the currency). Diogenes, like Socrates before him, thought that conventions needed to be confronted with knowledge of the true nature of things (*physis*), passion with reason (*logos*) (p. 40). He intended to improve the lives of the citizenry by encouraging the development of reason. In this sense, the cynics continued the Socratic tradition in their appreciation of education and the belief that virtue can be taught. Only then could true citizens participate well in a democracy, instead of blindly accepting the opinion or the will of the majority. To be ignorant was, and to some extent still is, seen as a sign of *irresponsibility* in the democratic context.

Still, cynicism has been portrayed by some, then as now, as a destructive cultural force. So, if Stewart's attitude fits so well into the mold of the ancient cynics, what does this say about him? Is he also destructive? Were the original cynics? Maybe if Stewart's message were that politics is pointless. But that's not the message. *The Daily Show* presents a different, in some ways more complete view of politics than is usually aired on the networks. Cynicism certainly can be destructive, but only in the sense of highlighting and undermining reckless practices, unreflective understanding, which, left alone, become detrimental to society. The Socratic teaching of a cynic, like Diogenes or Stewart, is that we should develop self-sufficiency (*autarkeia*) in our judgment of things and a willingness to question authority, particularly if the authority has been found less than reliable. When humor is mixed in, the cynic becomes a Socratic "gadfly," irritating society by poking fun at its failings and foibles, until it, at last, wakes up to itself.

Stewart is no philosopher, nor does he intend to be one. *The Daily Show*, however, delivers the undeniably philosophical message of just how important earnestness, honesty, and integrity are in the political sphere. I have no doubt that Diogenes would recognize Stewart as a fellow "dog." Sadly, though, some people are still put off, even outraged, by the cynic's form of humor, sometimes condemning it as an enemy of democracy, instead of seeing dog philosophy for what it is, democracy's best friend.[8]

Notes

1 Jody Baumgartner and Jonathan S. Morris, "*The Daily Show* Effect: Candidate Evaluations, Efficacy, and American Youth," *American Politics Research* 34 (2006), p. 360.
2 Diogenes Laertius, *Lives of Eminent Philosophers II* (Cambridge, MA: Harvard University Press, 2005). All translations are mine. All subsequent references made parenthetically in-text will be to this work.
3 For more, see Judith Barad, "Stewart and Socrates: Speaking Truth to Power," chapter 6 in this volume.
4 See Jon Stewart, Ben Karlin, and David Javerbaum, *America (The Book): A Citizen's Guide to Democracy Inaction* (New York: Warner Books, 2004), chapter 1.
5 "Newhouse School Press Breakfast," *American Perspectives*, C-SPAN (October 14, 2004).
6 "Jon Stewart's America," *Crossfire*, CNN (Washington: October 15, 2004).

7 In the *Poetics* (1452a) Aristotle spoke of this kind of transformation in the context of tragedies, in particular *Oedipus Rex*. But it's plausible to suppose such a phenomenon might also occur in comedy. The *Poetics* supposedly contained a second book dedicated exclusively to comedy, but there are no surviving manuscripts of that part of the text. Umberto Eco was in part inspired to write *The Name of the Rose* by speculating on the contents of Aristotle's second book and the conflict between Aristotle's defense of comedy and the doctrines of medieval Christianity.
8 Many thanks to Jason Holt and Robert J. Littman for comments on an earlier draft of this chapter.

REGULAR FEATURE:
CRITICAL THINKING AND THE WAR ON BULLSHIT

SEGMENT 3

9

PUBLIC DISCOURSE AND THE STEWART MODEL OF CRITICAL THINKING

ROBEN TOROSYAN

Tell me and I'll forget; show me and I may remember; but directly involve me, and I'll make it my own.

Confucius

With their unique brand of humor, Stewart and his *Daily Show* team inspire twenty-somethings and grandmothers alike by involving them in thinking critically to uncover underlying assumptions, logical fallacies, and dishonest arguments. One of the secrets of the show's success is that it taps a human longing for learning, questioning, and open conversation that is generally neglected in public discourse.

The Red (Herring) Menace

In a segment entitled "Are You Prepared?!?" (May, 2006) correspondent Samantha Bee begins: "Recent events have shown that Americans face certain death. Death that will kill you." Like many of the show's fake news items, the report caricatures the way the nation's leaders and television media tend to sensationalize stories, appealing to emotion rather than disciplined reason.

Bee interviews one suburban couple about their emergency preparedness:

Bee: Homeland Security says you need duct tape and plastic sheeting to protect your home. I assume you have that?

107

Couple:	No.
Bee:	Communications gear?
Couple:	No.
Bee:	(*lowering her voice as if embarrassed*) Do you at least have a large tarp with which to collect the corpses of your friends and family?

While exaggerated for comic effect, Bee's parody of loaded media questions conveys a serious message: civic discourse is often driven more by emotion and dogma than by reasoned dialogue. By reducing the entire issue of emergency preparedness to "either protect yourself or die," Bee lampoons how such false dichotomies (false either/or choices) do anything but promote safety (much less a *feeling* of safety), which requires even-tempered, reasoned planning, preparation, and prevention.

Hysteria makes a great red herring distraction. As Stephen Colbert says, "There's fear out there; someone's gotta monger it." A man evading pursuit once dragged a red herring across his trail to throw the hounds off his scent. The term now signifies attempts to distract audiences from the issue at hand. Today's media, for example, leniently allow politicians to use polarizing "wedge" issues to distract attention from corruption, wasteful government spending, and other serious problems.

After the 2005 London terrorist attacks, Stewart mused, "The attacks happened overseas, yet 62 percent of Americans are worried about similar attacks here. I wonder why Americans are so nervous about it." Glaring news headlines then flashed with ominous voiceovers: "London Terror," "Attacks in London," "Who's at risk? How prepared are we?" Wide-eyed, Stewart said, "Oh, I see. But I'm sure the on-air cable hosts will bring some perspective, context, and understanding to the coverage." Clips then showed hosts saying: "Are we next in America?" "How safe are we in America?" "Can we prevent a subway or a bus attack in the US?" "This is why I thought the Brits should have let the French have the Olympics." "Why are they doing this?" and "You have to wonder, will we ever *truly* feel safe again?" Such clips of alarming headlines and vacuous sound bites highlight the media's tendency to focus egocentrically on Americans' safety when people suffer elsewhere. They also show the failure of news organizations to act in the traditional, time-honored role of watchdog, arbiter, and protector.

Daily Show humor presupposes that news organizations have a responsibility to the public, much as Jean-Jacques Rousseau (1712–78) conceived a government and its citizens to be bound by a social contract. Government should provide people "a form of association which will defend and protect with the whole common force the person and goods of each associate."[1] News organizations, similarly, should function in ways that benefit people, not use scaremongering to gain audience share. Likewise, Stewart and company show how politicians appeal to voters' basest instincts to rally support for their own ideological positions.

"Diss" Ingenuous: Scapegoating and Leaping to Judgment (Day)

When the Republican-dominated House passed a resolution to continue the Iraq war ("Hearing Impaired," June 2006), Stewart underscored the event:

Stewart: Representative Tom Cole encapsulated how the Republicans had once again succeeded.
Cole: (*video clip*) Whether we are right or wrong on our side of the aisle, we do have a common position and it's expressed in this resolution.
Stewart: That's right: He's right. Or wrong. But either way, people agree with him.

Cole's assumption here seems to be that we shouldn't focus on whether such decisions would be better or worse, whether they would help or harm people. Rather, we simply need to agree – regardless of the consequences. Worse yet, we only need agreement among, and by extension *with*, the party in power, because the majority is presumed to represent the will of the people. Such an epistemology (or framework for knowing what's true) devalues thinking through decisions, compromises democratic deliberation, serves only the interests of those in power, and reduces everything to either-or absolutes.

As Stephen Colbert says (in one installment of "The Word"), "You're either for the war, or against America. There's no gray area." ("Or gray matter, apparently," as the explanatory side-text reads onscreen.)

Stewart has said most politicians probably do truly believe they'd do a better job than their opponents. But they tend to neglect making honest arguments to justify that belief. They don't consider enough information honestly to arrive at the best course of action. Instead, they often follow Niccolo Machiavelli's (1469–1527) advice "to learn how not to be good, and to use this knowledge and not use it, according to the necessities of the case."[2] Such reasoning leads to thinking that one's ends "justify" any means, no matter how destructive.

Stewart disagrees less with what politicians actually believe, and more with the way they suppress respectful and possibly fruitful exchange. Many leaders go from duplicitously manipulating rhetoric to outright dissembling and lying. Worse still, the media often appear to collude in the deception, failing to provide appropriate context or perspective. For example, when former Defense Secretary Donald Rumsfeld gave a speech ("Secretary on the Defensive," October 2006), he was interrupted by hecklers. Then he took a question.

Questioner:	I'm Ray McGovern, a 27-year veteran of the Central Intelligence Agency. Why did you lie to get us into a war that was not necessary, that has caused these kinds of casualties?
Rumsfeld:	First of all, I haven't lied.
Stewart:	Oh, he didn't lie. Well, that settles it. There's pound cake in the back, we can have a good time, and uh –
Rumsfeld:	It appears that there were not weapons of mass destruction.
McGovern:	You said you knew where they were.
Rumsfeld:	I did not.
Stewart:	See? He never said he knew where they were.
Rumsfeld:	(*earlier video from March 2003*) We know where they are. They're in the area around . . . Baghdad.
Stewart:	Well to be fair, Rumsfeld probably never saw that episode of *Meet the Press*.

Stewart begins his comments, as he often does, in the guise of a hopeful, if somewhat gullible, citizen. He then pretends to believe that the media will dutifully investigate such doubletalk: "So, the Secretary of Defense, caught, in a contradiction, about weapons of mass destruction. Surely that will be a big story." Clips instead show CNN's Paula Zahn accusing McGovern of having "an axe to grind," Tucker Carlson calling him "not just any heckler," and Anderson Cooper asking McGovern irrelevantly, "Were you nervous?" Carlson continued:

Carlson: Isn't it enough that he was wrong and had bad judgment? Why does he have to be a liar too?
McGovern: Well, that's the question you'll have to direct to him.
Stewart: But won't.

Stewart then showed clips from what he called "a Fox News unvestigative report" about Rumsfeld entitled "Why He Fights." The reporter interviews General Paul van Riper – who called for Rumsfeld's resignation – and asks accusingly:

Reporter: What are you trying to accomplish by doing this? And you don't think this debate threatens the civilian leadership of the military? Does that hurt the war effort?
Stewart: (*sniffing deeply*) Mmm, I can't tell if I'm smelling the fairness (*sniffs*) or the balance.

Alluding to the Fox News tagline "Fair and Balanced," Stewart draws attention to how loaded questions support a one-sided agenda, rather than providing an even-handed and honest investigation or forum for discussion. By allowing such contradictions, whether from politicians or the media, to speak for themselves, *The Daily Show* implicitly invites us to notice when we too resort to deception – keeping *us* honest when we believe, say, that we ourselves deserve to succeed by any means necessary.

In the Line of Ire: Reframing the Debate

One way to fight Machiavellian manipulation, the show implies, is to reframe the terms of debate. In interviewing William Bennett, author and former Secretary of Education under Ronald Reagan, Stewart questions the apparent inconsistency between Bennett's claim to affirm America's belief in freedom and his attempts to limit freedom by a ban on gay marriage:

> Stewart: Why not encourage gay people to join in in [sic] that family arrangement if *that's* what provides stability to a society?
> Bennett: Well I think if gay . . . gay people are members of families, they're *already* members of families.
> Stewart: And that's where the buck stops, that's the gay ceiling.
> Bennett: Look, it's a debate about whether you believe marriage is between a man and a woman.
> Stewart: I disagree. I think it's a debate about whether gay people are part of the human condition or just a random fetish.

Stewart rejects Bennett's framing of the debate. He doesn't just contradict him by saying, "Marriage isn't *necessarily* between man and woman." Rather, he suggests that the debate isn't about how to define marriage, but instead about who counts as human, and how to understand the human condition.

> Bennett: The question is how do you define marriage? Where do you draw the line? What do you say to the polygamist? What do you *say* to the polygamist?
> Stewart: You don't say anything to the polygamist. That is a choice, to get three or four wives. That is not a biological condition that "I gots to get laid by different women that I'm married to." That's a choice. Being gay is part of the human condition. There's a huge difference.

Stewart first shows that calling homosexuality a *mere* choice ignores that it's a much more basic condition of who someone is; he thus undercuts superficial versions of the determined/chosen dichotomy. Stewart then speaks to the larger question of what it means to be human. While Stewart seeks to foster respect for the freedom to be our fully human and different selves, Bennett treats differences of human condition as subject to choice and hence, regulation.

> Bennett: Well, some people regard their human condition as having three women. Look the polygamists are all over this.

Stewart:	Then let's go slippery slope the other way. If government says I can define marriage as between a man and a woman, what says they can't define it between people of different income levels, or they can decide whether or not you are a suitable husband for a particular woman?
Bennett:	Because, gender *matters* in marriage, it has mattered to every human society, it matters in every religion, uh, it has mattered in –
Stewart:	Race matters in every society as well. Isn't progress understanding?

Bennett's appeal resembles the warning of conservative orator Edmund Burke (1729–97) against interfering extensively with stability and habit. Stewart's suggestion, on the other hand, is that for real progress to occur, society must become more inclusive and accommodate greater variety and difference over time.

Stewart implies a belief in the fundamental value of learning and transformation over stagnation and tradition for tradition's sake. To learn first requires admitting that one's perceptions may be limited. As the *Tao Te Ching* puts it, "The mark of a moderate man is freedom from his own ideas."[3] To free our minds, we must either shift frames of reference ourselves or at least understand genuinely how others frame things differently.

Look Who's Not Talking Now: Going Beyond Experience

Our experience both opens and closes our perception of the world, like a lens that brings some things into focus while blurring others. As the philosopher Hans-Georg Gadamer (1900–2002) wrote, "If a person is trying to understand something, he will not be able to rely from the start on his own chance previous ideas."[4] If Bennett fails to question the source of his moral indignation – how, for instance, family influence or a distaste for gay sex may influence his viewpoint – he can't truly understand either the issue or his role in debating it.

In his interview, Bennett went on to target "activist" judges, saying that gay marriage is coming because "the courts have decided it." He continued by associating being gay with a devaluing of marriage in Western culture:

> *Bennett:* In Holland and Norway, marriage is taken less seriously. When you define it out, when you start to say it can involve anybody, then I think, any grouping, anybody who loves anybody, it has serious problems.
>
> *Stewart:* It has serious problems. And you know divorce is not caused because 50 percent of marriages end in gayness.

Deliberately associating being gay with "taking marriage less seriously" is a form of scapegoating. (Historically, the Jewish people symbolically burdened a goat with their sins.) Bennett's argument seems similarly aimed at blaming an innocent target (here, homosexuals) and gives no reason for his prejudice.

Stewart puts the obsession with the issue of gay marriage, and its abuse by politicians and pundits, in perspective by identifying divorce as not the result but the greater concern. As with all humor, the joke first gives a context (marriage), then sets up an incongruity or problem (what ends a marriage), and finally leaps to an unexpected resolution (marriage ends in gayness). The structure of such jokes resembles that of serious problem-solving. To make sense of a certain thing, we need to put it in appropriate context and build a new understanding. Stewart's juxtaposition highlights the absurdity of the view that homosexuality somehow mars the institution of marriage.

Show Me the Meta

America (The Book) contains an image of colonists meeting Native Americans.[5] The caption reads: "America's path to democracy was cleared by the colonists' generous giveaways, like the much sought-after 'Smallpox Blankets.'" The line makes us laugh at an agonizingly tragic fact about colonial history. Such sharply tinged satire in *The Daily Show* derives from the very nature of tragedy and comedy. According to Friedrich Nietzsche (1844–1900), tragedy combines both Apollonian and Dionysian tendencies, reason and recklessness, restraint and excess, going back and forth between the two, never resting at either.

Such a dynamic relationship is the theme of correspondent Ed Helms'
visit to one of the great battlegrounds of what *The Daily Show* terms
the "evolutionary" war. He stands in front of Ray County Courthouse,
in Dayton, Tennessee, the site of the infamous 1925 Scopes Monkey
Trial, where John Scopes was convicted for teaching evolution to high
school students. That trial "gave Dayton a reputation for closed-minded
ignorance," as Helms says. But, he then implies, it's really just a reen-
actment town.

Helms: (*voiceover*) Just like Colonial Williamsburg, the town is popu-
lated with costumed performers who reenact the quaint attitudes
of the good old days.

Helms: (*to resident June Griffin*) What is your take on the Scopes trial?

Griffin: Evolution is a total fabrication and a lie. Evolution distorts faith,
destroys faith, and builds an economic market that is contrary
to our American way of life.

Helms: That's good stuff.

Helms: (*voiceover*) In addition to the skilled actors, Dayton's attention to detail is staggering. The town has gone so far as to erect
this elaborate set of a fully functioning college. Named after
William Jennings Bryan, the prosecutor in the Scopes trial, the
college keeps things authentic. Store owner Tim Cruver, whose
daughter plays one of the college students, explains.

Helms: (*to Cruver*) What does their science department teach regarding evolution vs. creationism?

Cruver: Well it's a fact that they're going to be teaching creationism up
there because they don't believe in evolution.

Helms: When the tourists aren't, ya know, milling around, watching
the classes and stuff, then what do they teach?

Cruver: Well, the same thing.

According to a 2005 Pew Forum survey, nearly two-thirds of
Americans support teaching creationism alongside evolution. Yet
doing so treats faith and prejudicial belief on a par with scientific
truth. Science requires observation, testing, data, analysis, and verifica-
tion. And these can't simply be forced to fit one's values, important
as values are in deciding what questions to pursue.

Dayton's opposition to evolutionary theory, as Helms puts it,
"would be terrifying if it were real" – which it is! It rightly scares
us that so many people ignore or defame the scientific community's

consensus that humans evolved from non-human primates. An extra irony comes when Griffin says that she despises actors, apparently not realizing that Helms himself is an actor:

Helms: June, you're very good, you're very good. Do you have a back-ground in acting?
Griffin: No, I despise actors.
Helms: Really?
Griffin: Yes.

Griffin's "character" is unaware of the difference between a faith-based view (such as creationism) and a verifiable, scientific account of human origins (such as evolution), and is equally unaware that an actor has conned her into being the butt of a joke.

While the entire "Evolution, Schmevolution" series implicitly supports evolution, Stewart himself is usually concerned less with *what* people should think and more with how to engage in productive dialogue. In addition to reframing the terms of debate, he shows how to "go meta," or get above it all, and improve the process itself, be it political argument or media reportage.

For example, when interviewing Ramesh Ponnuru, author of *The Party of Death*, Stewart begins with meta-commentary:

Stewart: It seems like rhetoric like *The Party of Death* puts people on – I guess what I would call – the *defensive*, in some respects.
Ponnuru: Yeah. I can't really present the argument against things like abortion by pretending it doesn't have something to do with death. I guess that's part of the argument.
Stewart: Could you agree there is maybe sanctimony on both sides?
Ponnuru: Yeah, absolutely.
Stewart: Now, what's the sanctimony on your side?

By referring to sanctimony here, Stewart is targeting the false righteousness that's often involved in these debates. When pro-life advocates call abortion "genocide" and its defenders "murderers," they ignore important issues, such as women's right to protect their bodies. Likewise, when pro-choice advocates use language such as "products of conception" or "termination of pregnancy," they dehumanize the issue as one of cold, impersonal science. Ponnuru goes on to claim, "I try very hard to argue for a rational case," but rather than granting that his opponents have a reasoned defense, he reduces them to mere proponents "of death."

Stewart's approach to discourse, on the other hand, avoids the common attack-and-defend interview model, and instead endorses problem-solving values of conflict resolution.[6] As Stewart illustrates, this model prefers rationality to reactivity, sincerity to disingenuousness, authentic representation to dissembling, meaning to absurdity, and recognition to cynical suspicion. Of course, while the show implicitly values meaning over absurdity, it often amplifies the absurdity of public behavior, as with the Dayton story. *Daily Show* writers play up absurdity, however, not to get an empty laugh, but rather to affirm our right to more meaningful public discourse. In fact, critics often miss how the show targets precisely the sort of inaccuracy conveyed by empty jokes. When the show's writers use sarcastic or cynical humor, they arguably do so in response to the far graver cynicism of callous pundits and politicians who ignore their responsibility to society.

Self-Effacement and Good Faith

Stewart: I disagree with a lot of people. I think the whole problem with this debate is it's being waged on both extremes. If you extend it out it becomes: Do you condone what some would call rape to prevent what some would call murder? Because women are, I think rightly so, protective of what we call . . . their pussies. I don't know the scientific terms. But that's the part that's missing from the book. Can I tell you something?

Ponnuru: Yeah.

Stewart: I am very unprofessional.

No sooner does Stewart seriously summarize the abortion debate than he irreverently uses a word he knows will be censored and then derides his own behavior. Rather than take himself too seriously, Stewart often tries to make interviewees feel at ease, giving them a relatively free and uninhibited venue for speech and discussion. Adding unexpected taboo here, as elsewhere, provides lighthearted relief from the tension of serious discussion (which might go off track), for Stewart himself, his guests, and the audience alike.

Stewart is frequently self-effacing in this way, as when he reports that the show is now written by monkeys who complain, "Are we not sentient beings who deserve more than the relentless grind of ephemeral, topical, humor pabulum?" In this one line the *Daily Show* writers brand their *own* humor unfit for monkey, much less human, consumption, forgettably short-lived in its shelf-life, and so sophomoric as to be little better than baby food. Ironically, perhaps, to get the line's critical language, one needs more than basic sentience.

Further self-effacement comes when Stewart brings on guests like Bennett and Ponnuru, with whom he disagrees, and this often provides his guests with a face-saving out. For example, Stewart backed off Bennett at one point and said, "I'm just grasping at straws," acknowledging and taking responsibility for his own limited perspective, even putting himself down.

As he often does, Stewart also puts down audience ridicule. When Ponnuru hesitated and stumbled at one point, and the audience began to cheer, Stewart cut them off, saying, "No, no, no," then to Ponnuru, "And I want this, honestly, for us to have a conversation, because you're a smart guy, and you've made a lot of smart arguments." Stewart's shtick, even if it's an act, implies that one need not agree with someone in order to empathize with them or understand their viewpoint. In effect, Stewart extends a rarely seen presumption of good faith to those he interviews.

When actor Kevin Spacey told Stewart he wished "Congress and the Senate would go at [the President] every day" and added, "or maybe it should just be you . . . You should go, and every day ask him questions," Stewart replied, "I could barely get myself to work in the morning." As usual, Stewart portrays himself as a mere clown. When he himself is interviewed, he denies that *The Daily Show* is anything but comedy or at best, political and cultural satire. Such denials only reaffirm that Stewart's self-inclusive way of poking fun embodies a powerful way of being in the world – one of thoughtful, self-reflective, and modest engagement.

In the Ponnuru interview, for instance, Stewart's ultimate point is that we need lucid discussion, not heated provocation: "Isn't there a rational conversation to be had in the country . . . ?" Stewart's repeated call to overcome mutually exclusive oppositions often helps viewers to clarify their own thoughts and feelings, whether they agree or disagree with him or his guests. He seeks to find shared interest and common ground across political and ideological lines of debate.

Good faith, such as Stewart extends to most of his guests, relies on an implied promise that parties will participate sincerely in open dialogue and assume that progress can be made. By contrast, politicians and celebrities alike often act from bad faith, characterized by hidden agendas, closed discussion, and pessimism about, or indifference to, the genuine progress that open discussion might foster. Hence Matt Lauer delivers straight-laced reports like "Countdown to Doomsday," which Stewart called a "two hour investigation into your pants and why you should crap them."

When President Bush spent part of his vacation reading – and reportedly *liking* – Albert Camus' (1913–60) philosophical novel *The Stranger*, Stewart hinted at the irony of timing this choice during the Iraq war: Bush chose "a classic novel about a Westerner who kills an Arab for no good reason and dies with no remorse. Why that would strike a nerve, I don't know." *Daily Show* correspondent Jason Jones then "quoted" Bush's response to the work: "If the unexamined life is not worth living, then the soul not delved into is not worth being." Jones wishes that Bush were a kind of "philosopher king," Plato's ideal ruler, always acting rationally in the state's best interest.

Stewart similarly fantasizes about an ideal media and actually demonstrates how journalists would behave if they acted in good faith. For instance, he invariably adopts the persona of a serious reporter providing (and hoping for) much-needed perspective in place of mere sensationalism:

Stewart:	Obviously what is going on in the Middle East is awfully complicated. The fuel that fans the flames: The rival factions within Islam, both of them seem to have antipathy towards the US, Israel. It seems like there are some authoritarian regimes that are using proxy countries to fight their wars. It's a very difficult situation to grasp. Luckily, news organizations are on hand to give us context and ask the important questions.
Paula Zahn:	(*CNN graphic*: "Armageddon?") Are we really at the end of the world? We asked Faith and Values Correspondent Delia Gallagher to do some checking.

By juxtaposing the complexity of current international crises with the crassly commercial way cable networks cover them, *The Daily Show* lets misleading statements and images be their own undoing. The effect of Stewart's presentation is more immediate, and can be more powerful, than a pedantic, detailed, critique by an academic.

Not letting us rest content with taking in readymade perspectives uncritically, *The Daily Show* frees us from inert passivity and forces active viewing, as counseled by China's most famous philosopher (in the epigraph at the beginning of this chapter). The writers assume we can infer how reasoning has gone awry in public discourse, inviting us to wrestle with the rhetoric in order to get the joke. We try to keep pace with Stewart by leaping as he does through the roles of shocked viewer, confused inquirer, reasoned skeptic, and frustrated (because powerless) citizen. Yet while forcing us to reckon with what's most disturbing about the machinations of politicians and the media, *The Daily Show* also provides a cathartic laugh in the face of seemingly inevitable pain and disappointment.

Who knew thinking could be such fun?[7]

Notes

1 Jean-Jacques Rousseau, *The Social Contract*, trans. G. D. H. Cole (Amherst: Prometheus Books, 1988), p. 23.
2 Niccolo Machiavelli, *The Prince*, trans. Luigi Ricci, revd. E. R. P. Vincent (New York: McGraw-Hill, 1950), p. 56.
3 Lao-tzu, *Tao Te Ching*, trans. Stephen Mitchell (New York: Harper Perennial, 1992), p. 59.
4 Hans-Georg Gadamer, *Truth and Method*, trans. and ed. Garrett Barden and John Cumming (New York: Seabury Press, 1975), p. 238.
5 Jon Stewart, Ben Karlin, and David Javerbaum, *America (The Book): A Citizen's Guide to Democracy Inaction* (New York: Warner Books, 2004), p. 18.
6 Jay Rothman, *Resolving Identity-Based Conflict in Nations, Organizations and Communities* (San Francisco: Jossey-Bass, 1997), pp. 17, 40, and 47.
7 My deepest gratitude goes to Melanie Torosyan and Chris Worsley, without whose invaluable feedback I could not imagine writing. Thanks also to Ron Gross, Jack Kytle, Steve Sills, Rick Dewitt, and Jen Goldberg.

10

THE DAILY SHOW'S EXPOSÉ OF POLITICAL RHETORIC

LIAM P. DEMPSEY

In no area of human life is the purposeful misuse of reason more pervasive than in politics. Rhetoric, you might say, is the bread and butter of political discourse. It's also the mainstay of *The Daily Show*'s humor. Through purely informal means, the program brings to light various uses of political rhetoric for recognition and due ridicule. *The Daily Show*'s incisive satire makes these attempts at rhetorical manipulation (literally) laughable.

In this chapter we'll consider *The Daily Show*'s unique capacity to demonstrate, through satire, misuses of reason in political life. Most of the examples we'll consider are taken from the "Indecision 2004" segments originally broadcast on the show.[1] Some are taken from *The Colbert Report*. We'll begin by considering *The Daily Show*'s treatment of the more common logical fallacies employed by politicians and their exponents. Next we'll discuss various political appeals to emotion exposed by *The Daily Show*. Then we'll consider some of *The Daily Show*'s many forays into the alternative universe of political spin, the systematic, politically motivated use of persuasive language, including "talking-points." We'll conclude by briefly considering some of the different comedic devices used by Jon Stewart and Stephen Colbert to expose and satirize these kinds of political rhetoric.

A Cavalcade of Fallacies

Fallacies are errors in reasoning, which appear correct, and which often distract people, one way or another, from the real issues. Arguably the most common fallacy used in political discourse is the *ad hominem* argument. This fallacy is committed when, rather than addressing the argument or position a person offers, one simply attacks the person. Similarly, one might try to make a person's argument or position look good, not by giving reasons for it, but by praising its advocate.

Colbert gave a nice example of the *ad hominem* fallacy by "praising" partisan attacks on a ruling that the administration's warrantless wiretapping program was unconstitutional. Rather than addressing the merits or the details of the ruling, partisan attacks simply dismissed the decision on the grounds that the judge, Anna Diggs Taylor, was appointed by Democratic President Jimmy Carter. Of course, her political affiliations are irrelevant to the cogency of her arguments. Her decision stands or falls by the logical force of her reasoning, not some aspect of her personality or history. The reasons for her decision are (conveniently) ignored by partisan critics.

Also common in political rhetoric is the straw man fallacy, in which someone attacks a misrepresentation, a weakened version of an opponent's argument, preferably one casting the opponent in a negative light. Consider, for example, the claim that Democratic Representative John Murtha advocated a "cut and run" policy in Iraq. Not only is this claim demonstrably false – Murtha advocated a staged redeployment of troops out of Iraq while keeping them within the region broadly – it also trades on negative language. "Cut and run" is used to insinuate that he, and anyone who agrees with him, are irresponsible cowards. Note well that this phrase in no way addresses Murtha's *actual* position.

The Daily Show exposes a similar example of the straw man fallacy in its coverage of Democratic Senator Zell Miller's vitriolic speech against Senator Kerry (RNC, Day 3). Indeed, Senator Miller provides a number of examples of fallacies. Not only does he engage in *ad hominem* attacks, many of these attacks are attacks against straw men. Take, for example, his claim that, as president, Kerry would "let Paris decide when America needs defending."

The claim is, of course, preposterous. Other examples of the *ad hominem*/straw man blend are easy enough to find. After Hurricane Katrina, a popular administration talking-point was the plea that the press shouldn't "engage in the 'blame game'" by questioning the timeliness or adequacy of the government's response to the crisis.

Consider too the notorious "freedom fries" and "freedom toast" incident (unfairly targeting the French). When Capitol Hill cafeterias dropped "freedom" from their menus, Colbert bemoaned it in typical hyperbolic fashion, insisting that the change to "freedom fries" was the finest achievement of the Republican controlled Congress, that without it, we're left with "surrender fires." Or consider Governor George Pataki's speech in which he asks the audience, "What is this election about if it isn't about our love of freedom?" implying that only one party, the GOP, loves freedom, while Democrats and others don't (RNC, Day 4).

This brings up the false dilemma, the fallacy that there are only two choices when in fact there are more than two. Consider this remark on a cable news station. To paraphrase: "Sure it's not great having the government collect our telephone records, but it is better than having them collect our body parts!" The argument is, in effect, that we have two choices: either we allow possibly unconstitutional and invasive government surveillance, or we all die! Another famous example of false dilemma, "Either you're with us, or you're with the terrorists," trades on an appeal to patriotism. Satirizing this twisted logic on *The Report*, Colbert concurs with the President, insisting, "Either you're for the war [in Iraq], or you hate America. It's that simple!" (August 29, 2006). These false dilemmas have become quite laughable. With President Bush's declining poll numbers, it's especially absurd to think that over half the country supports the terrorists! Even so, the use of this sort of false dilemma continues. For instance, Stewart lambasted Vice President Dick Cheney for suggesting that anti-war Democratic candidate Ned Lamont's primary victory over Senator Joseph Lieberman was a victory for Al Qaeda (August 15, 2006). Again, the implication is that one either supports the war or one supports the terrorists, and so Lamont's criticism of the war puts him in league with the terrorists. Picking up on this ridiculous suggestion, Colbert began talking about Lamont as if he and Bin Laden were old friends!

It's worth noting that *Daily Show* correspondents often use false dilemma questions. Samantha Bee, for instance, satirizes the rhetorical theatrics of the 2004 Republican national convention with the following: "Is tonight the night that they exploit 9/11, or is tonight inspired by empty promises for the future?" (RNC, Day 3). It's fairly common practice on *The Report* for Colbert to ask the Congressional representatives he interviews (in his "Better Know a District" segment): "George W. Bush: *great* president or the *greatest* president?"

The slippery slope fallacy is committed when someone claims that a seemingly harmless action, if taken, will inevitably lead to a disastrous outcome. Noting a report of a woman in India allegedly marrying a snake, a Fox News commentator challenged gay marriage advocates to give principled reasons for why we ought to "draw the line" at snakes. The implication is that there's a slippery slope from gay marriage to *any* conceivable union, however ridiculous. There's also an *ad hominem*/straw man element here, as if homosexuals were no different from those who practice bestiality, implausible as it is to see a snake as a *person* capable of informed consent. Colbert's response to this argument was to "agree" that homosexuals *should* have to justify this purported marriage to a snake. Having said this, however, Colbert continued:

> I don't see gay marriage as a slippery slope down to people marrying snakes. I see people marrying snakes as a step up the slope from gay marriage. I've got no problem with people marrying snakes – as long as they're not marrying *gay* snakes. We must marry limbless reptiles of the opposite sex. Otherwise, it's just unnatural. (June 20, 2006)

The fallacy of equivocation is committed when someone uses a key word in two or more senses in the same argument and the apparent success of the argument depends on the shift in meaning. A statement from Presidential Press Secretary Tony Snow, satirized on *The Daily Show* (August 2, 2006), provides a humorous example. In response to questions about President Bush's medical exam, Snow proudly proclaimed that President Bush was "fit for duty." As a rhetorical device, this proclamation trades on an ambiguity between physical fitness, which a doctor assessed, and professional *competency*, which wasn't tested, and lies beyond the doctor's medical expertise.

Stewart illustrates this equivocation by displaying a picture of an overweight William H. Taft, who might have been fit for duty (competent) despite his apparent lack of physical fitness.

Finally, there's the fallacy of begging the question, which is committed when an arguer states or assumes the very things he or she is trying to prove as a conclusion. Consider *The Daily Show*'s satirical take on Senator Sam Brownback's argument against state-sponsored embryonic stem cell research (July 19, 2006). Brownback's presentation included a series of pictures following the development of a child, the result of a discarded embryo, a so-called *snowflake* baby. The first picture depicts the frozen embryo in question. During this presentation, Senator Brownback refers to the frozen embryo as the *same person* as in the other pictures. This reasoning is fallacious in that Senator Brownback assumes the truth of the very point at issue. He assumes that an embryo is a person in arguing that the state should treat it as a person. Thus, he begs the question against the proponents of embryonic stem cell research who don't accept the premise that embryos are persons. Indeed, Brownback goes even further, displaying pictures drawn by the child in question, of herself as a "happy" embryo – with a smiley face – juxtaposed with "sad" embryos that haven't yet been adopted. Not only does this beg the question, it also attempts to "tug at our heartstrings," trading on the very strong feelings we have for the welfare of children. As Stewart concludes with a chuckle, if research reveals that some embryos are capable of speech and emotions, they should, indeed, be exempt from research!

Tugging at the Heartstrings

It's common – all too common – for politicians to make direct appeals to listeners' emotions. These include appeals to fear, outrage, and patriotism. Since 9/11, fear has become a powerful rhetorical device in North American political life. Not surprisingly, fear-mongering – causing or using fear in your audience in order to persuade them – has become quite common. It's fear that often "justifies," in the public mind, both military interventions abroad and limitations on civil liberties at home.

Appeals to fear, outrage, and patriotism are brought out nicely in *The Daily Show*'s treatment of the 2004 Democratic and Republican national conventions. Both parties make ample use of these rhetorical devices to secure support. For example, as Stewart highlights, there were numerous references to Senator Kerry's (comparatively impressive) war record in an attempt to harness the fear, outrage, and patriotic fervor of post-9/11 America.[2] Recall Senator Kerry's salute to the audience and his exclamation: "I'm John Kerry and I'm reporting for duty!" The take-home message: the world is a very scary place, fraught with danger and hidden enemies, but John Kerry, a decorated war hero, will protect us from these dangers.

The Republicans, on the other hand, went so far as to have their convention in New York City, just miles away from Ground Zero. The *continual* references to 9/11 and the threat of terrorism in its delegates' speeches are difficult to overstate. As Stewart notes, not only were "September 11th" and "terrorism" frequent refrains in the speeches of the participants, "September 11, 2001" was displayed on the backdrop to the speaker's podium (RNC, Day 1). Colbert summed up these rather obvious – but apparently effective – rhetorical ploys as "crass-tastic."

Appeals to outrage can take at least two forms: trying to harness listeners' outrage in order to persuade them, and simply displaying outrage at something for the same purpose. In the latter case, outrage suggests conviction. If so-and-so is *that* upset about such-and-such, there must be something *really* objectionable about it. Democratic Senator Zell Miller's angry speech at the 2004 Republican national convention (RNC, Day 3) provides a nice example of the rhetorical use of outrage: "Today's Democratic leaders see America as an occupier not a liberator. And nothing makes this marine madder than someone calling American troops occupiers rather than liberators!"[3] Miller's suggestion is that it's outrageous, even unpatriotic, to describe the American military presence in Iraq as an occupation. The choice of "occupier" over "liberator" infuriates Senator Miller! But notice that Miller hasn't given us any *reason* to view "liberator" as more fitting than "occupier." He's just expressed patriotic outrage, without in any way justifying it, much less his conclusion. What's more, as Stewart humorously points out, President Bush himself had only recently referred to Iraqis as living under "occupation."

The ubiquity of fear-mongering and appeals to outrage and patriotism has also been picked up on by Colbert in his *Report*. In an exchange with Stewart at the end of one episode of *The Daily Show*, Colbert actually fear-mongers about fear-mongering, using fear to draw attention to the dangers of fear-mongering (August 16, 2006)! To take another example, Colbert satirized fear-mongering in cable news reports on the Middle East by enthusiastically embracing the potential outbreak of "WWIII," complete with graphics of explosions and allusions to Armageddon. Similarly, in his regular segment "The Threat Down" – introduced with a siren! – Colbert satirizes the popular use of fear-mongering with lists of *new* things (such as bears) to be afraid of.

Likewise, Colbert makes frequent appeals to patriotism, "wrapping himself in the flag," sometimes literally, in his rants against liberals.[4] Those who criticize the policies of the Bush administration are seen as part of the "blame America first crowd," and those critical of the Iraq war, or who want to bring American troops home, "refuse to support the troops," or in other words support "terrorists" against American forces.[5] According to Colbert's twisted logic, criticizing the Bush administration is tantamount to criticizing America itself and abandoning its troops to the terrorists.

Spin: The Systematic Use of Persuasive Language

Political spin relies primarily on the emotional impact of word choice and selectively highlighting some facts while ignoring others. To spin a political story in one's favor involves using language and imagery intended to produce the most favorable emotional response in the listener, regardless of the reality of the situation. One might recall *Daily Show* correspondent Ed Helms' look at the second Presidential debate between George Bush and John Kerry ("Extras"). As he shuttles back and forth between Democratic and Republican operatives looking for the truth about what happened in the debate, Helms becomes exasperated, recognizing that the he's being told contradictory things. After all, they couldn't have both won the debate! Eventually he comes to the "startling" revelation that their assessments were empty and manipulative attempts at persuasion.[6] In general, the numerous political "gunslingers" that now populate 24 hour cable news can be relied on to spin just about any development in favor of their preferred candidate or party.

Informed and educated citizens must be able to separate the logical force of a set of claims from the emotive force or "slant" provided by a political advocate's choice of words. This often involves recognizing the use of euphemisms (language which makes things seem better than they are) and dysphemisms (which makes them seem worse than they are). Euphemisms trade on positive associations, dysphemisms on negative associations.[7] For example, in the sphere of politics a homicide may be referred to as an "assassination" (with its negative connotations) or (with far less negative, almost clinical, if not positive connotations) a "neutralization." It matters whether people involved in political conflicts are labeled "terrorists," "insurgents," "guerillas," "partisans," "freedom fighters," or "heroes," whether a military action is referred to as "liberation," "invasion," or "illegal aggression." In many cases, some word choices are neutral, and so are more appropriate than others. To avoid being susceptible to the manipulations of spin, people must be able to distinguish the spin of a claim – positive or negative – from the logical force of the actual reasons given for it.

A closely related spin technique is rhetorical definition. Take for example the (rhetorical) definition of "abortion" as "the murder of an unborn baby." This definition attempts to smuggle in a *loaded* word. Defining "abortion" as the *murder* of a *baby* begs the question against those who deny that abortion is murder.[8] The question of whether or not abortion is murder is the very point in dispute, and so can't legitimately be assumed as a basis for debate. Loading a definition in this way can be a very effective rhetorical device despite being unjustified. After all, few would disagree that murdering babies is wrong.

The use of so-called talking-points is the *systematic* use of spin by a group or party. In the case of political parties, particular words, phrases, subjects, and emphases are disseminated to the party faithful. When presented with an argument that uses talking-points, we must be able to recognize and evaluate them to avoid being unduly influenced by them. *The Daily Show*, particularly through its use of montages, does a nice job of revealing the use of talking-points. By showing, in rapid succession, numerous political figures (and reporters) repeating the exact same phrases, the systematic and coordinated use of spin is laid bare. Having been exposed, their virtual vacuity revealed, the talking-points lose their rhetorical power.[9]

To demonstrate striking double-standards in policy and talking-points, Stewart displayed a montage of competing and contradictory rhetoric from President Bush concerning Iraq and North Korea (July 11, 2006). In the first case, the (arguably baseless) fear of Iraqi involvement in future terrorist attacks was said to warrant *immediate* military action – time had "run out" for Saddam Hussein. In the second case, the (actual) nuclear threat posed by North Korea was taken as a cue for *diplomacy, patience,* and international *consensus*!

In his 2002 State of the Union address, President Bush declared that he wouldn't permit the world's most dangerous regimes (the "axis of evil," including North Korea) to threaten the United States. It now seems clear, however, that the main target was Iraq. In the case of Iraq, Bush presented a false dilemma: "I had a choice to make: either take the word of a madman [Saddam Hussein] or defend America. Given that choice, I will defend America every time." But when faced with the arguably worse threat posed by the leader of North Korea, Kim Jong Il, President Bush doesn't present the situation in terms of this sort of dilemma. So while North Korea continues to threaten America with tests of ballistic missiles and nuclear warheads, the rhetoric about North Korea remains markedly different from the rhetoric that swirled around the invasion of Iraq. The talking-points on North Korea emphasize diplomacy and the need for patience, not the imminent threat of a "madman."

To consider another example, "Words Speak Louder Than Actions" presents the evolution of some of the administration's more inflammatory rhetoric, demonstrating a striking difference between the talk talked (rhetoric) and the walk walked (action) (RNC, Day 2). It begins with President Bush's now infamous declaration that his administration wanted Osama Bin Laden, and the other members of Al Qaeda, "dead or alive." Recall that he was "going to smoke them out of their caves" and bring them to justice. As the invasion of Iraq approached, however, the rhetoric changed. Capturing Bin Laden was marginalized – "the objective is not Bin Laden" – and the supposedly growing danger posed by Saddam Hussein was emphasized. Terrifying words and phrases were used: "anthrax," "rape-rooms," "weapons of mass destruction."[10] What's more, Hussein, who apparently wasn't at all involved in the 9/11 attacks, was increasingly and misleadingly associated with Al Qaeda. But with the failure to find weapons of mass destruction in Iraq, the administration's rhetoric once again changed. Rather than claiming that Iraq actually had "weapons of mass destruction," the administration claimed that Hussein was involved in "weapons of mass destruction related program activities." Note that the latter, rather ineloquent, characterization of the Hussein threat, while consistent with the lack of actual weapons of mass destruction, fails to convey the sense of imminent danger which was supposed to justify invasion in the first place.

Imagery and context can also play an important role in political rhetoric, as is illustrated by *The Daily Show*'s "Indecision 2004" coverage of both Democratic and Republican national conventions. Both parties display many examples of stagecraft and pageantry to move viewers to support them. Rather than relying solely on the content of their arguments and positions, both parties make ample use of marketing techniques to persuade the voting public. *Daily Show* contributor Lewis Black comments on the more ridiculous production details of the Democratic convention, like its numerous musical performances and its award-show-style format, with sometimes silly or inappropriate theme songs (RNC, Day 1). Then-correspondent Colbert, by way of trying to excuse his skipping out on the Democratic Convention, calls it "a farce, a scripted, stage-managed event. It's not news. It isn't even fake news!" (DNC, Day 3). In a subsequent episode, Colbert compares what he euphemistically calls his "protest" with what his executive producer refers to as "grounds for dismissal."[11]

Satirized for Your Protection

Exactly how does *The Daily Show* use humor to reveal political rhetoric? Does it use humorous editing techniques to expose attempts at rhetorical persuasion, or does the humor emerge from the rhetoric itself? If you've been paying attention, you should recognize this as a false dilemma. Among the various strategies in satirizing political rhetoric, the montage, as we saw, is ideal for exposing the use of talking-points. Half a dozen political operatives (or even reporters) using the exact same phrase is no coincidence, and when put together into a montage, this becomes all too obvious. We've also noted how montages are useful in charting the evolution of talking-points as rhetoric changes to suit changing political needs. In general, Stewart's careful selection of footage can reveal many chimaeras of reason. Rhetoric offends the intellect, and when highlighted, humor is the predictable result. Satirizing the excesses of personality-driven cable news show hosts with the most gratuitous examples of rhetoric, Colbert *embodies* the kind of bad reasoning that Stewart merely exposes. Colbert's character embraces the irrational fully, and makes explicit the biased agendas of those he satirizes.

Given the widespread use of political rhetoric, it's clear that many politicians have a rather cynical view of human nature. The popular use of manipulative persuasion techniques suggests that, from the perspective of the political elite, the average citizen shouldn't be trusted with the truth, but should rather accept beliefs handed down from on high. The democratic ideals that help shape and define Western culture reject this elitism, and so it's of the utmost importance that we avoid adopting and maintaining our beliefs uncritically, that we don't fall prey to the rhetorical machinations of our political leaders. A critically informed and thoughtful citizenry is essential to the health of the democratic institutions that are intended to ensure liberty. *The Daily Show*'s ability to expose and satirize political rhetoric makes it both enlightening and, oddly enough, enjoyable too.

Notes

1 These segments are collected in the DVD, *The Daily Show with Jon Stewart: Indecision 2004* (Comedy Central, 2005). References to coverage of particular conventions and days will be made parenthetically in-text.
2 Stewart also considers more familiar sorts of Democratic pandering. In an effort to "relate" to their working-class base, several speakers recounted stories of their difficult upbringings and working-class backgrounds, from being the son of a mill worker to being the son of a goat farmer.

3 After the speech, Senator Miller did an interview on Chris Matthews' show *Hardball* (MSNBC) in which he lamented that they didn't live in a time when he could challenge Matthews to a duel!

4 As viewers of the show will have noticed, the show's mascot is a bald eagle, and the stars and stripes, and other bits of patriotic symbolism, are ubiquitous.

5 More than one of his guests who are critical of the Iraq war has faced the (loaded) question: "Why do you hate our troops, sir?"

6 Post-debate spin has a significant impact on public perceptions of political debates. Winning a Presidential debate in the public's mind often means having advocates that effectively persuade the viewing public that the candidate has won or done a good job, regardless of whether this is so. Obviously the quality of a candidate's performance makes the job of spinning more or less difficult. But even disastrously poor showings can sometimes be effectively spun, and so it's important to recognize the influence of post-debate "spin doctors."

7 On the use of euphemisms and dysphemisms in political rhetoric, see Brooke N. Moore and Richard Parker, *Critical Thinking*, 7th edn. (New York: McGraw-Hill, 2004), pp. 124–8.

8 Alternatively, one might give a rhetorical definition of abortion which begs the question against the pro-life position by, for example, defining "abortion" as "the termination of a fast-growing tumor." A relatively neutral definition is "the termination of an embryo or fetus," which describes abortion without begging the question against either position on its moral status.

9 Likewise, a montage of different reporters who are, for example, leveling *loaded questions* against a person, party, or group brings to light potential biases in the press.

10 "Weapons of mass destruction" is a nebulous phrase including a variety of weapons which can differ widely in their potential destructiveness, while other weapons which seemingly possess the potential to cause mass or indiscriminant destruction (napalm, white phosphorous, depleted uranium munitions, and cluster bombs) may or may not be included. Note as well that large munitions (such as 2,000-pound "bunker busters") used on urban targets are quite capable of causing mass and, in some cases, indiscriminate destruction.

11 For a somewhat different slant on spin, see Kimberly A. Blessing and Joseph J. Marren, "Bullshit and Political Spin: Is the Medium the Massage?" up next.

11

BULLSHIT AND POLITICAL SPIN:
IS THE MEDIUM THE MASSAGE?

KIMBERLY A. BLESSING AND JOSEPH J. MARREN

Magician-comedians Penn and Teller have a show dedicated to it on Showtime. MIT (the Massachusetts Institute of Tauroscatology) publishes it as a weekly gazette. It can be played as a card game or a drinking game. Deflectors for it are available on the Web. It was recently found on the *New York Times* bestseller list. What is it? Bullshit. It was only a matter of time before Jon Stewart would wade in.

In March 2005 Ivy League philosopher Harry Frankfurt appeared on *The Daily Show* to promote his bestseller *On Bullshit*.[1] Stewart proved himself an able student of philosophy as he guided the discussion on the distinction between lying and bullshit. For Frankfurt, bullshit is more corrosive to society than lies because bullshitters don't care about the truth. Even though the liar intentionally distorts or misrepresents the truth (think of finger-wagging Bill Clinton: "I did not have sexual relations with that woman"), at least the liar knows, and by implication cares about, what is true. Bullshitters don't.

Philosopher-comedian Stewart followed up the discussion of the lie/bullshit distinction with the following question, which he posed to Frankfurt but never quite let him answer: "What is the difference between bullshit and political spin?" We'll take up Stewart's question, and consider how *The Daily Show* handles both bullshit and spin. First, let's examine bullshit.

133

The Essence of Bullshit

In a prior interview in *Rolling Stone* magazine, Stewart explained that the point of view of *The Daily Show* "is that we're passionately opposed to bullshit."[2] OK. Now fast-forward to the Frankfurt interview. In the first of several witty exchanges between host and guest, Frankfurt explains how his book came about:

> *Stewart:* When did you write it?
> *Frankfurt:* 1980 . . . 5.
> *Stewart:* Don't bullshit me.
> *Frankfurt:* No, well, '85 and a half?
> *Stewart:* Now, tell us how it came to be released as a book, only recently, no?
> *Frankfurt:* Yeah, in January. My editor at Princeton University Press got the idea of publishing it as a book. And when he brought it up I said, "What are you talking about? It's a 25 page essay. How can you bring it out as a book?" He said, "Well we can do lots of things with margins, and types of fonts, and page sizes," and that's what they did.
> *Stewart:* Really? That's lovely. [*Flips through book*] Boy, he's not kidding around here. They're like little affirmations. It's really interesting and very apropos for today.

It's too bad Stewart didn't pick up on the fact that the whole idea of playing around with font size on an already-published essay, in order to market it as a book, might strike some as another kind of bullshit. In other interviews, Frankfurt explains how he came to address the topic of bullshit in the first place, which he explains in terms of his training as an analytic philosopher. (Analytic philosophy is an Anglo-American movement that began in the twentieth century, focusing on the study of language and logical analysis of concepts.) Given what he viewed as the increasing volume of bullshit in the culture at the time, Frankfurt thought the concept worthy of analysis. In fact this delicious little book is a great illustration of analytic philosophy doing what it does best – clarifying concepts and the meaning of words.

To polish that gem of clarification, Stewart cross-examined his guest in a manner that would have made Socrates proud:

Stewart:	You say that bullshit is not lying.
Frankfurt:	No, it's not lying. Lying consists in believing that you know the truth, and saying something else.
Stewart:	It's willful.
Frankfurt:	It's willful. And the bullshitter doesn't really care whether what he says is true or false.
[Audience laughter]	
Stewart:	I should warn you that when they hear the word, it tickles them. They love the word.
Frankfurt:	I know, especially coming from an Ivy League professor. There's something special about that, I know.
Stewart:	For me, it's really. . . . It almost glasses me up.
Frankfurt:	I'm glad I could help.

Frankfurt spells out this distinction in more detail in his book. Liars care about what's true, which means they have a respect for the truth, if not always for telling it. By contrast, the bullshitter shows a lack of concern for the distinction between truth and falsity. With bullshitting the aim is to serve some purpose other than stating what's true or false, for example self-promotion, or promotion of some other person, program, or product. Since he's up to something else, the bullshitter doesn't really care about the facts, while the liar is deliberately trying to lead the listener away from them.

It is impossible for someone to lie unless he thinks he knows the truth. Producing bullshit requires no such conviction. A person who lies is thereby responding to the truth, and he is to that extent respectful of it. When an honest man speaks, he says only what he believes to be true; and for the liar, it is correspondingly indispensable that he considers his statements to be false. For the bullshitter, however, all these bets are off: he is neither on the side of the true nor on the side of the false. His eye is not on the facts at all, as the eyes of the honest man and of the liar are, except insofar as they may be pertinent to his interest in getting away with what he says. He does not care whether the things he says describe reality correctly. He just picks them out, or makes them up, to suit his purpose (pp. 55–6).

Let's return to the Bill Clinton example. In 1998, Clinton shook his finger at the American public and said, "I did not have sexual relations with that woman." He would later go on to state what he meant by "sexual relations." But clearly by the original statement Clinton intended to deny the reality of an event that had taken place.

Now imagine the following scenario: Hillary asked Bill whether or not Monica was in love with him. In order to spare his wife's feelings, Bill told Hillary that Monica was not in love with him, even though he believed that she was. Imagine further that Monica in fact was not in love with the President. Since Bill's statement corresponds to reality, his utterance is true. But he is still guilty of lying to Hillary because his intention was to deceive her, despite the fact that his statement ended up being true.

The Truth About Lies

Bullshit and lies have in common that they may or may not be true. While we can't distinguish bullshit from lies in terms of truth or falsity, we can distinguish them by speakers' different *attitudes* toward the truth and *intentions* in making the statements in question. Bullshitters are lackadaisical about the truth. They might be intellectually lazy, or perhaps they see simply their interests as better served by paying attention to something they *do* care about, like self-promotion. Liars aren't so lazy. They try to figure out the truth (even if they end up being wrong about it), and speak with the express intention of misleading their listeners, or turning them away from the truth.

To sharpen this contrast between bullshit and lies, let's imagine someone filling out a job application for a manager's position at Wal-Mart. When asked whether she has management experience, the applicant checks the "Yes" box on the application form, which let's suppose is false. Since she willfully stated a falsehood, she lied. Reviewing the application, the interviewer, believing the statements to be true, calls the applicant in for an interview:

Interviewer: It says here that you've had previous experience as a manager. Tell me how, as a manager, you motivate, say, a disgruntled employee.

Applicant: I would be *pro*-active, not *re*-active. I would map the teamwork environment to analyze interdependencies and then figure out how to match motivator to individual. Blah. Blah. Blah.

Being as good a bullshitter as she is a liar, our applicant lands the job. We notice that in the interview by stating that she *would be* proactive, and so on (as opposed to saying that at some point in the past she *was*) she avoids telling a lie. But by using phrases like "proactive" and "mapping teamwork environments," she is clearly feeding the interviewer a line of BS.

Not all bullshit is preceded by a lie. Our applicant could just as well as have told the truth and admitted to not having managerial experience, but been granted an interview anyway. (Of course then there would have been no need to bullshit, as the interview question wouldn't have come up.) We could also imagine another case in which the applicant told the truth about her lack of managerial experience, and was subsequently asked during an interview to imagine herself as a manager dealing with a disgruntled employee; at that point in the interview the applicant might or might not bullshit the interviewer.

These different considerations suggest that lies and bullshit aren't necessarily connected, and that it isn't the truth or falsity of the statements in question that determine whether a person is lying or bullshitting. Rather, the difference between lying and bullshitting has to do with differences in speakers' attitudes about the truth. In order for a liar to lie, or succeed in a dupe, she must know or at least *believe* she knows what's true and then state the opposite, which means she must already have some stake in knowing what's true. While the lying job applicant takes the trouble to form a belief about what's true and then states the opposite, the bullshitting interviewee says whatever is necessary to get the job, regardless of the truth. In order for the "shit to fit," all that's necessary is that the bullshit artist disregard or disrespect the truth in the interest of serving some other end, like landing a better-paying job.

The Origin of Bullshit

Having penetrated the essence of bullshit, Stewart asks Frankfurt about the relative harm of lying and bullshit:

Stewart: Which do you think is more corrosive to society, the lie or bullshit?

Frankfurt: Well, I claim that bullshit is a more insidious threat to society, because it undermines respect for the truth, and it manifests a lack of concern for the truth. It therefore undermines our commitment to the importance of truth. The liar is concerned for the truth, he just doesn't want it. He is taking care to avoid it.

Stewart: But he has to know it. To be able to lie, you need to know what the truth is, to go the other direction.

Frankfurt: Or at least you have to think you know what it is. Right.

Stewart: But the bullshitter . . .

Frankfurt: Doesn't care.

Stewart: At all.

Frankfurt: He's engaged in a different enterprise.

Stewart: When you say "he," you're looking at me, and it's not right.

Frankfurt: I didn't say *you*.

Stewart: No, but I see the eyes, with the "he" and the "hmmm" [*looks at Frankfurt*].

Frankfurt: I'll try to be more careful.

Stewart: I appreciate it.

Stewart then asks about the relative amount of bullshit and lying:

Stewart: Which is more prevalent, do you think?

Frankfurt: There's a lot of lying, but I think probably bullshit is even more pervasive.

Stewart: Tons and tons of bullshit.

Frankfurt: Tons and tons of bullshit.

Frankfurt attributes the large and increasing amount of bullshit to the growth of marketing in American culture. Everyone's trying to sell something, and what matters is to get the customer to believe whatever is needed to make the sale. For example, a used car salesman will sell you any bill of goods to get a car off the lot. It might be that some things he'll tell you are lies, but more likely he won't take the time or trouble to learn the exact condition of the car. Instead, he'll tell you whatever it is you want to hear. Bullshit. Ka-ching.

Unfortunately it's not just in used car lots where we find unsavory characters. We're being sold bullshit bills of goods in politics, higher education, advertising, and journalism, to name a few. For example, sports writers during the so-called "Golden Age" fell into two camps: the "gee whiz" types who glorified athletic prowess (think Babe Ruth and Bobby Jones), or the hard-bitten cynics who saw through the bull (think Ring Lardner and baseball's "Black Sox" scandal). Sure, there was bullshit, and lots of it, but along the way the truth sometimes came through. What the bullshitter wants is more or less analogous to "gee whiz" reporting. But whether to convince you of an athlete's greatness, get you to vote for a certain candidate, or persuade you to buy a used car, you can be sure you're being fed lines and lines of bullshit. It's just easier than lying.

Frankfurt is intrigued by the observation that we seem to tolerate bullshit more than lying, and the media play right along. The way a story is "framed," or presented in print or broadcast, sometimes depends on the agenda of the news organization. Think way back to 1972 (maybe before you were born). Democratic Presidential candidate Edmund Muskie wept outside the office of a New Hampshire newspaper that he said had defamed his wife. Or think more recently of Presidential hopeful Howard Dean's "yawp across the airwaves" in 2004. Each of those stories was framed in a way to imply that the candidates weren't in control of their emotions, that they'd be unfit for office. During the Cold War, it wasn't uncommon for news organizations to trivialize news from behind the Iron Curtain. Back then, coverage focused on what we wanted to read, see, and hear. Stories about what our enemies did wrong made headlines, which helped disparage Cuban, Chinese, and Eastern European governments. We were rarely told that their leaders were, in many ways, little different from ours.

That's perhaps why Frankfurt suggests that our tolerance of bullshit might depend on the inevitability of bullshitting. We just can't help it. We seem inescapably drawn to the tawdry and the scandalous. Everywhere we turn, publications and broadcast stations bombard us with ne'er-do-well content: "If it bleeds, it leads." As responsible citizens, we're expected to know something about the more important stuff, but the sheer amount of information in a 24/7 news world makes it impossible to have informed views on all matters. So when push comes to shove, we're forced to bullshit our way through, so too for government officials. Maybe, just maybe, bullshit is a necessary evil in this "Golden Age of Information."

A New Spin on an Old Art

Having clarified the distinction between lying and bullshit – isn't ana-lytic philosophy fun? – Stewart asks Frankfurt about political spin. Stewart seems to think he already knows the answer to his own question:

> *Stewart:* Let me ask you – political spin. What would you categorize that as? You know, the spin that has enveloped political discourse.
>
> *Frankfurt:* Yeah, I've thought about that. I haven't got very far, but it is a form of bullshit. I think it's a—
>
> *Stewart:* A subcategory.
>
> *Frankfurt:* A subcategory, a subset, right. And I haven't been able to put my finger on the distinguishing characteristics of spin, but it's an interesting question.
>
> *Stewart:* Is spin a subset of bullshit, but because there's an agreement not to call "bullshit" on it? In other words, within the media, they go to Spin Alley. After a debate, they all go to Spin Alley. They would never say, "Hey, let's go over to Bullshit Street." Is maybe the difference that there is sort of an implicit agreement with those who are all bullshitting each other not to call it?

Frankfurt takes up Stewart's question and, in a good natured way, allows his protégé to put him through his Socratic paces:

> *Stewart:* Do you think that the people in political spin think they're lying? Do you think they care about the truth, or do they care about the result of what their spin gets them?
>
> *Frankfurt:* Yeah, it's the last I think. They don't care particularly about the truth. They care about producing a certain impres-sion in the minds of the people to whom they're addressing their speech. And they're engaged in the enterprise of manipulating opinion, they're not engaged in the enterprise of reporting the facts.

In ordinary language we use the words "facts" and "truth" inter-changeably. If you're speaking the facts, you're speaking the truth. However, strictly speaking, facts aren't true or false. There's no such thing as a false fact. Consider the claim, "Water freezes at 35 degrees Fahrenheit." The fact is that water freezes at 32 degrees Fahrenheit, and facts are what we appeal to in determining whether beliefs or statements are true or false. Journalists, for example, are in the business of simply reporting the facts. They're supposed to avoid editorializing and avoid inserting their opinion or subjective point of view into the story. Failing to do so is what gives rise to spin. We can distinguish people engaged in reporting the facts – the who, what, where, when, why, and how of a story – from those who spin the truth, such as a spokesperson for a Presidential candidate who's trying to create a certain impression in the minds of voters. Journalists are supposed to be engaged only in reporting the facts, so they're supposed to be devoted to, and thus have a respect for, the truth.

Earlier we picked on Bill Clinton. To be fair, and to examine Frankfurt's claim about spinners, let's turn some attention to George W. Bush. We'll frame our discussion with the liberal assumption that Bush and Cheney are masters at bullshit and spin, the morass in Iraq being a case in point. Assuming this, and focusing on Iraq, we might ask, "Where was the watchdog press?" Weren't the "good guy" journalists supposed to be in wait and ready to pounce on the spin, penetrate the bull, and proclaim truth throughout the land? Well, strangely, they were relatively quiet and acquiescent, at least according to the liberal spin.

This example would buttress Frankfurt's claim that spinners care about producing certain impressions in the minds of the public. In the case of Bush-Cheney and the war in Iraq – and unlike Clinton's extramarital affair with Lewinsky – it seems the government didn't even go to the trouble of lying to the American public. It also seems that, with the "watchdog media," we didn't care enough about what the government was up to.

Sleeping with the Enemy

Frankfurt seems to want to claim that spinners and bullshitters share indifference toward truth. Liars, by contrast, care about the truth, and willfully express the opposite of what they know or believe to be true. But don't spinners, unlike bullshitters (and like liars), *have* to care about the truth?

In the case of a lie, the aim is to deceive people about what's true. For this to happen, the liar must have formed a belief about what's true, even if she ends up being wrong. Likewise the bullshitter aims at deceiving the listener about what the bullshitter does or doesn't know, yet can succeed without actually going to the trouble of forming a belief either way. The same can't be said for the spinner. Like the liar, the spinner must know what's true in order to be able to spin it. Moreover the spinner, again like the liar, aims at making it very difficult, if not impossible, for listeners to figure out the truth. Contrary to Frankfurt's claim, then, the spinner doesn't seem to share the bullshitter's lackadaisical attitude toward the truth, which calls into question Frankfurt's contention that spin is a subset of bullshit. So lies and spin can be distinguished by the spinner's aim to avoid telling a falsehood (or at least getting caught telling a falsehood). Having gone to the trouble of forming a belief about what's true, good spinners go to the further trouble of manipulating a listener's opinion to persuade the listener that their spin is true. This tactic is clearly much more involved, and requires much more finesse, than mere bullshitting.

Spin seems to grow well in the area of public relations. Take a tobacco company CEO who wants to hire someone in PR whose job will be to convince the public that smoking is pleasurable or cool. The CEO doesn't want to get the company in trouble (read litigation) by having a spokesperson lie, stating for example that there's no causal connection between smoking and lung cancer. To avoid telling a lie, the PR agent needs to know what's true – that there is a connection between the two. If called to action, the spinner might actually be able to convince people, without coming right out and saying so, that lung cancer is just a matter of bad luck, so smoke away!

To be fair to PR folks – and to avoid being spinners or bullshitters ourselves – let's revisit President Clinton. Back in '98, when he assured us he didn't have sex with Lewinski, his loyal minions spun all sorts of anonymous stories accusing her of being what the Brits would call "chav" (trailer park trash). In the end, there were losers all around. But a PR person who cared about the truth could have tried to stop the smear campaign by reminding colleagues that spin is, ultimately, the enemy of PR, even if it's hard to see the long-term losses over the short-term gains of keeping up appearances. A PR person devoted to the truth would first stop the spin, and then reassure us that what they are saying is true, before trying to convince us how hunky-dory the world is. Still, in the public's mind, spin is part and parcel of PR as well as journalism. What's more, we do seem to tolerate spin even more than bullshit, just as we tolerate bullshit more than lies.

Let's put this all together. Spinners, like liars but unlike bullshitters, must know what's true in order to spin their tangled webs. Given what was suggested earlier, this implies that spinners do, if only of necessity, care about, and so respect, the truth. And this might mean that Stewart is on to something when he suggests that the difference between bullshit and spin is that we're more willing to call spin "spin" than bullshit "bullshit." Maybe we tolerate spinners more than bullshitters because at least the spinner cares enough about the truth to know (or believe to know) what it is, and then goes to the added trouble of manipulating our opinion about it. But why should liars and not spinners be more vilified than bullshitters if both spinners and liars share a concern for the truth? An appeal to the facts might prove helpful. Spinners are required to know what is and is not true and then try to *color* the (commonly known) facts; unlike liars, they don't try to use this knowledge to *deceive* us about what the facts are. Mere bullshitters would never even bother with the facts. It's not that spinners are engaged in reporting the facts, as if they were journalists, but at least they do care about what is and isn't true. Their purpose isn't to change our sense of what the facts are, but to put their own particular slant on the relative significance or meaning of those facts.

Ridding the World of Evil

What happens to a culture that bandies bullshit as artistry and promotes spin to the ranks of medicine? (After all, we call them spin doctors, not spin artists.) We end up being more easily confused about distinctions between true and false, right and wrong, reality and appearance. Look at *Crossfire*. They chastised Stewart for not asking Presidential candidate John Kerry tough questions during Kerry's "Indecision 2004" appearance on *The Daily Show*, to which Stewart understandably retorted: "That's not my job. I work for

Comedy Central." Many viewers might not have known what to make of Stewart's response. If not his, whose job was it?

Well, journalists', of course. Unfortunately, often failing as watchdogs, they've become the mere instruments of able spin doctors. So where can we go for even a snippet of truth? Many young people get their news from alternative sources such as *The Daily Show*. But this seems problematic, since in Stewart's view, providing politically relevant information isn't his job. Instead he says his job is to comment on the news media – to watch the watchdogs. Hillary Lipko makes this point in a 2005 article in the *Financial Times*. Lipko highlights one skit in particular that satirized the short attention span of the major news organizations, revealing how ripe they are to be manipulated by spin. The skit suggested that the media should still be exploring the Scooter Libby indictment instead of quickly moving on to report about Supreme Court nominee Samuel Alito's chances of being confirmed by the Senate. In the skit, Stewart asked his so-called Senior White House Correspondent, Rob Corddry, if the timing of the nomination was meant to be a distraction. Corddry's answer, as his attention is diverted by a huge ball of tin foil on the White House lawn and bubbles floating around him, is that the Libby indictment was "practically last month."

By bringing up the issue of political spin to his guest expert on bullshit, Stewart points to the near-failure of political systems in which image means more than message, a lesson learned from Marshall McLuhan, the "Oracle of the Electronic Age." Frankfurt and Stewart agree that there's a growing and pernicious prevalence of both bullshit and spin. We need the media as an institution – and individual reporters, broadcasters, editors, directors, producers, and publishers – to take responsibility and renew their commitment to discovering and transmitting truth. For example, to return to President Bush, could it be that the media were blindsided by propaganda that convinced enough of us that Iraq was (as many believe it still is) hiding weapons of mass destruction? If so, when the media quoted so-called "senior officials," shouldn't the reporters have told the audience beforehand that they'd be getting the administration's point of view, not necessarily an objective one?

Today's bullshit artists and spin doctors are the figurative descendants of the sophists, who were teachers of rhetoric, the art of manipulating public opinion. Back in ancient Greece, before journalism as we know it ever existed, ordinary citizens relied on another group to keep the sophists in check. They were the philosophers, doggedly devoted to, and respectful of, the truth. Seeking neither fame nor fortune, Socrates helped found a discipline that would be devoted to seeking truth and calling out bullshit, and Harry Frankfurt serves as an exemplary heir to this tradition. But in a culture and age that little respects philosophers and intellectuals in general, we turn to the media to be our gadflies, only to find they too have feet of clay. The youth, "corrupted" by Socrates over two thousand years ago, today see no alternative but to turn to *The Daily Show* and look to comedian Jon Stewart to be the gadfly to those who should be the gadflies. Parody has become reality. And *that* is bullshit.

Notes

1 Harry G. Frankfurt, *On Bullshit* (Princeton: Princeton University Press, 2005). Subsequent references will be made parenthetically in-text.
2 John Colapinto, "The Most Trusted Name in News," *Rolling Stone* (October 28, 2004), quoted in Rachel Joy Larris, "The *Daily Show* Effect: Humor, News, Knowledge and Viewers," MA Thesis, submitted to the Faculty of the Graduate School of Arts and Sciences, Georgetown University (May 2, 2005).

12

BULLSHITTING BULLSHITTERS AND THE BULLSHIT THEY SAY

ANDREW SNEDDON

Harry Frankfurt, the author of *On Bullshit*, was a particularly appropriate guest on *The Daily Show*. One of the show's basic assumptions seems to be that bullshit is always a bad thing, and that identifying it is always morally and politically significant (and sometimes funny). Frankfurt explicitly shares this assumption, calling "bullshit" a generic term of abuse[1] and a term of condemnation.[2] In this chapter we'll examine what bullshit is, where it's found, and how it functions, all to see whether it's always really such a bad thing.

Frankfurt on Bullshit

In common speech, "bullshit" is often used as a synonym for "lie." Witness Stephen Colbert's June 27, 2006 interview with Chris Matthews. At one point Matthews says he thinks he's winning the debate. Later, after joking that they've been off the air for three minutes, Colbert remarks, "I'm certainly cutting out that bullshit about you beating me." The implication here is that Matthews' claim was a deliberate misrepresentation, a lie. Frankfurt, however, thinks that we can usefully distinguish bullshit from lies. For both lies and bullshit to be successful, the speaker's intentions must be hidden from the audience (p. 54). But the intentions of the liar are importantly different from those of the bullshitter. For Frankfurt, the liar and the bullshitter are distinguished by their attitudes concerning truth. The liar is concerned with what the truth is: lies are intentional efforts at misrepresenting something false as true. To lie, the liar must keep track of the relevant truths and the relations between them and her utterances. By contrast, the bullshitter doesn't care about truth. Bullshit is aimed neither at accurately conveying truth nor at misrepresenting it (p. 55). The bullshitter's aims are altogether disconnected from the issue of the accuracy of her assertions.

Both *The Daily Show* and *The Colbert Report* exploit the lies of public figures to great comedic effect. Arguably, however, they make even more fertile use of bullshit. In part this might be due to the burden of proof: it's probably easier with brief video clips and quips to show that someone has no interest in the truth than to demonstrate that the same person is attempting to misrepresent the truth. This may also be due to the relative prevalence of bullshit. The high frequency of bullshit is Frankfurt's starting point: "One of the most salient features of our culture is that there is so much bullshit" (p. 1).

The Daily Show and *The Colbert Report* focus on bullshit in political and journalistic speech. The following are just a few examples from the summer of 2006.

(1) On June 26, 2006, *The Daily Show* presented a story about government and media coverage of a purported "terror cell" in Miami. Attorney General Alberto Gonzales held a press conference to announce that seven men had been arrested for conspiring to support Al Qaeda by targeting the Sears Tower. This press conference was, in part, to justify FBI surveillance of bank accounts, which had been recently revealed in the *New York Times*. Questions from reporters at the press conference revealed, contrary to the appearances presented by the Bush administration, that the seven men had neither contact with Al Qaeda nor weapons, and that the evidence for the alleged Sears Tower "plot" was a brief reference to the tower combined with one of the group member's history of living in Chicago and correlative familiarity with the landmark. The group that the government represented as international terrorists was actually unarmed, unorganized, and unconnected. After Stewart asked what harm could be done when the government exaggerates threats in this manner, the show ran footage of a Chicago woman reporting renewed post-9/11 anxiety after having experienced a return to normalcy. Overall, the government's aims were not primarily about security but about image. They were largely unconcerned with

truth. A combination of mere appearance and exaggeration to the point of dishonesty was used to achieve their true end. To the extent that this incident is characterized by government officials' lack of concern for the truth of their statements and instead by other ends, this is an example of political bullshit.

It's also an example of media bullshit. Besides press conference footage, Stewart briefly commented on CNN's hyping of the same non-emergency. *The Daily Show* portrayed the 24 hour news network as relatively uninterested in the truth of its reports and instead interested in ratings and advertising revenue. To the extent that Stewart's portrayal is apt, CNN's reporting is revealed to be journalistic bullshit.

(2) On June 27, 2006, *The Daily Show* examined direct government response to the *New York Times* story about government surveillance of banking information. In a June 23 speech, Vice President Dick Cheney said, "Some in the news media take it upon themselves to disclose vital national security programs, thereby making it more difficult for us to prevent future attacks against the American people. That offends me." Stewart skewered this rhetorical posturing by affecting the vocal mannerisms of a stereotypical Southern belle, saying, "I do declare! My delicate sensibilities have been violated! Get me my rosewater mist before I swoon!" The point was to show that making a true report of his feelings wasn't the primary purpose of Cheney's speech. The purpose instead was to rally opposition to the efforts of the *New York Times*. If the truth or falsity of what he said didn't matter to him, Cheney was bullshitting.

An interesting part of this particular segment is Stewart's own admission of bullshitting. Both the admission and the original bullshit play important roles in the humor. *The Daily Show* presented a chart purportedly recording things Cheney finds either offensive – "natural light" – or not offensive – "Abu Ghraib." About the chart, Stewart laughingly noted that people who pay attention to it will see that "we just threw shit in there." That is, their primary aim was to be funny, and if monkeying with the truth will accomplish that, no matter. If indicating their own bullshit is also funny, so much the better. We'll return to *Daily Show* bullshit in the final section of this chapter.

(3) *The Colbert Report* paid close attention to the Joe Lieberman/ Ned Lamont Democratic Primary in July–August 2006. The show

quoted conservative commentator David Brooks, who wrote, "What's happening to Lieberman can only be described as a 'liberal inquisition.'" Accordingly, *The Colbert Report* dedicated a segment of "The Word" to "inquisition." Colbert joked that since incumbent senators such as Lieberman have such a high winning rate, Connecticut Democrats were overstepping their authority by responding so positively that Lamont might beat Lieberman. If this sort of thing continued, incumbent politicians all over the country would have to run by defending their records. "There is only one word for that," said Colbert. He completed this with "inquisition," but the sidebar read "democracy." The point of the segment was that Brooks had thrown the word "inquisition" around in an effort to influence a democratic election through rhetoric that paid little attention to the real and historical connotations of "inquisition" or to the mechanisms of democracy. In other words, in hopes of keeping in office an incumbent Democrat supportive of many of George W. Bush's policies, Brooks was bullshitting.

Besides these particular cases, one of the most pointed comedic tactics of *The Daily Show* is the juxtaposition of video clips of public figures making incompatible statements at different times, such as denying that one ever said X when one said exactly X on camera in front of a crowd of witnesses. For example, in "Bush v Bush," available through *The Daily Show* website, the show juxtaposes clips of George W. Bush in an official debate format. Bush is shown saying one thing, then as rebutting himself by saying something incompatible with it. Another example was broadcast on August 8, 2006. Donald Rumsfeld was shown testifying to a Senate committee. Against Hilary Clinton's claim that Rumsfeld had misrepresented the war in Iraq to the Senate, Rumsfeld protested that he had always spoken carefully and moderately about the war. *The Daily Show* juxtaposed this with footage of Rumsfeld speaking recklessly about the war, such as dramatically underestimating the amount of time the US would be involved. We might be tempted to interpret such cases as instances of lying. However, this is a hard case to make. For one thing, it involves attributing a specific motive to the speaker on the basis of scant evidence. For another, it involves crediting these speakers with remarkable cognitive abilities. For them really to be lying, they must have the ability to recall exactly what they said, often months before, on the same topic. They also must have the ability to misrepresent themselves in moderately convincing fashion. To many people, including many prominent public figures, the attribution of such cognitive abilities is a bit hard to swallow (or, I'm tempted to say, "Bullshit!"). Instead, it's much more convincing to see these juxtapositions as revealing that these speakers often don't care what the truth is. They're concerned to represent the truth neither accurately nor inaccurately. Their aims are something else altogether, and one of the products of such aims is bullshit.

So bullshit, as Frankfurt and *The Daily Show* conceive it, is an assertion without concern for the truth. Frankfurt and *The Daily Show* are right to think that bullshit is *often* problematic, but is it *always* a problem? Can bullshit serve laudable functions, at least sometimes? What desirable flora might this sort of speech fertilize? To answer these questions we'll turn from political and journalistic speech to academic speech. Then we'll pay closer attention to the relationships between bullshit as a thing, bullshitting as a process, and the bullshitter as a person who bullshits.

Academic Bullshit

Political speech and journalistic speech are complex. They *might* have accurate conveyance of truths as their aim, but they might just as well aim at attaining and maintaining power, selling papers, or increasing ratings. Academic speech is also complex. The fact that academics are often guests on *The Daily Show* and *The Colbert Report* suggests that the producers see academic speech as an effective mode of counteracting bullshit. And it is. But power and sales are issues in this context too, although the overarching aim of academic speech is the discovery and transmission of truth. While disciplinary methods differ, this aim is shared by every single academic discipline. We might be tempted to think that if bullshit is unwelcome anywhere, it must be so in academic contexts. How can speech devoid of concern for truth possibly have a place in a context where truth is the fundamental aim?

Once upon a time I might have thought that there's no place for bullshit in the academy. But experience has taught me otherwise. Of course, a lot of academic bullshit isn't justified. But academic bullshit is justified, even by academic standards, when it serves the overarching academic end of discovering and conveying truth.

To see how, consider one place academic bullshitting happens: the classroom. Here's an experience I've had many times, and one I suppose that's common to other teachers as well. After I've been lecturing for a while on some topic, a student asks me a question, and I'm not exactly sure what the answer should be. Perhaps I haven't thought about the particular issue the question raises, but have thought about many related issues. I find myself standing in front of a crowd who expect me to speak intelligently about this topic, but I don't yet have a worked-out response. So to stall for time *and* to work out just what the answer should be (and to maintain a confident appearance, to retain intellectual authority over the class, and other things), I start to talk. I don't think my initial utterances are sufficient to answer the question, nor do I think that they amount to a lie. Instead, they are a way of *stabbing* at the answer, of *figuring out* what the answer should be. As these utterances are devoid of a concern for *immediate* representation or misrepresentation of the truth, they're bullshit. But they're justifiable, since they're part of a larger process that does aim at truth, and sometimes produces it. In this way, bullshit and bullshitting can be a useful part of the process of uncovering and transmitting truth.

So far my focus has been on the process of bullshitting. Similar reflections apply to bullshitters, that is, people who bullshit. Consider people training to work in academic fields. Fundamentally, their jobs will be to uncover and communicate truths. Most people don't arrive at university with well-developed skills for this sort of work. Instead, they spend years learning and polishing them. Among these skills are those used to trace connections between ideas and to communicate persuasively. These skills are also of use to the bullshitter. For bullshit to be effective, the bullshitter must be skilled at putting ideas together in a coherent way and at conveying this to others. These are exactly the skills involved in the justifiable bullshitting we've already seen. Although at the time of the awkward question these skills are used to produce bullshit, they're valuable academic skills nonetheless. Newsflash: universities produce bullshitters! The real news, of course, is the role the skills of the bullshitter play in pursuit of valuable academic aims, and the correlative positive light this shines on some kinds of bullshit.

Back to Political Bullshit

The lesson of the reflections about academic bullshit is that bullshit can be justified when it's part of an overall process that aims at the truth. Is this defense available to the kinds of bullshit targeted by *The Daily Show*? Let's focus on political speech. The fundamental value which gives academic speech its rationale is truth. Political speech is different. Political speech is a central mechanism in running a civil society, presumably by aiming at individual and collective wellbeing. So what's the political significance of truth? This is a complex issue, about which only a little can be said here.

The Daily Show operates within a liberal democratic political landscape, and in a liberal democracy, political authority stems from the individual autonomy of its citizens, from individuals' capacities and rights to rule themselves.[3] Effective self-rule requires the ability to exercise control over one's life. Among other things, such control requires a reasonably accurate view of one's situation. For example, I can't control my viewing of *The Daily Show* if I don't know when it's on or how I can gain access to a television. For the exercise of political autonomy, people require an accurate view of many aspects of the world in general, of the political situation in particular, and of the mechanisms and stakes of political participation. The kinds of political speech relevant here are those that transmit information from political figures and institutions to the citizenry. Distortion of people's perceptions interferes with their ability to control their political lives. So such distortion undermines individual autonomy to a greater or lesser extent. This means that truth is of great political significance in liberal democracies.

Bullshit is speech produced without a concern for truth, so political bullshitting exhibits a lack of concern for a crucial aspect of liberal democratic political legitimacy. For political bullshit to be defensible in the same way that academic bullshit is, it must ultimately serve the end of discovering and transmitting truth. While political figures might sometimes find themselves in a position analogous to the lecturer, having to buy time and fumble for an answer to a tricky question by bullshitting, it's reasonable to think that political speech is often different from academic speech. Political bullshit in the form of unprepared responses to probing reporters (which we might call "flying bullshit") is one thing. Calculated political bullshit, perhaps in the form of so-called talking-points (which we might call "prefab bullshit"), is quite another. The first kind of bullshit could be part of an attempt to discover and communicate truths. Prepared bullshit, however, the kind *The Daily Show* targets most, is fundamentally divorced from efforts to reveal and pass on accurate information. It *might* do this, but given that such speech is deliberately produced without a concern for truth, this would be a lucky coincidence. Overall, the defense of some academic bullshit has very limited application to the greater part of political bullshit.

Might political bullshit be justifiable in some other way? Although truth is a precondition for individual political autonomy in normal circumstances, circumstances are not always normal. The pursuit of other goals, such as security, sometimes calls for special measures. This raises the question of whether such goals can provide the basis for a different and distinctly political defense of political bullshit. In times of emergency, public figures often face a tricky decision: respect individual autonomy by speaking truthfully, which might compromise efforts to maintain security, or pursue security by overriding individuals' right to self-rule. Choosing the second option is "paternalism," acting in someone's interest regardless of their wishes.[4] Stop signs, fluoride in public drinking supplies, and seatbelt laws are all examples of paternalistic measures. Political paternalism is a natural place for bullshit. The informative aspect of political speech becomes secondary at best; what matters is that this speech contributes to the given goal. Public figures can be expected to develop an increasing taste for bullshit when pursuing paternalistic policies.

Even if paternalism and bullshit are sometimes justified on their own, there are fundamental issues which, when seen clearly, strongly suggest that paternalistic political bullshit (a combination of the two) is *never* justifiable. We can see why by focusing on a simple practical question: Can the desirable end be accomplished without bullshitting?

Suppose that we give this question a *positive* answer. This strongly suggests that paternalist political bullshit isn't justifiable. The reason is the fundamental importance of individual autonomy in the justification of political authority in a liberal democracy. The greater the extent to which government actions can be tied to the autonomous will of the people, the greater the extent to which they are justified by liberal democratic standards. Paternalistic political bullshit blocks this connection. In a liberal democracy, if political ends can be achieved without bullshit, it's reasonable to think that bullshitting means of achieving the same ends are ruled out.

So, in order for paternalistic political bullshit to be justified, it must be that the goal can't be achieved without bullshitting. When the end is desirable, however, this is *never* the case. Suppose that pursuit of a desirable end requires many details about the government's activity to be concealed. To think that bullshit is called for here is a mistake. In such cases, it's *crucial* that the truth be concealed: whether or not political speech accurately represents the truth must be monitored and controlled. But bullshit is speech without regard for truth; as such, it can be *either* true *or* false. True bullshit is counterproductive when it's vital that things be concealed. Either deception or the frank and open admission of secrecy is called for here, not bullshit. The upshot is that not only is bullshit not the only way to accomplish the end in question, it's probably a poor way. Clearly, it's not justified.

The Daily Show focuses much of its attention on political bullshit. As political bullshit erodes the foundations of liberal democracy, efforts to combat it function to safeguard these foundations. So the *modus operandi* of *The Daily Show* is spot-on: the bullshit on which they focus is morally problematic. This is one of the functions of a free press as well. The more effective the American media are at calling out political bullshit, the less important *The Daily Show* is. However, the more that conventional journalists lose their concern for truth – the more they themselves become bullshitters, that is – the less they're able to call out political bullshit effectively. While one might think that the humor of *The Daily Show* undercuts its efficacy at serious bullshit-watchdoggery, it's also reasonable to think that this affords the show certain opportunities unavailable to conventional news outlets.

Jon Stewart: Bullshitter?

If we stand back from the preceding discussion, one lesson is that the significance of bullshit depends on the kind of bull that produces it – that is, on its context. In academic contexts, bullshit is justifiable when it serves the overall pursuit of truth. The skills of the bullshitter are sometimes useful in this pursuit. But bullshit is rarely if ever justifiable in political contexts, where the skills of the bullshitter become dangerous.

What about *The Daily Show* itself? Is Jon Stewart a bullshitter? If so, how should we characterize the speech context of *The Daily Show*? Put bluntly, the point of academic speech is truth, the point of political speech is power, and the point of *The Daily Show* is humor. We barely need ask whether the pursuit of humor invites bullshit. Of course it does! Again, while the liar has the goal of misrepresenting the truth and of keeping this misrepresentation hidden, the bullshitter has no such goals. The bullshitter doesn't care at all about the truth or falsity of her assertions, so long as it contributes to achieving her other goals. Just as bullshit can serve academic or political goals, it can also serve comedic goals.

We hardly need academic reflection on the nature of bullshit to realize this. All we need do is to pay attention to the jokes on *The Daily Show*. Many of them are funny precisely because they're bullshit. Moreover, they're funny because they're *obviously* so – winking bullshit, to mix images. Stewart himself sometimes admits as much, as we've already seen in the Cheney Offense Chart example. Some of the humor in such cases depends on presenting the joke in a way that makes clear how it's disconnected from the truth of its content. There's a whiff of paradox here, as the wink in question amounts to an admission of falsehood while the joke's success depends on its being presented as minimally truthful speech. But this amounts, I think, to the familiar smell of bullshit. Neither lies nor frank and open testimony is being offered, and the truth/falsity of *The Daily Show* jokes are, semantically, beside the point. Humor is the ultimate end here, whether it's served by truth, falsehood, or both. Hence Jon Stewart is a bullshitter. Stewart's kind of bullshit stands as another counterexample to Frankfurt's concept of "bullshit" as exclusively pejorative.

There's some reason to worry, however, that the odor of Stewart's bullshit isn't as wholly pleasant as this makes it seem. The crucial question is whether humor is the only objective of *The Daily Show*. Although humor is clearly the primary goal, at times Stewart also flirts with political speech. Consider, for example, that during the 2004

Presidential election campaign, Stewart jokingly implored viewers to vote for John Kerry so that Stewart and his writers could have a rest. The Bush administration had been an exhaustingly rich source of comedic material. As another example, on August 2, 2006, while interviewing Vali Nasr, Stewart said that he thought that, since so many different faiths have a stake in Jerusalem, the city should be taken out of the hands of particular states and instead be made international. The military expenditure of the US and of other countries could then be spent protecting Jerusalem and ensuring that the surrounding states were left alone to attend to their own internal affairs.

Given the importance of bullshit to Stewart's brand of humor, and given that political utterances are interwoven with his jokes, it's reasonable to expect political bullshit from The Daily Show on occasion. The primary commitment to humor might seem to minimize the risks here. Although political bullshit is rarely if ever justifiable, perhaps The Daily Show shouldn't be taken as a serious venue for political discussion. At the same time, there's reason to see the humorous aspect of The Daily Show as enhancing its political power and, correlatively, the bad smell of its political bullshit. Witness the size and nature of its audience, with special attention to the proportion for whom it's an important source of political information.[5] I suppose it's not surprising to learn that those who work with so much bullshit sometimes put their feet in it, along with ours. But given the much greater amount of political bullshit about which The Daily Show has warned us, perhaps we shouldn't begrudge them the occasional ruined pair of shoes.

Notes

1 Harry G. Frankfurt, *On Bullshit* (Princeton: Princeton University Press, 2005), p. 2. Subsequent citations will be made parenthetically in-text.

2 Harry G. Frankfurt, "Reply to G. A. Cohen," in *The Contours of Agency: Essays on Themes from Harry Frankfurt*, ed. Sarah Buss and Lee Overton (Cambridge, MA: MIT Press, 2002), pp. 342–3. His target, in the same volume, is G. A. Cohen, "Deeper Into Bullshit," pp. 321–39.

3 For good discussions of autonomy, see Gerald Dworkin, *The Theory and Practice of Autonomy* (Cambridge: Cambridge University Press, 1988); Marilyn Friedman, *Autonomy, Gender, Politics* (Cambridge: Cambridge University Press, 2003). I discuss autonomy in connection with specific

issues in Andrew Sneddon, "What's Wrong with Selling Yourself into Slavery? Paternalism and Deep Autonomy," *Criticá* 33 (98) (2001), pp. 97–121; Andrew Sneddon, "Advertising and Deep Autonomy," *Journal of Business Ethics* 33 (1) (2001), pp. 15–28; Andrew Sneddon, "Equality, Justice, and Paternalism: Recentering Debate About Physician Assisted Suicide," *Journal of Applied Philosophy* 23 (4) (2006), pp. 387–404.

4 Gerald Dworkin's "Paternalism," *The Monist* 56 (1972), pp. 64–84 is a well-known discussion of paternalism. See also his "Paternalism: Some Second Thoughts" in *The Theory and Practice of Autonomy*, pp. 121–9. My views of paternalism are most fully developed in my "Equality, Justice, and Paternalism."

5 "National Annenberg Election Survey" (press release), *Annenberg Public Policy Center* (September 21, 2004).

INTERVIEW:
RELIGION, GOD, AND DARWIN

SEGMENT 4

13

THE CHALLENGE OF RELIGIOUS DIVERSITY IN "THIS WEEK IN GOD"

MATTHEW S. LOPRESTI

What's so funny 'bout peace, love, and understanding?
Elvis Costello

The God-Machine and its avatars – Praise be unto that which is both many and one! – have revealed the three major philosophical responses to religious diversity: exclusivism, inclusivism, and pluralism. These *isms* reflect distinct philosophical attitudes and presuppositions held by religious zealots, secular heathens, and all those wimpy fence-sitting agnostics in between. To make their significance available to the uninitiated, let's explore these philosophical positions through the wisdom of the God-Machine's high priests: Stephen Colbert, Rob Corddry, and Ed Helms. By examining the philosophical responses to religious diversity, we can begin to understand how the responses often hinder – but sometimes help – attempts to reconcile contentious differences between the world's major religious traditions.

A quick look at the philosophical problems presented by religious diversity might incline us to seek some sort of integration of the various religions. However, merging the different traditions into one mega-religion, where everyone is welcome and everybody gets saved, regardless of whether they follow Jesus, Buddha, or the Flying Spaghetti Monster, is not a plausible solution. Despite the warm, cuddly feeling we might get imagining people of all creeds holding hands and singing "Kumbaya," any attempt to unify the religions of the world under one banner would do tremendous violence to the individual traditions themselves. Such violence would not be physical, of course, but intellectual. The philosophical differences that separate religious traditions are far too complex to allow full integration, and many of the differences are fundamental to the identities of the individual traditions.

The distinct lineages and teachings of different religions should be respected and honored for the unique insights into human existence that they provide. Some religions address facets of human existence that do not concern other religions. For example, we can't just say that each religion is a different response to the divine, because some religions have neither gods nor a concept of transcendence. People who wish for interreligious harmony too often overlook such details, for while the ideal of harmony may suggest unification, it absolutely *requires* difference. Nothing would be more detrimental to promoting harmony *among* world religions than to eliminate the defining differences between them. Identity isn't harmony. However, if we do preserve the integrity of these various religions and their respective claims to truth, this will give rise to significant philosophical problems. To help resolve these differences, let's *bring out the God-Machine*!

"Who's your daddy!?" [*Smack!*]
["*Bebobobebobobebobobebobobebobobebo . . . be . . . bo . . . bo.*"]

Exclusivism! – There Can Be Only One

You know what that means, people. Oh yeah! Time for a "faith-off!" In "This Week in God: Alt God-Machine," Ed Helms offers play-by-play commentary on two religious practices as if they were pitted against each other in head-to-head competition. Helms calls it a "faith-off," guided by the simple exclusivist dictum: "Only one can be right!" The contenders: Hindus in India celebrating *Holi* (the Festival of Colors) and the descendents of the Ancient Mayans in Mexico welcoming the new spring. Now religious exclusivists aren't so meek as to stake some small claim of truth and stand silently by while others hold ostensibly competing views. On the contrary, exclusivists claim that one tradition alone exhausts any and all religious truth – coincidentally, *theirs*. Hence the name "exclusivism." They claim *exclusive* rights to religious truth, declaring the claims of all other religions to be false, and hence the faith-off where *only one can be right*.

In a side-by-side camera shot the Mayans and Hindus begin their rituals rather timidly. Both practices seem pretty dull until, as Helms comments, the Hindus make their move: "Oh, Doctor! The Hindus throw some kind of colorful powder! There's more! Colors just keep comin'. The Mayans cannot hold on! This is over people! It is over. Hinduism wins! Down goes Maya! Down goes Maya!" Both the humor and the exclusivist rules of the faith-off rely on this being a zero-sum competition, where only one practice can be effective, only one tradition true, meaning that all other practices are ineffective, and all other traditions false. This kind of exclusivist view really lays an intellectual smack-down on other religions, claiming title to what I call here the triple-crown of religious truth. This triple-crown consists of the following major categories of religious dogma: religious praxis (rituals, practices), soteriology (theories of salvation), and religious ultimates (objects of greatest religious worship or concern, such as God, Brahman, Dao, and so on). It's difficult to sort the pretenders from the contenders here. Naturally, we would need to evaluate what Stephen Colbert would call the "truthiness" of each, yet there seems to be a remarkable lack of objective evidence favoring one religion over others in these areas.

The most prominent philosophical problem that arises whenever different religious traditions are compared, and which serves as a setting for the three jewels in the triple-crown, is the problem of conflicting truth claims.[1] Religious pluralism, which will be discussed later, questions whether different religious traditions actually produce conflicting truth claims in these areas, while religious exclusivism, and to a lesser extent, religious inclusivism (see below) affirms that if one is true then all the others are false. However, even if exclusivism is right and it's true that only one religion could be right, this should in no way lead us to believe that any one of the religious traditions that exist in the world today is *the* one.

It's difficult to imagine interreligious conflict occurring if those involved didn't think that they *alone* were in the right. The implications of such monopolistic claims can clearly make interreligious communities divisive and hostile to one another. While most religions don't operate as spectator sports where faith-offs determine what's true or what's right, exclusivist followers are much more likely to work to convert and assimilate or marginalize others. The former is hardly ever benign, and the latter can easily foster ill-will and intolerance. But religion is about much more than being nice to one another; it's unavoidably and unmistakably invested in being *true*! Clearly this concern for truth can be the root of more than just academic disputes. These difficulties can be exacerbated when exclusivists take a zero-sum approach to truth when comparing their tradition to others. But this also seems to be cause for laughter when the issue is presented as a literally competitive faith-off. For a slightly more enlightened reaction to perceived competition for the triple-crown, we must, once again, *bring out the God-Machine*!

"The power of Colbert compels you!" [*Whack*!]
["*Bebobobebobobebobebobobebobobebo . . . be . . . bo . . . bo.*"]

Inclusivism! – One of Us

One of the hallmarks of a genuine Christian is a determined commitment to the salvation of others. This goes for both exclusivist and inclusivist Christians. Both are forms of religious absolutism, considering their own version of religious truth to be the only correct one. The difference is that while an exclusivist may attempt to convert everyone to her precise way of thinking, the inclusivist will consider conversion unnecessary for those who hold different but sufficiently similar views. These sufficiently similar views and practices can be explained as deficient manifestations of Christianity. For example, one can argue, as Catholic theologian Karl Rahner (1904–84) has, that members of certain religious traditions are actually, unbeknownst to them, "anonymous Christians." The benefit of this way of thinking is that one doesn't have to feel bad for people who've never even heard of Jesus going to hell as a result of not accepting him as the alleged "one true God" he's supposed to be for Christians. So long as these Godless heathens are good *anonymous* Christians, they can still make it through the pearly gates without ever having to say "Amen." I like to think of this view as "armchair evangelism." Academic theologians are particularly adept at this, saving souls without ever having to leave the ivory tower by merely redefining what it is that other religions *actually* believe and whom they're *really* worshipping. This often means holding views and beliefs that are completely detached from reality.

Although this explanation of religious diversity might avoid the hands-on cultural imperialism that comes from overzealous evangelical missions, it still results in harmful intellectual imperialism, since it forgoes a genuine attempt to understand and appreciate other religions, seeing them instead from a limited if favorable perspective. Though now a High Priest Emeritus of "This Week in God," Stephen Colbert employed just this sort of absurd reasoning in his witty and insightful roast of President Bush during the 2006 White House Correspondents' Dinner. Colbert's witty repartee lit the way of his evangelical ministry when he spoke from the pulpit: "Though I am a committed Christian, I believe that everyone has a right to their own religion. Be you Hindu, Christian, or Muslim, I believe there are infinite paths to accepting Jesus Christ as your personal savior."[2] Displaying great confidence in the power and truthiness of his own religion, Colbert's is a very thoughtful and sweet gesture, trying to make room for the salvation of Hindu and Muslim souls. But how can this inclusion be achieved? Are Colbert's views to be broadened so as to accept the teachings of others as conveying truthiness too? Not quite. We can see at the close of his statement of faith that his is a naïve religious inclusivism, reducing other traditions to different manifestations of Christianity itself.

Colbert's satire of Bush's naïvely simplistic view of the world demonstrates an inclusivist attempt to co-opt or explain unique traditions solely in terms of something familiar, in this case Christianity. Inclusivist claims that other religions are "OK" often result from an incorrect understanding. The thought for instance that "Christians and Buddhists worship the same God" is false. They don't. In fact, most Buddhists are *atheists*. The ideas that inform Buddhist atheism, like *impermanence* and *no-Self* (Emptiness), are central and unique to the Buddhist tradition. So too are *Atman* and *Brahman* unique to South Asian traditions, *Dao* to Daoism, and so on. These religious concepts are unique, and tend to be completely foreign to other traditions; they tend not to be understood by off-the-cuff inclusivists, and are essentially ignored by intellectually irresponsible inclusivists who are better informed. These inconvenient facts don't discourage well-intentioned armchair evangelists from casting entirely different traditions as variations on their own. For example, Colbert's description of Hinduism as a path to accepting JC as one's personal Lord and savior assumes that Hinduism is, at base, just another type of Christianity – although one that's several millennia older, with a pantheon of divinities, both male and female, and a multiple-life system of karma and rebirth instead of a one-chance shot to avoid sin and eternal damnation.

Implying that another tradition is only right or true to the extent that it resembles one's own denies the native version of the tradition a legitimate explanation of itself.[3] If successful, however, the inclusivist approach could conceivably reduce religious violence motivated or rationalized by perceived differences, but it fails utterly at even approaching a true understanding of other traditions. This failure would rightly be seen as offensive by adherents of these religions, and would lead to blatantly erroneous interpretations of their traditions, beliefs, and intentions.[4] At its best, such inclusivism is a naïve attempt to cast other religious traditions as having access to the truth, the way, and the light *as you and your religion define it*. At worst, this sweet, seemingly innocent intention can be a form of intellectual imperialism, attempting a hostile takeover of an entire belief system.

The ultimate irony of inclusivism is that, despite its seemingly good-natured intent to be *a uniter, not a divider*, it actually works to marginalize and isolate religious traditions by the very means by which it intends to be more open to them. No one wants to be subject to some "triumphalist" philosophy that reduces their identity and professed self-interests to something they think, believe, and dare I say, *know* they're not. Yet so many seem eager to do this to others as a way of demonstrating the alleged universality of their own beliefs. As a result, religious inclusivism tends, in spite of itself, to antagonize and exacerbate the tensions that may already exist between religions.

Religious exclusivism and inclusivism are types of religious absolutism, which judge other religions solely in terms of their own values, goals, and dogmas. The move towards genuine and mutually open dialogue isn't so obvious a step if one has either of these attitudes. After all, what need is there to learn from or about other religions when one's own is presumed to be the correct cipher for interpreting the meaning and value of all others? From an exclusivist point of view interreligious dialogue is an even less obvious step, since interreligious engagements would be warranted only for the purpose of conversion. Jeffery Long, a Hindu religious pluralist, writes that "the problem with both inclusivism and exclusivism is that they do not take with sufficient seriousness the possibility that other religions may teach important truths that are not already contained within their own traditions." Both ultimately deny the "*legitimacy* of all other religions . . . *as* other religions."[5] Naturally, these philosophical responses to religious diversity tend to problematize interreligious harmony and squelch any genuine attempt at interreligious dialogue. If dialogue is to take place at all, then all sides must be open to the possibility of change while remaining confident enough in their own positions to avoid feeling intimidated or threatened by other traditions.

Given the unquestionably vast history of interreligious violence, it's nice every so often to hear about the ways that people of different faiths can come together under the banner of dialogue and moral unity. To help us figure out more appropriate responses to religious diversity, we once again *bring out the God-Machine*!

"You are healed!" [*Thud*!]
["*Bebobobebobobebobebobobebobobebo . . . be . . . bo . . . bo.*"]

Pluralism! – Interreligious Harmony (Against Gays) in Jerusalem

Over the centuries various religious groups have been able to cooperate in forming societies of great learning, wealth, and power. It seems that a similar kind of peaceful dialogue is desperately needed these days, and so it seemed to be cause for celebration when Stephen Colbert reported in "This Week in God: The Manife-station" that such pluralistic unity may have already begun in the Middle East, when religious leaders sat down together to discuss their common interests. What motivated such an unprecedented display of unity between religions that preach compassion and love in one of the most religiously violent places on Earth? Good ol'-fashioned intolerance, of course! Jews, Christians, and Muslims of the holy city of Jerusalem banded together in a show of solidarity – not for peace, social justice, or some other wacky idea, but *against* a gay-pride parade. Despite the wide swath of social justice issues these PRIHCs could have addressed,[6] I suppose in some demented way that their coming together to face the supreme domestic terror of the day for religious conservatives – their own homophobia – could still be cited as a step in the right direction as far as interreligious harmony is concerned. This is because interreligious dialogue is more than just a good idea, it's necessary for the development of a satisfactory response to religious diversity. But is this really the kind of harmonious pluralism we need?

Scholars and theologians have discussed shared interests between religions for centuries, and so finding common ground among various traditions (for good or ill) on external issues isn't all that uncommon. The superficial ecumenical harmony Colbert brings to our attention is light years away from having anything to do with developing interfaith understanding, much less offering the possibility of a common ground of doctrine and belief. It's thus unfortunate, but also unremarkable, that these PRIHCs are only superficially pluralistic and don't go any further to explore how their foundational beliefs or practices might complement one another.

By "religious pluralism," we don't simply mean a tolerant attitude towards the many different religious traditions of the world. Religious pluralism abandons the zero-sum view of religious truth found in religious absolutism, attempting to account for the world in such a way that many religious claims from various traditions might be able to be simultaneously true. This is a pretty tall order. First, one has to respect (and therefore understand) individual traditions' belief systems, theories of salvation, objects of worship, rituals, and practices, so as to avoid conflating those that are distinctly unique. At the same time one must be able to explain how these vastly different systems might still be simultaneously true without falling into the pitfalls of a debilitating relativism. Religious relativism is the view that all religions are equally true, but this also means they're all equally false. Relativism is practically meaningless, since it's incapable of offering a standard for determining truth, and so lacks meaningful explanatory power altogether.

The most basic minimum standard that distinguishes pluralism from relativism is the former's basic adherence to the law of non-contradiction. David Ray Griffin writes that in its generic form, religious pluralism is even further distinguished from other *isms* by its adherence to two basic assumptions, one negative, the other positive:

> The negative affirmation is the rejection of religious absolutism, which means rejecting the *a priori* assumption that [one's] own religion is the only one that provides saving truths and values to its adherents, that it alone is divinely inspired, that it has been divinely established as the only legitimate religion, intended to replace all others. The positive affirmation, which goes beyond the negative one, is the acceptance of the idea that there are indeed religions other than one's own that provide saving truths and values to their adherents.[7]

Many philosophers of religion argue that there's no good reason to think that any one religion has a monopoly on truth; indeed, there seem to be elements of truth in many different aspects of divergent religious traditions.[8] This *doesn't* imply, however, that all aspects of all religions are somehow correct. Rather, it means that no *one* religion has the *whole* story. Pluralism walks the middle ground between relativism and absolutism by suggesting that there are elements of truth to be found throughout the landscape of religious thought. Does this mean that all religions are somehow equally false? The absolutist might object to his particular tradition losing its luster of pure, complete veridicality under the pluralist hypothesis, but just because another tradition might be appropriately sensitive to some truth that isn't emphasized in one's own, this doesn't mean that one's own tradition is false, even in part. Despite undeniable areas of overlap, it is quite clear that the problems of human existence that religions address vary significantly from one tradition to the next.

A Plurality of Pluralisms

The Hindu Festival of Color and the Mayan welcoming of spring in Ed Helms' faith-off are two entirely different rituals. Both celebrate the change of seasons. But celebrating the cycles of the earth needn't be tied to any specific doctrine or religious intentions beyond a basic awareness of life, death, and renewal. These celebrations needn't conflict with the doctrines and dogmas of other religions, nor does the one religious celebration challenge or negate the validity of another. This goes double for partaking in the Christian sacraments or practicing Buddhist meditation. These are neither competing nor necessarily conflicting responses to the divine. Rather, they are two entirely different practices that have entirely different aims. The effectiveness of one would in no way diminish the possible efficacy of the other.

In "This Week in God: Voodoo," Rob Corddry (incidentally, my frat brother) endorses the effectiveness of different practices in his "Thank you Lord, may I have another" sketch, in which he briefly presents Shinto, Russian Orthodox, Indonesian Muslim, Thai Buddhist, and Shiite Muslim rituals, all meant to "please God" through spiritual purification. Though it too is a superficial type of pluralism (after all, this is comedy), Corddry's example offers an excellent transition between praxis and salvation. More often than not, the practices of different traditions, when properly understood, are *not* in conflict, so long as it isn't assumed (as an exclusivist would), that at most only one of the various rituals could be effective.

The brand of religious pluralism developed by the contemporary philosopher John B. Cobb, Jr. can account for multiple theories of salvation, arguing that "there is no contradiction in the claim of one that problem A is solved by X and the claim of the other that problem B is solved by Y. . . . The claims are complementary rather than contradictory."[9] Cobb uses this basic logical truth to attempt to reconcile contradictions that ostensibly plague interreligious dialogue between Christians and Buddhists in particular.[10] Christians can seek transcendent salvation through Christ, while Buddhists can realize immanent epistemic awakening. These aren't mutually exclusive, because the salvation sought in each case is of a *different* kind. According to this type of pluralism, not only are there different ways of achieving the same religious objective, there are also different legitimate goals. To see how this might work, we'll turn to what's often called "process" metaphysics, which also allows for obeisance to a plurality of different religious ultimates.

The process metaphysics of Alfred North Whitehead (1861–1947) describes the world as being in a constant state of flux, and ruled by two ontological "ultimates." Creativity is the universal force that propels dynamic change. The other ultimate is a personal being who works with the world, guiding its creative flow towards ever-increasing moral and aesthetic ends. Neither ultimate is in complete control. Instead, the two work together to carry the world forward. This generic notion of a deity differs in important ways from other characterizations of God in the Abrahamic tradition. Among other changes, the meaning of "omniscience" and the manner in which God can act in and react to the world are altered in ways that make God a bit less fantastic and thus more plausible than the deity of traditional Western theology, which is wrought with con-tradictions. Traditional theists are loath to accept this "process" conception of God, even though it's still a uniquely powerful and omniscient, good and caring being. It is, to this extent, compatible with the sacred texts of the three major theistic faiths of the West (though not necessarily with all of the hundreds of widely diverse sectarian dogmas of every single denomination that stems from these faiths). Creativity, on the other hand, works as a generic category that can include non-theistic, non-personal, non-dualistic religious ultimates such as the nameless, formless *Dao* of Daoism, the blissful Emptiness (*sunyata*) of Buddhism, and the unqualifiable *nirguna Brahman* of Hinduism. Creativity drives "the becoming of the world," the divine being shapes it, and inspires us towards moral and aesthetic improvement. In Whitehead's philosophy, the world couldn't exist as it does without both of these ultimates working together, and Cobb argues that it's precisely these *two* ultimates that underlie the objects of religious worship or concern of the various traditions around the world.

"The God Exchange" is Now Closed

In "The God Exchange" Rob Corddry highlights the triumphs and woes of the world's religions in terms every capitalist can understand – fluctuating stock prices. In a jaded consumer market where reli-gious recruitment and retention is almost as paltry as US military reenlistment rates, it's important for religious leaders to keep abreast of the almost daily fluctuations of "religious market value," the highs and lows of religious morale, and "convert-futures" rocked by scandals, natural disasters, and religiously fueled political unrest. It's a competitive market of ideas and religious lifestyles these days, and forces that push and pull people to identify with (or against) certain faiths are a sad indication of just how fickle some people are when it comes to reality.[11] It should be a great relief that reality itself isn't subject to change from person to person, faith to faith, or due to the whimsical market forces dictated by whatever religious ideas are currently in vogue. The validity of a pluralistic view of religion greatly depends on the underlying theory of reality (or metaphysics) that informs it. Fortunately, Cobb's deep religious pluralism offers us a metaphysical platform with broad enough explanatory power to accommodate widely divergent belief systems. No matter which religious robe we don, we can see all of them as being cut from the same metaphysical cloth. Hopefully this view can help the competitive and combative emotions that have dominated interreligious relations for so long to slowly become a thing of the past.

The satire of *The Daily Show* not only amuses but also enlightens its audience. Often the comedy, especially in the case of religion, stems from the fact that the subject matter itself often resists full comprehension.[12] It should be no mystery why competing notions of the sacred can be so damned funny. Where understanding stops in a subject such as religion, emotion fills in the rest. Be it anger and even hatred of the zealot, the righteous indignation of the evangelical, or the amusement and LOL reaction of the un-indoctrinated, these responses – the destructive and the creative – are natural, human. The destructive ones can be eschewed, however, by a greater understanding of philosophical solutions to the problem of religious diversity, as outlined in this chapter and illustrated by "This Week in God." The response that best enables genuine interreligious dialogue and harmony is pluralism.

If, for whatever reason, pluralism *doesn't* turn out to be viable, it's my sincere hope that people, fallible and far from omniscient as they are, will increasingly abandon monopolistic answers to questions about the meaning of life, our place in the universe, and how we ought to orient ourselves in the face of life's mysteries. A good sense of humor at our own expense, and recognition of the often palpable absurdity of being thrown into the mystery of this world, goes a long way in helping us attain the healthy degree of humility required of us when making claims and arguments about religious truth. In the end, I'm in agreement with Whitehead:

> There remains in the final reflection, how shallow, puny, and imperfect are [our] efforts to sound the depths in the nature of things. In philosophical [or religious] discussion, the merest hint of dogmatic certainty as to finality of statement is an exhibition of folly.[13]

Indeed, it's only with such overt humility that any attempt to understand the world's religions must begin.

Notes

1 The challenge posed by the diversity of religious or mystical experience comes in a close second and is intimately related.
2 White House Correspondents' Association Diner, C-SPAN (April 29, 2006).
3 It would be similarly absurd to reduce the humor of all Comedy Central programs as being humorous to the extent that they resemble the satire of *The Daily Show*, even if they preceded its existence or rely on entirely different kinds of humor.
4 Imagine a Buddhist being so daft as to try to explain to a Christian that the teachings of Christ are really just skillful lies to help him develop as a better (anonymous) Buddhist until he becomes wise enough to be receptive to the teachings that all things are Empty and that there really is no God or soul after all.
5 Jeffery Long, "Anekanta Vedanta: Towards a Deep Hindu Religious Pluralism," in *Deep Religious Pluralism*, ed. David Ray Griffin (Louisville, KY: Westminster John Knox Press, 2005), p. 140.
6 These religious leaders are members of an informal organization I like to call the Pan-Religious Israeli Homophobia Coalition, or PRIHC, formally known as No-NAMB.
7 David Ray Griffin ed., *Deep Religious Pluralism* (Louisville, KY: Westminster John Knox Press, 2005), p. 3.
8 Along with Griffin's *Deep Religious Pluralism*, see, for example, John Cobb, *Beyond Dialogue: Toward a Mutual Transformation of Christianity and Buddhism* (Philadelphia: Fortress, 1982); John Hick, *A Christian Theology of Religions: The Rainbow of Faiths* (Louisville, KY: Westminster John Knox Press, 1995); Paul F. Knitter and John Hick eds., *The Myth of Christian Uniqueness: Towards a Pluralistic Theology of Religions* (Maryknoll, NY: Orbis Books, 1987).

9 Leonard Swidler, John B. Cobb, Jr., Paul F. Knitter, and Monika K. Hellwig, *Death or Dialogue? From the Age of Monologue to the Age of Dialogue* (Philadelphia: Trinity Press, 1990), p. 14.

10 Griffin discusses two very helpful quotes from Cobb on this very point in *Deep Religious Pluralism*, p. 48. See John B. Cobb, Jr., *Transforming Christianity and the World: A Way Beyond Absolutism and Relativism*, ed. Paul F. Knitter (Maryknoll, NY: Orbis Books, 1999), pp. 74, 140.

11 As if the moral quality of publicly declared adherents to one faith or another implied anything about the religion itself. For example, pedophiliac priests and the Spanish Inquisition in no way invalidate the teachings of Christ, nor do the actions of terrorists who wrap themselves in the cloak of jihad in any way diminish the teachings of the prophet Mohammed.

12 For more on the humorous aspect of nonsense, see Alan Richardson, "Tractatus Comedo-Philosophicus," in *Monty Python and Philosophy: Nudge Nudge, Think Think!* ed. Gary L. Hardcastle and George A. Reisch (Chicago: Open Court, 2006), pp. 217–29.

13 Alfred N. Whitehead, *Process and Reality: An Essay in Cosmology*, ed. David Ray Griffin and Donald W. Sherburrne (New York: Free Press, 1978 [1929]), p. xiv.

14

CONTINGENCY, IRONY, AND "THIS WEEK IN GOD"

BRAD FRAZIER

Contingent things aren't necessary; they can change, they often *do* change; they could have been otherwise, and need not have existed at all. Contingency makes things seem arbitrary, meaningless. Note how *The Daily Show*'s God-Machine conveys a powerful sense of contingency when it comes to religion.

Religious practices offer us an interesting view into the way people cope with contingency and the threat of meaninglessness. Presenting an idiosyncratic moral code as the command of an eternal, omnipotent, and omniscient being, or as the expression of a divinely created law woven into the fabric of reality, can make the moral code's socially constructed nature invisible to many people and thereby give it credibility and an air of inevitability. If threats of punishment, death, and eternal damnation for lawbreakers are added, that's all the better, since such threats tend to stifle skepticism and dissent. In turn, the code may provide greater stability and cohesion to a tenuous social order by giving it a cosmic grounding.

In the process, however, what is merely human comes to seem non-human, immutable, and beyond critique. This is problematic not least because it's alienating, but also because human beings have a propensity to use religious legitimations of their social practices and rules to justify violence against those unlike themselves. So, a perspective on religion that discloses its human qualities, while alleviating the pain of this revelation with a touch of irony and comedy, can be both helpful and humanizing.

The humorists of *The Daily Show* offer us this sort of approach with their ironic take on religion, most prominently in "This Week in God." Here they reveal utterly wild contingency in religious practices and beliefs that purportedly reflect transcendent and sacred realities that are anything but contingent. The humor that emerges in these moments largely turns on recognizing this palpable incongruity. As a result, the often powerful grip of religion and God-talk is loosened, and we are more apt to see the thoroughly human features of that which we previously took to be non-human.

Ironist Philosophers

There's a longstanding tradition in philosophy, dating all the way back to Socrates (470–399 BCE), of critiquing and taking an ironic stance toward religious beliefs, institutions, and practices. This esteemed tradition includes religious philosophers such as Michel de Montaigne (1533–92) and Søren Kierkegaard (1813–155), and in our time the Italian philosopher Gianni Vattimo, and non-religious philosophers, such as David Hume (1711–76), Karl Marx (1818–83), Friedrich Nietzsche (1844–1900), Sigmund Freud (1856–1939), Albert Camus (1913–60), and now, the American philosopher, Richard Rorty, to name just a few.

In *Contingency, Irony, and Solidarity*, Rorty sketches irony as a stance that facilitates the recognition of contingency in human practices and beliefs, as well as ways of understanding and evaluating both the world and the human condition. The main weapon of an ironist, so construed, is redescription. Redescriptions simply are alternative takes that usually challenge, satirize, or critique a prevailing view of something. Consider, for instance, Stephen Colbert's redescription of the "Grand Old Party" (GOP) as "God's Own Party." Or consider the "swiftboating" of John Kerry, the Democratic nominee in the 2004 Presidential election, which scurrilously redescribed Kerry's decorated military service in Vietnam as a sordid combination of hype and fiction. Nothing in life, furthermore, is immune to redescription; *anything* can be made to look good or bad by being redescribed.[1]

When the *Daily Show* humorists turn their withering ironic gaze and considerable powers of redescription toward religion, what appears other-worldly, divinely ordained, and infallible is unmasked as local and thoroughly human. Consider, for instance, Stephen Colbert's redescription of the sacred ritual of apostolic succession – Pope picking – on display in the selection of a new vicar of Christ to succeed Pope John Paul II. In his coverage of this hallowed process, Colbert describes a contest of "Popefuls" who had dropped by the Vatican, "the city that never sins," to fill out carefully their "paplications," since the (omniscient) "human resources guy" at the Vatican (and everywhere else, presumably) is *very* thorough. Drawing out the alarming implications of this period of transition, he reports to Jon Stewart, "Do you realize that no one on Earth is infallible right now? The whole thing is being run by human beings." Some time later, after the selection of Cardinal Ratzinger (now Pope Benedict XVI), Colbert observed that the "new Pope smell" was fading at the Vatican.

Social Legitimation

If there's a direct antithesis to this sort of sarcastic stance toward religion, it's the stance of the fundamentalist, not that there's just one such specific stance. Fundamentalists tend to see necessity and immutability where ironists see contingency and social construction. Most fundamentalists, moreover, are completely serious about shaping the human social world into the mold prescribed by their particular religion. Given the ravaging effects of fundamentalism in the world today, it's clear that we need an antidote for it (other than "the Decider"). One such cure is irony. To see more clearly how ironists are able to use redescription to uncover contingency and social construction, let's briefly examine an old saw about religion with new teeth.

The Freudian idea that religion is a kind of psychic crutch, a pining for a Cosmic Father, for people who can't bracingly accept the sufferings and injustices of human existence (wimps), is well known. What's not as well known is a less controversial view among sociologists that religion is the most widespread and effective means of legitimating social and political orders and the rules and practices that constitute them. The basic idea is rather straightforward and fairly plausible. As the renowned sociologist of religion, Peter Berger, explains:

If one imagines oneself as a fully aware founder of a society, a kind of combination of Moses and Machiavelli, one could ask oneself the following question: How can the future continuation of the institutional order, now established *ex nihilo*, be best ensured? . . . Let the institutional order be so interpreted as to hide, as much as possible, its *constructed* character. . . . Let the people forget that this order was established by men and continues to be dependent upon the consent of men. Let them believe that, in acting out the fundamental programs that have been imposed upon them, they are but realizing the deepest aspirations of their own being and putting themselves in harmony with the fundamental order of the universe. In sum: Set up religious legitimations.[2]

In other words, the simplest recipe for shoring up the tenuous foundations of an emerging social and political order is to hitch it to a cosmic, non-contingent framework, to make it seem as if it's the expression of an infallible divine blueprint.

Modern religionists who employ such legitimations, at least those who aren't Southern Baptists, tend to avoid the flat crassness of claiming "We do things this way because God told us to," but not always. Consider, for instance, the religious rhetoric sometimes used to justify policies that discriminate against homosexuals: "It was Adam and Eve in the Garden of Eden, not Adam and Steve." Or, as Colbert likes to put it, "We are the children of Abraham, not *Gay*braham." Here the Hebrew Bible's poetic depiction of human origins in divine sources is used to sanction heterosexual marriage and to condemn and outlaw same-sex marriage.

Politicians of the religious right, such as Rick Santorum, have a somewhat subtler approach. They argue that same-sex couples will merely destroy the divinely ordained institution of heterosexual marriage and human civilization as we know it, and then introduce legalized bestiality. (At that point, the apes take over and the last humans place Charlton Heston in a time capsule and blast him into outer space to preserve the Platonic form of heterosexual manliness for posterity. It's all in the original *Planet of the Apes*. Check it out, young people.) This kind of rhetoric invites us to believe that the decision to organize our social, legal, sexual, and religious practices in a way that discriminates against homosexuals isn't really a matter for careful deliberation and civil debate in view of our most basic *shared* ideals, since God, who hates gays, has spoken on the issue.

Now it might seem as if the suggestion is that religious leaders *deliberately* fabricate legitimations for the social practices and rules that they prefer, in order to put one over on the people who accept these stories, and to render them sufficiently docile and malleable. In fact, it's a much more complicated process than that. Most people hear these justifications frequently as they grow up, so much so that they come to seem natural, intuitive, and commonsensical to them over time. Regarding those unique few, like Moses (if he even existed), who *establish* societies or social institutions, presumably most of them believe the religious rhetoric they employ to legitimize their endeavors. In some cases, they may even be unaware of the social utility of the practice.

Religion and Alienation

This brings us to a major problem that helps to explain why we need to be able to laugh at religion and subject it to ironic redescription. Think of it this way: whatever we make of the *ultimate* merits of religious legitimations that aim to give our customs, practices, and institutions a cosmic foothold, their tendency has been to shroud these very human entities in mystery and to conceal from us our own vital contributions to them and responsibility for them. As a result, what is, at least in principle, comprehensible and analyzable in human terms comes to seem incomprehensible and unapproachable. Philosophers and sociologists have a name for the state of being oblivious to and cut off from this knowledge of ourselves and our world-building and stabilizing activities: mystification.

Besides leaving us in the dark about ourselves in crucial respects, mystification fosters alienation. The term "alienation" has multiple uses. Here I have in mind what happens to us when the merely human is made to seem to us as if it isn't, and, as a result, we're mystified and perhaps even terrified and tyrannized by it when we shouldn't be. To be estranged from our very humanity and its effects in this way is to experience or suffer from a potentially harmful kind of alienation.

But before we get to more serious forms of alienation, let's consider a common silly manifestation of it. If you're a sports fan, think of all the times you've heard American athletes give sole credit to

Jesus or God for their athletic performances and victories (but curiously never blame for their losses or blunders). In "Spiritual Heritage," an installment of "This Week in God," Colbert observes, "If Super Bowl speeches have taught us anything, it is that God personally determines the outcome of everything on Earth." Colbert then cues up the game, "Praised or Hazed," to see how the Lord micromanaged the previous week's sporting events. It turns out that the Kentucky Derby winner Giacomo, a 50–1 long shot before the race, won because "Jesus loves a long shot." After all, Christianity is, according to Colbert, "the religion of the original comeback kid." (Take that, Satan.) The pre-race favorite, Bellamy Road, came in eighth, leading Colbert to observe, "God hates him so much." But apparently not as much as some human beings in sub-Saharan Africa, where carnage from civil wars and famine dominated that week's news. These people were hazed by God, according to Colbert, but on the plus side, their weather was sunny and mild.

The 2006 NBA Finals provided an occasion for Rob Corddry to explore similar themes related to the deity's sports preferences in "Spiritcenter." Before the deciding game of the Finals between the Miami Heat and the Dallas Mavericks, Jason Terry of the Mavericks was interviewed about the upcoming game. For all of us neophytes, Terry reduced the players' talents, strategies, home crowd advantage, and determination down to a fundamental and most obvious question: "Who do you believe in?" In other words, for Terry, the deciding game and hence, the NBA Championship, came down to the question of belief in God – as Mavericks fan! Apparently Terry and the Mavericks, in an unintended homage to Moses, trusted God to deliver them victory; it just remained for them to lift their hands, play the game, and have God orchestrate the preferred outcome. Unfortunately, as Corddry points out, Terry was unaware of the fact that several months earlier, under the guise of what appeared to be a resurrected and steroid-bloated Jerry Garcia, God was spotted at the NBA all-star game wearing a Heat jersey. In the midst of a celebration following the Heat's victory, Dwyane Wade (yes, that's how his first name is spelled) of the Heat noted, inadvertently correcting Terry, that God deserved all the praise for the Heat's victory. Clearly, Wade's own MVP performance had nothing to do with it.

Look, I confess, I don't know which teams are God's favorites. They seem to change fairly often, except when God's in the mood for a dynasty. It's clear as I write this, however, that God now loves Tiger Woods (sorry, Ku Klux Klan). But what does all of this have to do with a silly, but still real, form of alienation? Simply this: when athletes talk as if God personally determines the outcome of their games, they may be attempting to be humble (or to make sure that the divine gloryhound gets his props so he'll hook them up next time too). But by doing this they mystify a very ordinary, if extraordinarily performed, human activity. A thoroughly human event with winners and losers becomes an occasion for silly God-talk that distracts us from the human drama and sense of play in sports. We're also invited to wonder why God gave victory to one side and not the other.

The Divine Blame Game

This sort of alienation is trivial, however, in comparison to the sort that occurs when more significant features of human experience are rendered alien and otherworldly by God-talk. Is it a natural part of the human condition, for instance, to be subject to death and destruction from natural disasters? It certainly was for our ancestors. But religious leaders then and now have used these catastrophes as occasions for verbally lacerating and scapegoating the "sinful" among us, who often are the *victims* of these disasters, or at least are thought to be by the very persons who lacerate and blame them.

For instance, some evangelical Christians argued that hurricane Katrina was directed by God at New Orleans (like a divine bunker-buster) in order to destroy the French Quarter, which was "infested" with homosexuals and, according to one evangelical organization, was scheduled to hold a gay pride parade on the day the city's levees broke. (Other Christian groups blamed the abortionists in New Orleans.) In "Katrina," a truly brilliant installment of "This Week in God," Stephen Colbert draws out the unexpected logical implications of this reasoning. It turns out that the French Quarter wasn't flooded and destroyed, but townships around it were, leading Colbert to observe, "God loves gays, but hates the gay-adjacent." Here Colbert simply uses the incredibly asinine reasoning pattern of a leader of the evangelical group "Repent America" – If x is destroyed in a natural disaster, then x must be hated by God – but with the *actual* facts of the destruction to New Orleans in view (a gumptious *reductio* of this group's perspective).

I suppose it could be argued in response to Colbert that he overlooks the fact that "Repent America" (or "NAMBLA," the North American Militant Biblical Literalists Association) actually reasons this way – If *x* is destroyed in a natural disaster, *and we hate x*, then *x* must be hated by God. That additional clause keeps "Repent America" from having to accept that God hates anyone that they don't already hate.

If it seems that Colbert is picking on a rather crude form of Christianity here, rather like beating up a straw man, let me assure you that blaming "sinners" for the destruction to human life that occurs in natural disasters isn't something that only coarse religionists do. A much subtler form of this religious "blame game" is prominent in philosophical discussions of the problem of evil. (Colbert refers to this as the "age-old" question, "Why do bad things happen to . . . well, why do bad things happen?")

One leading Christian philosopher, for instance, speculates that the very first human beings might have had "preternatural powers," such as a kind of advanced Doppler radar as part of their original hard-wiring (my description, but I'm not kidding about the idea – check it out).[3] This helped them avoid natural disasters. But then they disobeyed God in that momentous act now known simply as "the Fall" and ruined things for the rest of us. It's unclear, by the way, whether these super powers also included GPS or perhaps inbuilt cellular service. But presumably these people never ventured on a hike, picnic, or trip to Bourbon Street that was ruined by bad weather.

Whether we have in view God's furiously crashing gay parades with hurricanes (with, let's face it, a pretty dismal crashing average) or severely downgrading the hardware of our Doppler-wielding superhuman ancestors because of their disobedience, the basic point is the same: being subject to death and destruction from natural disasters isn't a *natural* part of the human condition. From this perspective, meteorologists, who trade in scientific explanations of destructive weather patterns, can appear as a kind of "sect," as Colbert ironically notes.

This religious casting of *natural* disasters as harbingers of divine wrath is both deeply alienating and especially cruel. In its basest versions, it directs us to blame certain groups, usually minorities long-despised by conservative religionists, for the destruction wrought on them and others by these disasters. In its subtler forms, it instructs us to blame the first human beings who ever lived. Consequently, an awful but inevitable part of being a human animal is mystically transformed into divine terrorism.

In *On the Genealogy of Morality*, Nietzsche unmasks the deeply human motivation that underlies this dehumanizing and callous religious rhetoric: the need for meaning. Nietzsche argues that people cultivate religious explanations for human suffering, explanations that implicate themselves or other human beings, because this is a way of making apparently *gratuitous* human suffering *make sense*. Nietzsche thinks that the worst part of suffering is its seeming pointlessness. For many people, this is psychologically unbearable. As an antidote, religions provide myths, moral codes, and other narratives to give suffering a point. Unfortunately, usually the point is that we suffer because we *deserve* to suffer. And sometimes there's collateral damage – occasionally, a pious, pro-life heterosexual is killed or maimed by God in a natural disaster (another way the divine godhead parallels the Bush administration). If this somehow seems unfair, Colbert is quick to remind us, paraphrasing the "theologian" Donald Rumsfeld: "Sometimes you have to worship the God you have, not the God you want."

Religion and Bodily Fluids I: Homophobia

Religion tends to mystify and alienate by making people uncomfortable in their own skin, uneasy with their bodily existence, not to mention their bodily fluids and their inclination to share (or not share) them. Religion has long been a main source for norms regulating sexual behavior. Its track record, however, is, well, spotty, on this issue.

For starters, in modern liberal democracies such as the United States, conservative religion, especially fundamentalist and evangelical Christianity, is by far the main sponsor of hatred for and discriminatory policies against homosexuals. In fact, contempt for homosexuality is one of the few things that bring together believers from disparate religious traditions in efforts to promote discriminatory policies against homosexuals, a phenomenon Colbert refers to as "manotheism." This hostile expression of paranoia and xenophobia is rationalized as a divinely sanctioned stance that is necessary for the preservation of the family (as God designed it, of course) and individuals' moral purity. Accordingly, when questioned, those who foment such hatred usually pass the buck to God. However, homosexuality is just another way, a non-heterosexual way, of being human. So, religious people who persecute and vilify homosexuals and make them feel ashamed and guilt-ridden for simply being who they are, are purveyors of alienation.

Religion and Bodily Fluids II: Masturbaphobia

Religiously inspired guilt about human sexuality often takes the form of guilt about masturbation too. I'm not suggesting that this form of guilt rises to the level, so to speak, of that associated with homophobia. This is a more private matter, which, ironically, affects all of us. But it's clear that concerns about masturbation get much of their psychic punch from religion.

For instance, just about every male who was socialized into any sort of conservative Christian tradition knows about the sin of Onan. In case you missed that, Onan is a figure in the Hebrew Bible (or *Old* Testament, as some Christians pejoratively put it, as in "That's *so* Old Testament"). Onan, we're told, was put to death by the Lord for spilling his semen on the ground (old school birth control) in defiance of the practice of levirate marriage (getting hitched to the brother of your childless dead husband to produce offspring, see Genesis 38: 8–10). Some religious leaders have seized on the story of Onan as a reliable method for instilling guilt in adolescent males, otherwise known as masturbataholics, who'd prefer not to be slain by the Lord, but are nonetheless ready to risk their lives for Jessica Simpson at least a few times a day.

Here we get a clear, albeit silly, view of the art of grounding a socially constructed sexual stricture in a cosmic framework. Think about it. The *Lord* – not the father or mother who's tired of thirty-minute bathroom visits and sticky socks – is prepared to kill teenagers who are fond of exploring through fantasy their newly discovered (and presumably, God-given) sexual nature. Maybe the Lord's just jealous that he can't get a boner like a teenage boy anymore. If indeed he did appear at the NBA all-star game in the guise of a steroid-bloated Jerry Garcia, this would explain the problem.

Somehow some human beings make it through adolescence without getting struck down by the Lord. They may wonder how they survived, but as a divine compromise, they're given a guilty conscience. If *this* Lord's way with masturbators seems harsh, and yet you find yourself still inclined to be religious, Stephen Colbert has a recommendation for you. Join the "First Church of Constant Masturbators."

According to Colbert, for these religionists, masturbation isn't a sin, but is, on the contrary, fundamental to their religion. In fact, as Colbert notes, "their Messiah was masturbated to death by the Romans." Masturbation for them, in fact, is sacramental. As an aside, this burgeoning church boasts the strongest youth appeal of any religious movement today, even outpacing the Catholic pedophilia movement in the United States.

Religion and Delegitimation

I've argued that when religion legitimates, it simultaneously alienates. But many religions claim to save human beings by putting them in touch with their *true* selves (their *non-primate* selves). I won't even try to determine whether there's any sense in which any religion could make good on this claim. However, I readily acknowledge that religion can also *delegitimize* social orders, and so can offset, by redressing social injustice, for instance, at least some of the alienating effects it otherwise has.

Consider, for instance, Martin Luther King, Jr.'s use of biblical narratives to *de*construct racist policies of segregation that were partly grounded in religious justifications that made white supremacy seem "natural." Here the process of legitimizing racist social practices via white Christian readings of the Bible was thrown in reverse. Biblical narratives and ideals were used to *expose* the merely human and grossly unjust practices that were incongruent with them. Citizens then were encouraged to take responsibility for the dehumanizing effects of these practices, not to chalk them up to divinely ordained prejudice.

Regrettably, however, religionists of this sort tend to be assassinated or imprisoned for their critiques, often by fellow believers who bristle at the thought of overturning social practices that they take to be established by God. It was white Southern *Christians*, after all, who mounted the fiercest opposition to King, and who perpetrated the worst violence against fellow Christians, who were African-Americans, during the Civil Rights Movement. Unfortunately, one man's religious legitimation can simultaneously be another man's religious *de*legitimation (and yes, I do mean one "*man's*," since this almost exclusively has been a male and patriarchal enterprise). As the American political philosopher, John Rawls (1921–2002) reminds us, that's one reason why it's better to avoid religious foundations altogether in a pluralistic democracy. Still, revolutionary religionists, such as King, show us that religion doesn't have to be used to justify the status quo (especially if the Democrats are in power). In this respect, at least, they're in league with ironists.

Revival

Growing up as I did in a Southern Pentecostal church (think of Colbert holding snakes up to his neck and chanting in tongues and that about captures it), I became quite aware that religious passions can dissipate for a while, only to be rekindled when the traveling evangelist, usually a loudmouth blowhard, comes to town. Pentecostals, along with some other Christians, call this phenomenon "revival." Especially for the men of the church (the local "Deciders"), it's a kind of spiritual viagra, which, as Colbert observes, is "crank that makes your jimmy thicker," in this case, your spiritual jimmy. The question I now wish to address is whether we can have revival right here and right now.

Don't get nervous. There aren't any sweaty, blathering evangelists preparing to mount the pulpit. What I have in mind is this. If anything can be made to look good or bad by being redescribed, then the argument I've given about religion's role in promoting human alienation itself can be made to look bad too. So, in honor of all those preachers who used to scare the hell out of me with their talk about the rapture, let me give it a shot (or two).

A religionist might point out that human beings are inherently religious, that nearly as long as there have been human communities, there also have been human beings worshipping gods of some sort and performing peculiar religious rites to appease or inflame them. In that case, being religious is a very human thing to be, and so it isn't alienating at all.

Far from suggesting that to be religious is to be something other than human, I've argued that religion is *utterly* human. Furthermore, I've argued that religious practices, beliefs, and myths are responses to profoundly human needs for cultural stability and meaning. This position leads to a mild paradox: throughout much of our history, in order to fulfill very human needs, many of us have unwittingly embraced practices and beliefs that are alienating and that actually frustrate those needs.

Must we do this, though? The claim that we must because religion is an *essential* feature of human nature is wrongheaded. It conflates frequently occurring, but nonetheless contingent traits of an evolving animal with a fixed, unalterable, and timeless essence. What we *are*, both collectively and individually, is what we have been *so far* and are in the process of *becoming*. And so far, while it's true that many human societies have grounded their social institutions in religious legitimations of some sort, for several hundred years now some, including our own, have been experimenting with *non-religious* ways of bringing cohesion, stability, and even meaning to their central institutions and everyday life. A crucial part of this experiment, furthermore, is the granting of basic freedoms to all citizens to be as religious or non-religious as they desire to be, within the constraints set by the core values that make possible our democracy. So, it's misleading to construe this experiment in pluralism, which is a fragile and ongoing endeavor, as an ineluctably *irreligious* venture.

The revival isn't over yet, however. Some people argue that an ironic perspective on religion inevitably distorts it to such an extent that one is left with a fundamental choice: either be religious or be ironic about religion, but if you choose irony, you thereby forego your chance to understand religion. But is it necessary to be religious in order to understand religion? Are ironists bound to have a blinkered view of religion? Why think that irony and religious faith are incompatible anyhow?

Clearly, people who try to be completely ironic about *everything* aren't going to understand people who are blindly devoted to their religion, and vice versa. However, while there are plenty of people who fall into the latter category, it's more difficult to locate those who belong in the former. The humorists of *The Daily Show* don't belong in this category. At least several of them grew up in religious traditions and clearly have an *internal* perspective on many of the religious practices they satirize. Indeed, this is one reason why Colbert, who's Catholic, is so incisive and savage in his religious humor. (This is also why the new home, if not in name, of "This Week in God" is, in fact, *The Colbert Report* on any night that Colbert has religion in his sights, especially if "The Word" is a religious topic.)[4]

Furthermore, many things that may seem incompatible in theory are *practically* reconcilable, that is, can be brought together in a multifaceted human life. This holds true for irony and religion. Some complicated people are *both* religious *and* ironic about religion at the same time (sorry, James Dobson). So, it just doesn't follow that ironists inevitably come to a distorted view of religion.

Irony as Ritual

If irony isn't circumscribed by solidarity with other human beings and affirmation of the human condition, it too can produce alienation by fostering cynicism and disengagement. But unlike some critics of *The Daily Show*, I don't think that the show has this effect. On the contrary, the nightly irony baths that we get from watching *The Daily Show*, not to mention *The Colbert Report*, help to reaffirm the reality before our eyes, the reality that many of our political and religious leaders don't want us to see. They also expose the silliness and inhumanity of so much religion in our time, and the crass and moronic uses to which God-talk is often put by religious and political leaders. We respond by considering again the merely human qualities of it all, and laughing about it. And that helps make things better. That's our way of coping with religion.

Notes

1 Richard Rorty, *Contingency, Irony, and Solidarity* (Cambridge: Cambridge University Press, 1989), p. 73, italics added.
2 Peter Berger, *The Sacred Canopy: Elements of a Sociological Theory of Religion* (New York: Anchor Books, 1967), p. 33.
3 Peter van Inwagen, *God, Knowledge, and Mystery: Essays in Philosophical Theology* (Ithaca: Cornell University Press, 1995), pp. 105–6.
4 Consider, for instance, Colbert's riff during an installment of "The Word" entitled "Old School," in which he discusses the return of Yahweh, the warrior god of the Hebrew Bible, in the devastation of hurricane Katrina, and the subsequent decentering of the meek and mild Jesus. It's almost as if Colbert seeks to provide a shockingly funny set of "Cliffs notes" to Harold Bloom's recent book, *Jesus and Yahweh: The Names Divine* (New York: Riverhead Books, 2005).

15

EVOLUTION, SCHMEVOLUTION:
JON STEWART AND THE CULTURE WARS

MASSIMO PIGLIUCCI

"Are we characters in a dubious fairy tale written thousands of years ago in the depth of human ignorance, or random globs of cells who got a little luckier than the fucking slime that grows on our shower towels?" This was the opening question in *The Daily Show* series "Evolution, Schmevolution," one of the most daring attempts at exploring a serious and controversial issue in the history of fake news TV. *The Daily Show* appropriately timed the series to air during the momentous trial that took place in Dover, Pennsylvania in the fall of 2005. The plaintiff in the case *Tammy Kitzmiller vs. the Dover Area School District* contended that the theory of "intelligent design" (ID) shouldn't be taught in public schools on the grounds that it's a form of creationism, and that teaching it would amount to a clear violation of the separation between Church and State.[1]

Stewart's opening question goes straight to the heart of why there's a controversy between creationists and evolutionists and not, say, between creationists and quantum physicists: people have an intuitive understanding of the philosophical implications of the idea of evolution, while the consequences of quantum mechanics in this context are much more nuanced (another reason why quantum mechanics is usually left alone is that, as Nobel physicist Richard Feynman reminded us, nobody *really* understands quantum physics, not even quantum physicists). Stewart's framing of the problem is reminiscent of another famous source of popular scholarship, Monty Python, in their immortal opus *The Meaning of Life*: "Why are we here? What's life all about? / Is God really real, or is there some doubt? . . . What's the point of all this hoax? / Is it the chicken and the egg time? Are we just yolks? / Or, perhaps, we're just one of God's little jokes." And so on and so forth.

Of course, phrasing the question as an either/or choice may in itself represent a classic example of <u>logical fallacy</u>, the false dichotomy, in which someone presents two options as exhausting all possibilities, when in fact there are more positions that can be reasonably taken. During the "Evolution, Schmevolution" series, Lewis Black, a regular *Daily Show* commentator, points out that presenting an issue as an either/or choice may not be the wisest thing to do, and indeed may lead to rather silly outcomes:

> The scientific method has taken us pretty far: we've cured diseases, sent men to the moon, given erections where before there were none. . . . Religion has also inspired man to do some pretty great things [*showing image of the Sistine Chapel's ceiling*]. The problem is, when you try too hard to apply science to religion, both come off looking ridiculous.

So, what's the real status of the scientific theory of evolution? And what do people mean by "intelligent design?" More generally, what's the proper relationship between science and religion, not to mention politics, in early twenty-first century America? This chapter will examine these and other weighty questions through the inquiring minds and sharp tongues of Jon Stewart, Lewis Black, and *Daily Show* "correspondent" Ed Helms. While the four episodes of the "Evolution, Schmevolution" special may have changed few minds on this topic, the series represents a good example of humorous yet engaging intellectual discourse, addressing complex philosophical questions, even peppered with instances of logical fallacies committed by the host, his correspondents, or some of the guests.

Evolution: The Fundamentals

Scientific theories are complex statements about the workings of the natural world, and they're notoriously difficult to frame in straightforward and understandable terms. This explains why scientists are famously inept at communicating with the general public (with few remarkable exceptions such as Carl Sagan, Stephen J. Gould, and Richard Dawkins).[2] This ineptness was on display during Ed Helms' interview with primatologist Dan Wharton at the Bronx Zoo. The guy managed to remain as stiff and humorless as the quintessential ivory tower intellectual even when Helms launched into a discussion of the comparative anatomy of human and chimpanzee penises (although, to be fair, *The Daily Show*'s editors did their best to accentuate the effect on poor Dr. Wharton)!

Nonetheless, in the opening monologue to the "Evolution, Schmevolution" series, Stewart gave a succinct but substantially correct summary of the Darwinian theory, using a diagram portraying the classic example of giraffes with necks of different lengths, one of which was clearly more adapted to reaching high tree leaves than the others (there was also a "really cool" but alas unlikely mutant version which could spit fire from its nostrils). Essentially, Darwin's theory is based on two fundamental insights: on the one hand, all living creatures are related to each other by common descent; on the other, organisms differentiate from each other and adapt to the ever-changing conditions of their world.[3] The main mechanism for this latter process is natural selection. Natural selection, in turn, is simply the result of the fact that animals (and plants) differ from each other (because of mutations in their DNA) in transmissible traits that affect their survival and their ability to produce offspring. Those that manage to survive and have more babies will pass more of their winning characteristics to the next generation, where the game will start all over *ad infinitum*. That's pretty much it, though there are a few additional complications, and the whole story can be told in much more precise (and quite a bit more complicated) mathematical terms.

Philosophers of science have sometimes debated the scientific status of Darwin's theory. Karl Popper (the father of "falsificationism," the idea that scientific theories can't be proven correct, but must be capable of being proven wrong) at one point stated that "Darwinism is not a testable scientific theory, but a metaphysical research program."[4] This pronouncement is often quoted by creationists, although Popper later admitted that his earlier views on the subject were mistaken: "I have changed my mind about the testability and logical status of the theory of natural selection; and I am glad to have an opportunity to make a recantation."[5] If only such intellectual honesty were more common in these sorts of debates! Popper's error aside, the consensus among philosophers of science is that the theory of evolution is a legitimate scientific theory, characterized by a mix of historical claims (common descent) and experimentally verifiable natural processes (mutation and selection). As Patricia Cleland effectively sums it up, it isn't rocket science, but it's very solid science nonetheless.[6]

What sort of evidence can scientists possibly muster in support of their statements about life forms that are now extinct? In part, the evidence is the sort of inferential logic based on fossil records that Lewis Black highlights in his "Evolution, Schmevolution" commentary. As he puts it:

> Scientific theory is based on observations made in the real world. . . . [For] little creationists there is '*D*' is for *Dinosaurs*, where kids are taught that before the Flood all dinosaurs were vegetarian. Makes sense, especially when you look at this early dino-skeleton [*points to a fossil of a meat-eating dinosaur*]: those 80 dagger-shaped teeth and huge claws were perfect for chasing down and killing any plants that try to run away!

That, in a nutshell, is the scientific method.

Why, Then, Is There a Problem?

While watching "Evolution, Schmevolution," one could be forgiven for concluding that the theory of evolution ought to be uncontroversial for the simple reason that it makes sense. This would be the same sort of mistake that a politically liberal viewer of *The Daily Show* might make when concluding that, say, it's pretty obvious that the United States shouldn't have invaded Iraq (Stewart's ongoing series "Mess O' Potamia" is probably worth a book in and of itself). But the fact is that evolution is highly controversial in the United States. More than 50 percent of Americans surveyed in various Gallup polls reject the theory entirely, and many more accept it only with the proviso that God is somehow controlling the process. Explanations for the predominant American view include a long and complex history of anti-intellectualism peculiar to the US and the sorry condition of scientific literacy in the population at large.[7]

The "problem" was clear for everyone to see when Ed Helms visited Dayton, Tennessee, the site of the original "monkey" trial of 1925, during which substitute science teacher John Scopes was tried and eventually convicted of teaching the "false doctrine" of evolution (the only time evolutionists have actually lost a court case).[8] Helms interviewed locals while pretending that they were actually impersonating characters from 1925. As he put it: "So come on down and enjoy Dayton, safe in the knowledge that it's all pretend. Because if it were real, it would be fucking terrifying." Indeed, a woman interviewed by Helms candidly stated an astonishingly common position among the American public: "Evolution is a total fabrication and a lie. Evolution destroys faith and builds an economic market that is contrary to our American way of life."

Of course, the creation-evolution controversy, while not a scientific debate, has several root causes – not just scientific ignorance and religious bigotry. Stewart's crew subtly brought to the public's attention the political element at work. The controversy has been exploited politically ever since three-time Presidential candidate William Jennings Bryan volunteered to be on the prosecution team against John Scopes in 1925, facing the famous (or infamous, depending on your point of view) liberal lawyer Clarence Darrow, activist and prominent member of the then newly established American Civil Liberties Union. During the "Evolution, Schmevolution" series, Stewart brought in Chris Mooney, author of *The Republican War on Science*, to weigh in on the broader issue of the relationship between politics, science, and religion. Stewart pointed out that putting a political spin on scientific findings is nothing new, and that Republican and Democrat administrations alike engage in such practice. Mooney replied that the current situation is different because "The scientific community [is] coming out and releasing strong statements saying that the [Bush] administration abused science across the board. And I would trust the scientific community to diagnose whether science has been overly politicized." The second President Bush actually came out in favor of creationism as a competing theory, stating on August 3, 2005 that "That decision [about teaching creationism in public schools] should be made by local school districts, but I [feel] like both sides ought to be properly taught. . . . I think that part of education is to expose people to different schools of thought." This is the standard (and rather disingenuous) ID line of "teaching the controversy."

Mooney, addressing the broader contention that disagreement within the scientific community implies that we should seriously consider all positions on an issue, said that no matter how well supported, "Scientific knowledge is by its nature tentative, so you can selectively say 'Oh, we don't know enough about global warming,' when in fact we know a heck of a lot. . . . It's the same about evolution. . . . The war on science is compelled by corporate interests and religious conservative interests."

Stewart then pursued this general line by presenting the possibility of a postmodern position on truth: "Will scientific debate, then, become in the same way that a court case becomes, in that . . . if you hire the right experts you'll do better. . . . In the way, let's say, OJ Simpson puts together a nice team and hires guys who say 'DNA means nothing!'" This point about the alleged relativity of truth and knowledge is a serious one that philosophers have discussed ever since the ancient skeptics argued that there can't be certain knowledge of any kind. The long tradition of rationalism in philosophy, from Plato (ca. 427–ca. 347 BCE) to Descartes (1596–1650), argued for the milder position that while empirical knowledge (based on what the senses tell us) is unreliable, the mind can access truth by using logic and applying it to first principles (culminating in Descartes' method of "radical doubt"). Then again, empiricists like David Hume (1711–76) pointed out that there's very little, if anything, about the outside world that we can come to know in this way, and the best we can hope for are rather tentative conclusions based on admittedly incomplete empirical evidence. As a result, science – which emerged as a blend of rationalism and empiricism – is a messy business yielding rather tentative conclusions. According to Mooney, this situation doesn't sit well with the need for relatively simple answers in both the political and religious arenas. In this respect, it's interesting to note the awkward and philosophically untenable position in which religious fundamentalists put themselves when they resort to claiming that scientific knowledge is relative. Surely they don't want to go as far as claiming that *all* knowledge is relative to one's culture or ideological position, since that would undermine their own religious stance. The same applies to the extreme postmodernist position, which is often attacked on the ground that if no point of view has any special claim to truth, why should one regard the postmodern position itself as having any more value than any of the many possible anti-postmodernist positions?[9]

What is Intelligent Design, Anyway?

The "Evolution, Schmevolution" series was prompted, as mentioned earlier, by the trial in Dover. That trial was important in the history of the controversy because it was the first time that the idea of "intelligent design," and not just standard "the earth is 6,000 years old" creationism, was being tested in a court of law. But what exactly is ID? Once again, Stewart and his collaborators did a surprisingly good job of getting to the bottom line in a clear and entertaining way. As Stewart said: "Put simply, Intelligent Design says life on earth is too complex to have evolved without some kind of guiding hand. They are not saying it's God, just someone with the basic skill-set to create an entire working universe." This captures the alleged (and clearly disingenuous) distinction between creationism and ID, the very same "distinction without a difference" that made Judge Jones impatient at the Dover trial: "The evidence at trial demonstrates that ID is nothing less than the progeny of creationism. . . . Compelling evidence supports the Plaintiff's assertion that ID is creationism re-labeled."

To further probe this matter, Stewart convened a panel discussion featuring leading ID proponent William Dembski, historian John Larson, author of *Summer for the Gods*, and New Age spiritualist Ellie Crystal.[10] Dembski opened the discussion with an interesting philosophical move: according to him, ID proponents don't deny natural selection, since "it's not either/or – there can be design that's implemented through [natural selection]." This suggests that evolutionary biologists are guilty of committing the fallacy of false dichotomy that we already encountered at the beginning of this chapter. Of course, strictly speaking, Dembski is correct: science can't rule out supernatural oversight of natural processes, simply because the supernatural is outside the purview of science. Since by definition the supernatural can't be subjected to empirical investigation and experimentation, the possibility advanced by Dembski – usually referred to as theistic evolution – can't be excluded on scientific grounds. This, however, is a somewhat Pyhrric victory for ID.[11]

ID's proponents, beginning with Dembski himself, repeatedly claim that ID is good science. Stewart highlights the contradiction when he brings up the following example: "Let me ask you this: Intelligent Design, the scrotum, the most painful part of my body. This intelligent designer chose to put it in a bag that anyone can walk across and hit with a baseball bat." To this Dembski could only reply with a rather evasive "ID is not committed to every aspect of reality being the result of intelligence." Well, then, how do we know which bits of reality ID *is* committed to explaining?

While Stewart clearly meant the scrotum reference as a joke (indeed, he thanked Dembski for considering the question seriously enough to attempt to address the point), he was actually right on the mark. If a supernatural (or, for that matter, natural) intelligent agent is directing evolution from behind the scenes, then that agent is responsible not just for the marvels of biological complexity and success, but for the apparent stupidity and inefficiency that plagues the biological world.[12] This is why I said theistic evolution results in a Pyhrric victory for ID. Let's not forget, as evolutionary biologist Ernst Mayr observed, that 99.99 percent of all species that ever existed are now extinct. Not exactly a record to be proud of if one aspires to the title of creator and engineer-behind-the-scenes of the universe!

Of course, a weaker interpretation of Dembski's claim of non-mutual exclusivity is that religion and science aren't inherently incompatible, contrary to what has been asserted on various occasions, for example, by biologist Richard Dawkins.[13] Stewart posed precisely that question to the historian on the panel, John Larson, who pointed out that "we are talking about science here, the problem with divine intervention, a miracle, is that it's not repeatable, it's not testable in a laboratory, it's not falsifiable." In other words, ID proponents simply can't have it both ways: either there's a supernatural designer who works outside of the confines of natural laws – in which case ID isn't science and shouldn't be taught in public schools as such – or ID has to make some claims that are empirically verifiable and so be open to the possibility that such claims may be shown to be false. Once again, Dembski's rebuttal is rather weak: "I'm not talking about the big G, I'm saying that there are organizing principles." But of course no scientist has ever claimed that there are no (natural) "organizing principles" generating the order and complexity that we see in the universe. Natural selection is supposed to be precisely one such organizing principle!

Stewart saw through Dembski's rhetoric, and promptly asked him, "What came first [for you], the religion [*sic*] conversion or the evidence convincing you?" to which Dembski admitted "the religious conversion came first." Now, strictly speaking, Stewart was very close here to committing the genetic fallacy, rejecting an argument not on the grounds of its weakness, but because of where it comes from. One might also diagnose this as coming close to the *ad hominem* fallacy, rejecting the view because of the view holder. Just because, say, a racist biologist publishes a paper purportedly showing evidence of genetic differences in the cognitive abilities of different ethnic groups, one can't reject the paper simply on ideological grounds. Proper scientific analysis requires the evidence presented in the paper to be assessed on its own merits, regardless of the ideological positions of the author. Nonetheless, the fallacy occurs only if one concludes from the character of a given individual that his ideas are *necessarily* flawed. Stewart obviously stopped far short of that, simply hinting at the curious fact that while the scientific community includes people of all religions, ID proponents are invariably committed to a narrow range of Christian (or Muslim) conservative positions. It doesn't follow that ID proponents are wrong, but it would be disingenuous or naïve not to be suspicious of their motives and possible biases.

So, Evolution or Schmevolution?

Jon Stewart began the "Evolution, Schmevolution" series by promising (obviously in jest) that the public would finally know the answer by the end of the week. Again this is analogous to Monty Python's promise in the title song of *The Meaning of Life*: "So just why, why are we here? / And just what, what, what, what do we fear? / Well *çe soir*, for a change, it will all be made clear / For this is *The Meaning of Life*." Just as Monty Python didn't really "solve" the meaning of life, neither did Jon Stewart solve the evolution-creation controversy. Perhaps figuring out the meaning of life is a personal matter, something that's up to particular individuals to work out for themselves. One might be tempted to see an analogy between the two questions, and argue that the solution to the evolution-creation controversy is also a personal matter, not an issue that can be resolved by objective external evidence. In a sense, this may be the case; let me explain, by way of a short digression.

Meaning in life is not to be found in external, objective mandates (unless one believes that such meaning can come from a god, and one also has reason to believe that that god's message has been transmitted loud and clear). Rather, individual human beings construct meaningful lives out of their physical possibilities and limits, their cultural biases and practices, and their innate desires. As Aristotle would have put it, "happiness" (although the Greek word *eudaimonia* really has a broader meaning than the roughly equivalent English term) is a work in progress, and we can't assess the outcome until death puts an end to the quest. It's for this reason that it makes little sense to ask the simplistic question: what is *the* meaning of life?

Similarly, it might seem to make equally little sense to seek a resolution to the evolution-creation controversy. Scientists and philosophers of science have convincingly argued that there's simply no *scientific* controversy here.[14] From a philosophical standpoint, ID isn't science, because it doesn't include empirically verifiable statements, and because it invokes a supernatural intervention which is by definition outside the realm of scientific investigation. From a scientific perspective, there's just about as much disagreement among professional biologists on the modern theory of evolution as there is among physicists on the mathematics of quantum mechanics – pretty close to zero. Of course, both theories may eventually be superseded or significantly altered in the future, but certainly not by vague statements about intelligent organizing principles. In this sense, the evolution-creation debate is similar to the debate on global warming, as Chris Mooney pointed out to Stewart: the scientific community increasingly converges toward one answer, but the public is divided on the issue because of the political and ideological muddling that seeps through the media's treatment of it. Ironically, Jon Stewart's approach to the evolution-creation controversy ranks as one of the best media treatments of the debate in recent memory.

In another – non-scientific – sense, however, the "solution" to the controversy is and can only be personal, in that individuals have to make up their minds about whether they're willing to fully accept a scientific-rationalist worldview, or whether they'd rather pick and choose which aspects of a pre-Enlightenment mentality they wish to retain. One can certainly enjoy the benefits of science – from laptop computers to air travel to modern medicine – while still engaging in mystical thinking about intelligent designers and worldwide floods that never happened, but this comes at the risk of much cognitive dissonance and social strife, not to mention philosophical untenability. Although we're free to choose either side, we may not be free to choose either wisely.

The Daily Show series on evolution ended on a semi-sober note, with a brief outline of the matters that should really concern us. Forget supernatural intelligent design, the real problem is that humans have now learned enough about genetics and evolution to actually start tampering with the basic structure of life itself. Stewart and company take aim at genetic engineering and cloning while depicting scientists as aloof, out of touch with what's important to humanity, engaging in intellectual games for their own sake (as in the case of efforts to clone cats, which Stewart characterizes as "making copies of something no one needed to begin with"). Indeed, a basic problem with the creation-evolution controversy is that in one camp we have an army of anti-intellectuals who distrust science, and in the other a small elite band of intellectuals who largely think it beneath them to explain to the general public what they're doing and why (despite the fact that it's the general public that pays their bills). Stewart introduced the "Evolution, Schmevolution" series by saying, "The stage was now set for an epic debate between the forces of science on one side and religion on the other. One side says 'You're backwards, and primitive,' the other side says 'You're godless, and love Satan.' Sadly, the debate itself has not evolved in over 150 years." Indeed.

Notes

1 The trial ended with a resounding victory for the evolution (Plaintiff's) side. Judge Jones, presiding over the case, concluded: "We find that ID fails on three different levels, any one of which is sufficient to preclude a determination that ID is science. They are: (1) ID violates the

centuries-old ground rules of science by invoking and permitting supernatural causation; (2) the argument of irreducible complexity, central to ID, employs the same flawed and illogical contrived dualism that doomed creation science in the 1980s; and (3) ID's negative attacks on evolution have been refuted by the scientific community."

2 For example, Carl Sagan, *The Demon-Haunted World: Science as a Candle in the Dark* (New York: Random House, 1995); Stephen J. Gould, *The Panda's Thumb* (New York: Norton, 1992); Richard Dawkins, *The Blind Watchmaker: Why the Evidence of Evolution Reveals a Universe Without Design* (New York: Norton, 1996).

3 Charles Darwin, *The Origin of Species by Means of Natural Selection: Or, The Preservation of Favored Races in the Struggle for Life* (New York: A. L. Burt, 1910 [1859]).

4 Karl Popper, "Darwinism as a Metaphysical Research Program," in *But Is It Science? The Philosophical Question in the Creation/Evolution Controversy*, ed. Michael Ruse (New York: Prometheus, 1996), pp. 144–55.

5 Karl Popper, "Natural Selection and the Emergence of Mind," *Dialectica* 32 (1978), pp. 339–55, and his letter to *New Scientist* 87 (August, 1980), p. 611.

6 Patricia Cleland, "Historical Science, Experimental Science, and the Scientific Method," *Geology* 29 (2001), pp. 987–90.

7 For a discussion of the various causes and forms of creationism, see Massimo Pigliucci, *Denying Evolution: Creationism, Scientism and the Nature of Science* (Sunderland, MA: Sinauer, 2002), especially chapter 3.

8 For a discussion of the history and aftermath of the Scopes trial see Pulitzer Prize-winner Edward J. Larson, *Summer for the Gods: The Scopes Trial and America's Continuing Debate over Science and Religion* (New York: Basic Books, 1997).

9 For example, philosopher Paul Feyerabend famously argued that astrology and rain dances have as much a claim to being a source of knowledge as science, and that their dismissal by scientists is motivated by intellectual elitism or downright racism. It's hard to encounter a more irrational view of science and knowledge among professional philosophers. For a more balanced treatment of the positive and the nonsensical in postmodernism's attitude toward truth, see Ian Hacking, *The Social Construction of What?* (Cambridge, MA: Harvard University Press, 1999).

10 Why the panel didn't feature an evolutionary biologist is a mystery that shall go unsolved until Jon Stewart reads this chapter and writes to me about the inner workings of his mind. I won't mention Crystal again,

since her rambling was so incomprehensible even Stewart didn't quite know what to do with her!

11 The term refers to the ancient king Pyrrhus of Epirus, who attacked and defeated the Roman legions on two occasions in 279 BCE. However, his losses were so great that they eventually made it impossible for him to continue the war, which was eventually won by the Romans (who had home field advantage, and could more readily count on fresh troops). According to the Roman historian Plutarch: "The armies separated; and, it is said, Pyrrhus replied to one that gave him joy of his victory that one other such would utterly undo him."

12 This "argument from bad design" is essentially the same that has plagued Christian apologists since Thomas Aquinas, and is a particular version of what is known in theology as the problem of evil.

13 Dawkins' most complete attack on religion can be found in *The God Delusion* (Boston: Houghton Mifflin, 2006).

14 For example: Niall Shanks and Karl H. Joplin, "Redundant Complexity: A Critical Analysis of Intelligent Design in Biochemistry," *Philosophy of Science* 66 (1999), pp. 268–82; Elliott Sober, "The Design Argument," in *The Blackwell Guide to Philosophy and Religion*, ed. William E. Mann (Oxford: Blackwell, 2001), pp. 117–47; and Matt Young and Taner Edis eds., *Why Intelligent Design Fails: A Scientific Critique of the New Creationism* (New Brunswick: Rutgers University Press, 2004).

CHECKING IN WITH STEPHEN COLBERT/YOUR MOMENT OF ZEN:
BEYOND *THE DAILY SHOW*

SEGMENT 5

16

AMERICA (THE BOOK):
TEXTBOOK PARODY AND DEMOCRATIC THEORY

STEVE VANDERHEIDEN

The Daily Show has emerged as one of the most influential media sources for political information, despite the show's status as "fake news." Scholars have observed that the show increases cynicism about politics and the news media, but that it also assists viewers in understanding politics, and so performs an educative as well as critical function.[1] The same reliance on satire and parody as a means of social and political critique is on display in the show's spin-off book, *America (The Book)*,[2] which ostensibly takes the form (in parody) of an American government introductory textbook, promising an analysis of democracy through history and as embodied by contemporary politics. Like the show, the book's primary aim is humorous and playful, but its secondary aim is serious and critical, developing a theory of democracy that warrants examination in its own right, especially given the powerful effect that soft news now has on shaping ideals and influencing social and political opinions.

Both the book and television show aim to hold up a mirror to the contemporary United States. *America* reflects an America whose self-image is often in sharp contrast with its very real shortcomings, absurdities, vanities, and hypocrisy. The book reminds us of our aspirations and illuminates various ways we fall short of our ideals, and does so with a keen sense of humor and critical edge that's anathema to real news programs and many textbooks. The parody and satire *America* relies upon can only work if the objective is something more than pure entertainment and if its target is also something quite serious. To understand the use of humor in achieving this end, we'll look at the philosophy of humor before turning to democratic theory.

Humor with a Point

As Israel Knox notes, "humor is a species of liberation, and it is the liberation that comes to us as we experience the singular delight of beholding chaos that is playful and make-believe in a world that is serious and coercive."[3] Such playful chaos is on abundant display in *America*, as is a thinly veiled recognition of the seriousness of the subjects it parodies but doesn't disown. *America* relies upon the most potentially emancipatory of all forms of humor, satire, letting us laugh at political figures and institutions that palpably affect our lives in ways that are often "serious and coercive."

With political satire in particular, humor can't be disconnected from the broader social project of liberation, and *America*'s subtext contains far more than an attempt to make us laugh at "a jarring incongruity between form and content."[4] We must be able to stand at some critical distance, or we'll fail to appreciate the joke. But we must also feel some sympathy for the thing satirized, Knox suggests, or the sense of indignation that satire contains "would have neither purpose nor direction, and would vent itself in some form of action or invective rather than express itself in some form of art" (p. 546).

The "fake news" format of *The Daily Show* lends itself especially well to political satire, as does *America*'s textbook parody. Geoffrey Baym notes: "Unlike traditional news, which claims an epistemological certainty, satire is a discourse of inquiry, a rhetoric of challenge that seeks through the asking of unanswered questions to clarify the underlying morality of a situation."[5] The conventional textbook conveys a similar certainty, typically only asking questions that are answered elsewhere (as in study questions at the end of a chapter), while *America (The Book)* is replete with unanswered questions (or those answered only with a contrived ignorance that's subversive in its ironic naïveté) that likewise offer the same kind of "rhetoric of challenge." The questions are hard and can't be answered adequately without serious and sometimes disturbing reflection on the current state of the world. But they're questions that must be asked.

Baym concludes that the news satire format should be characterized not as "fake" news (as it conveys much factual political information), but rather "as an alternative model of journalism." In an observation that applies equally well to *America* (which, like the show, seeks a kind of moral clarity through the cognitive clash between familiar form and unexpected content), Baym suggests that satire is here being used "to interrogate power, parody to critique contemporary news, and dialogue to enact a model of deliberative democracy" (p. 261). Not only does *America* "enact" such a model by encouraging a more critical examination of some basic political ideals, its central serious point is a plea for more avenues of deliberative democracy in American government. *America* practices what it preaches.

Unlike the "fake news" of *The Daily Show*, *America*'s target isn't the medium it mocks (the American government textbook). The joke is rather on the state of American political education more generally, which all too often fails to call adequate attention to the gulf between the ideals of freedom and democracy and the much less exalted practice of democracy in the contemporary United States. As Tom Carson notes in his review of *America*, "the book's ultimate joke – on our educational system, if not us in general – is that it's not only more informative about how American government and culture work than the textbooks it burlesques, but gives us a keener sense of having a stake in both."[6] Our stake is made clear in the book's dedication, which reads: "To the huddled masses, keep yearnin'!" In this epithet lie two key thematic messages: that Americans aren't yet able to breathe freely (as the obstacles to liberty and democracy are many and varied), and that this elusive goal (invested with the distinctly American conception of liberty) is still worth striving for.

The contrast between *America* and the conventional textbooks it mocks reveals the book's method. Whereas many social studies textbooks approach their subjects with awe and reverence (the result of which is often an unfortunate lack of critical perspective on the current state of the union), *America* pulls no punches and leaves no sacred icons untouched. Just as it figuratively strips away the shrouds of timid reverence that usually surround textbook discussions of governmental institutions, it *literally* strips away the robes of the Supreme Court justices in "Dress the Supreme Court" (pp. 98–9). *America*'s authors are unafraid to say which part of the empire has no clothes, or to use a doctored photograph of nude justices if necessary in order to make this clear to the rest of us.

Reversing Democracy Inaction

The book's ironic subtitle (*A Citizen's Guide to Democracy Inaction*) calls attention to the disturbing lack of meaningful citizen input into the contemporary political process, and implicitly recommends a far more robust form of democracy than it finds in actual practice. Suppose democracy is merely a process by which citizens occasionally select representatives to govern them. This is a "thin" conception of democracy, where the power of ordinary citizens is limited to a periodic choice between competing slates of elites, to be contrasted with "thick," more participatory forms of democracy.[7] According to *America*, the American system ("which neither needs nor particularly wants voters") doesn't come off as particularly democratic, composed as it is of "a president freely chosen from a wide-open field of two men every four years; a Congress with a 99 percent incumbency rate; a Supreme Court comprised of nine politically appointed judges whose only oversight is the icy scythe of Death" (p. 1).

Under "thin" democracy, elections provide the only means of citizen direction and oversight of government, but this assumes at least some popular ability to replace governing elites with their challengers. With elections seemingly unable to perform this role effectively, American democracy might be described as one of "inaction" rather than action. In a mock infographic on the first page of *America* (supposedly explaining the decline in democratic participation in the US), 23 percent of citizens say that they're "too tired" to participate, 17 percent that the "game was on," and 8 percent that they "had a thing." A further 52 percent cite the fact that the monetary rewards are unsatisfactory. These excuses are funny because they're not far from the truth. The impression is that we have cause to worry about democracy, as many of our nominally democratic processes struggle to count as even thinly democratic.

Diagnosing the health of contemporary American democracy, declining voter participation is identified as merely a symptom of a larger malaise, yet one that suggests a coming crisis if its underlying causes aren't addressed. Although historians and political scientists have long speculated about the "life cycles" of states, such theories rarely find their way into introductory government texts, given the unsettling prediction of inevitable national decline. Relying on the analogy of human development (from "infancy" through "old age"), *America* presents a two-page graphic of the life cycle of democracy in a remarkably cogent (and humorous) analysis of the growing pains of maturing societies, along with advice for managing them: "Tip: You may also notice dissidents where you formerly had none. Don't worry; this is normal, and they can always be arrested" (p. 13). The reader is implicitly invited to consider in what stage American democracy is now, and what comes next. A little thought leads to the conclusion that we are in the "middle age" category, which *America* characterizes as follows:

> Voter turnout is thinning, your welfare system is bloated, you're completely dominated by corporate interests, and you haven't had a proper election in years. When this happens, a nation may go through a mid-life crisis, seeking solace in superficial "toys," like satellite-based lasers to shoot down missiles or action stars turned politicians. (p. 12)

The satirical tone can't conceal the serious warning: when democracy advances into "old age" (the stage immediately following "middle age"), it becomes dysfunctional, as "the best and the brightest of your nation shun public service," and "by the end, you can't even recognize your own ideals." But such processes are reversible: there is, so to speak, a fountain of youth for democratic regimes that reverses the aging process, breathing new life into areas where genuine democracy is now almost entirely absent. In this way, *America* can be read as a call to *action*, an antidote for "democracy inaction."

More robust forms of citizen participation in public life are widely viewed as an antidote to the sort of decline identified in *America*'s life cycle graphic. The political scientist Robert Putnam describes the processes in question as creating "social capital," an essential ingredient for making democracy work.[8] Without meaningful outlets for civic engagement (including many forms of participation that go far beyond voting and so belong to a "thick" conception of democracy), citizens can lose the capacity to see beyond their narrow selfish interests to a view of the public good. As a result of such interests, public life suffers (as when citizens withdraw from participation). Putnam finds social capital to correlate not only with healthy political institutions, but also with educational quality, economic vitality, and public safety. His research not only agrees with *America*'s assessment of American democracy in decline, but identifies increased citizen participation as the necessary remedy for reversing this decline and restoring public confidence in democratic institutions. Perhaps the projected slide into "Constitutional Robocracy" and other possible post-democratic futures may yet be averted, if Putnam is correct.

Similarly, the political theorist Benjamin Barber notes of our current "thin" version of democracy that "community without participation first breeds unreflected consensus and uniformity, then nourishes coercive conformity, and finally engenders unitary collectivism of a kind that stifles citizenship and the autonomy on which political activity depends."[9] It's only when citizens are able to genuinely participate in self-governance, in a thick, *deliberative* democracy, that democracy can yield the benefits in justice and legitimacy it promises. Deliberation involves the process of interacting with others, attempting to justify one's policy preferences and to persuade others to likewise endorse them as in the public good, rather than merely registering those preferences privately and without interaction or justification (as in voting), and this process of deliberation characteristic of "thick" democracy is widely seen as providing a uniquely legitimate or fair means of resolving disagreement over political issues.[10]

Only when citizens actively participate in democratic deliberation can they acquire the resources to overcome the most divisive conflicts among them. When citizens withdraw from politics the result is intensified and highly polarized conflicts (as *America* recognizes and bemoans). The goal in politics shifts from a search for common ground to a competitive gamesmanship where both sides try to exclude their opponents from power, wresting a temporary advantage at the cost of social stability, reciprocity, and trust. America (the country) has witnessed an upsurge in divisive partisanship, and the diagnosis of its principal causes and likely effects in *America (The Book)* closely tracks those of leading contemporary political theorists.

Indeed, the lack of effective outlets for genuine citizen participation in shaping contemporary American politics resounds as a theme throughout *America*. At various points the text alludes to the power void left by the absence of popular control over institutions of government being filled by such non-democratic (and occasionally anti-democratic) forces as corporate lobbyists. In the chapter on Congress, for example, declining voter turnout is posed as a possible problem for the notion that the legislative branch is beholden to the will of the people. The – ironically suggested – solution is that responsiveness to organized economic interests, rather than public opinion, is identical to democracy itself. Corporations are "the white knights of democracy" that make up for the lack of strong public involvement: "These altruistic entities hire lobbyists whose sole job is to insure, through persuasive argument and financial remuneration, that Congress never forgets the people's wishes" (p. 58). Of lobbyists, the authors satirically point out: "these professionally concerned private citizens can assist our representatives in any last minute changes in language, content, or intent necessary to insure their reelection funds" (p. 69), alluding to the corruption often associated with such interests.

Not only are elections charged with failing to provide a means by which the people's wishes can be communicated to their representatives in Congress, they can't even provide a basic check on politicians' past performance, given the uncompetitive nature of most elections (in which 96 percent of incumbents are typically reelected).[11] The authors ironically suggest that this anti-democratic feature was designed to "allow Americans to enjoy the benefits of a lawful and functioning society while only having to think about it once every two to four years – if at all!" (p. 58), and that "it is perhaps a sign of the strength of our republic that so few people feel the need to participate" (p. 117). This repeated dismissal of worries about declining participation betrays a serious concern with the problem.

Government of, by, or for the People?

The lack of meaningful public participation in self-governance isn't *America*'s only critique of contemporary American democracy. A second theme is the narrow range of demographic groups making up the government. A government composed almost exclusively of rich white men tends to reflect the interests of only that small cross-section of the public, and will consequently often fail to appreciate the problems and aspirations of other groups, who may have very different experiences, different challenges, and different political perspectives. Taking aim at such an easy target, *America* is able to emphasize humorously the wide gap between ideals of equality and meritocracy and the reality of privilege and exclusion: "By placing no explicit race, gender, or religious requirement on the presidency, the Founders opened the door to true meritocracy. Why no women, blacks, or non-Christians have answered the Founders' challenge is a mystery, though most indications point to some inherent genetic flaw" (p. 40).

Demographic representation of Americans hasn't been much better in the Senate, which *America* calls attention to in its "Senate Color by Numbers" exercise, where readers are invited to compare the original 1789 Senate with its larger but no more racially diverse 2004 counterpart, a fact further emphasized by the ironic quip: "As the nation grew in ethnic and cultural diversity, the Senate responded by getting bigger" (p. 68). Indeed, the absence of legal restrictions on female or minority candidates paradoxically calls attention to what is widely seen as an inherent flaw in US-style representative democracy. The door to meritocracy may be open, but electoral rules that cater to the majority (single-member districts, winner-take-all elections) ensure that minority electoral preferences, whatever their merits, are granted no real voice within political institutions.

Democracy depends on the ability of political institutions to be responsive to the full range of citizen preferences, not merely to those fitting neatly in the relatively narrow ideological spectrum of the two major political parties. Democratic theorists often call for reform of such electoral rules for just this reason, and describe the two-party system that such rules reinforce as posing an unhealthy constraint on democracy. Among the reforms suggested are replacing single-member districts with multi-member proportional systems, using instant run-off voting systems to allow for preference ordering among candidates, and the related formation of viable third parties.

Although *America* doesn't explicitly mention any such reforms, it tacitly endorses them by bemoaning the two-party system: "together, the two parties function like giant down comforters, allowing the candidates to disappear into the enveloping softness, protecting them from exposure to the harsh weather of independent thought"

(p. 107). Likewise, "the two-party system elegantly reflects the bichromatic rainbow that is American political thought" (p. 108). If that "rainbow" is to include more than two colors, it must allow for a more inclusive array of political voices within the institutions of government, rather than maintaining electoral rules stifling true electoral competition. If it fails in this regard, it's sure to add more permanent residents to the political graveyard pictured in *America* in a two-page spread where headstones mark the passing of various short-lived third parties, and where a sign on the garbage can at the graveyard entrance reads "Please place wasted votes here" (pp. 110–11).

Mediating the Media

As in *The Daily Show* itself, *America (The Book)* reserves some of its sharpest criticism for the media. The news media are often characterized as a kind of go-between linking the citizenry and the government, transmitting popular preferences and concerns to government officials and keeping citizens informed on public issues. For this reason, the press is often called the "fourth estate" or "fourth branch" of government. Given the relentless skewering of the US news media through the "fake news" format of *The Daily Show* and mock punditry of alum Stephen Colbert on *The Colbert Report* (not to mention important public appearances by both Stewart and Colbert), one might conclude that no further satire of the mass media is necessary.[12] And indeed, the book's indictment of the press offers the only case of pointed criticism where the contrast between ideals and reality isn't cloaked behind a veil of ironic humor, but is instead presented in a tone of exasperated sarcasm: "A free and independent press is essential to the health of a functioning democracy. It serves to inform the voting public on matters relevant to its wellbeing. Why they've stopped doing that is a mystery" (p. 131).

Unlike the "mystery" of race and gender uniformity among US presidents, the authors offer several explanations for the media's abdication of this mediating role in democracy. Following several academic and popular studies of recent changes in the mass media, *America* identifies media conglomeration as a prime contributor to this problem, detailing the ever-increasing concentration of media own-ership in text and graphics, in which "thousands of uncontrollable, perilously independent media voices were finally organized into a more manageable five" (p. 151). As John Stuart (not Jon Stewart) Mill wrote, competition within the "marketplace of ideas" is necessary for dis-covering truth,[13] and decreasing competition within the news media bodes ill for the "watchdog" function of the press.

With media ownership concentration comes a disappearing firewall between news content and advertising, increasing editorial control exercised by corporate ownership, declining media independ-ence from powerful corporate interests, and disinvestment from investigative reporting in favor of "synergy" (where putative news content is used to promote advertisers' products). Since citizens rely on the press for the political information that forms the basis for the democratic deliberation characteristic of "thick" democracy, philo-sophers draw causal links between the development of autonomy (or the capacity of self-governance) and the competition between oppos-ing political ideals that mediating institutions supply in well-functioning democracies.

As Joshua Cohen and Joel Rogers argue, "satisfying the conditions of reasonable deliberation requires that public discussion proceed against a background of alternative coherent views,"[14] but these altern-ative views are not typically presented by the mass media. Because of changes in media ownership and structure, as *America* notes (fol-lowing academic critiques), the press can no longer reliably perform the truth-seeking role described by Mill or the oversight function noted above, and is instead a propaganda arm of the government relying, not on its own reporting, but rather on official sources and press releases: "The public remains informed of the good things that the government is up to, and the media is freed up to use its entire arsenal for the next photogenic child's disappearance" (p. 154).

Putting Knowledge to Work

While its obvious purpose is to entertain the reader, *America*'s final chapter reinforces the book's emancipatory ideals. Purporting to compare the United States to other political systems and cultures (collectively referred to as an "international house of horrors"), the authors reveal their project with surprising candor (given the loads of irony elsewhere). They remark: "some of our book's more astute readers may have noticed that in detailing the complex and bewildering institutions that comprise our government, we inadvertently called attention to some slight imperfections in our otherwise perfect Union – inefficiencies, inequities, injustices, absurdities, hypocrisies, and an overall failure to live up to the lofty ideals expressed in our nation's founding documents" (p. 183). The over-the-top ethnocentric portrayals that follow convey another thematic message: the flaws observed in the American system aren't unique, but rather seem endemic to politics everywhere. The proper focus of critical enterprises such as *America*, then, isn't to throw out the imperfect in search of a perfect democracy (which exists nowhere), but to follow the advice of the book's dedication and keep struggling for greater freedom and equality.

The moral of citizen empowerment and action is repeated in the Afterword, which reminds the reader that "democracy, for all its flaws, still offers you and your fellow cold and huddled masses the best chance of improving your lot in life" (p. 220). On the final page, readers are awarded a "Certificate of Completion" that declares them "fully qualified to practice, participate in, or found a democracy." Explaining the last option, *America* points out that, although there's no land available for founding a new democracy from scratch, there are several "fixer-uppers" one might improve. *America* then ends on a strikingly sincere inspirational note: "Now go out there and make your Fathers proud."

Notes

1 Jody Baumgartner and Jonathon S. Morris, "The *Daily Show* Effect: Candidate Evaluations, Efficacy, and American Youth," *American Politics Research* 34 (2006), pp. 341–67.
2 Jon Stewart, Ben Karlin, and David Javerbaum, *America (The Book): A Citizen's Guide to Democracy Inaction* (New York: Warner Books, 2004). Subsequent citations will be made parenthetically in-text.
3 Israel Knox, "Towards a Philosophy of Humor," *Journal of Philosophy* 48 (1951), p. 541. Subsequent citation will be made parenthetically in-text.

4 G. D. Kiremidjian, "The Aesthetics of Parody," *Journal of Aesthetics and Art Criticism* 28 (2) (1969), p. 232.

5 Geoffrey Baym, "*The Daily Show*: Discursive Integration and the Reinvention of Political Journalism," *Political Communication* 22, p. 267. Subsequent citation will be made parenthetically in-text.

6 Tom Carson, "Last Comic Standing," *New York Times* (October 3, 2004), Section 7, p. 20.

7 See Joseph Schumpeter, *Capitalism, Socialism, and Democracy*, 3rd edn. (New York: Harper Perennial, 1962).

8 "Social capital" is defined as "features of social organization such as networks, norms, and social trust that facilitate coordination and cooperation for mutual benefit," in Robert D. Putnam, *Bowling Alone: The Collapse and Revival of American Community* (New York: Simon & Schuster, 2000), p. 67.

9 Benjamin Barber, *Strong Democracy* (Berkeley: University of California Press, 1984), p. 155.

10 See Amy Gutmann and Dennis Thompson, *Democracy and Disagreement* (Cambridge, MA: Belknap Press, 1996).

11 Although *America* claims (quoted above) that 99 percent of congressional incumbents are reelected, the actual percentage has varied from a low of 87 percent in 1962 to a high of 98 percent in 1998, with 96 percent typical of recent elections (the last is also noted in *America*, p. 58).

12 See Rachael Sotos, "The Fake News as the Fifth Estate," chapter 3 in this volume.

13 John Stuart Mill, "On Liberty," in *Utilitarianism, On Liberty, Considerations on Representative Government*, ed. H. B. Acton (Rutland, VT: Everyman's Library, 1972), pp. 90–1.

14 Joshua Cohen and Joel Rogers, "The Principle of Democratic Legitimacy," in *On Democracy* (New York: Viking Penguin, 1983).

17

THE *DAILY SHOW/COLBERT REPORT* GUIDE TO NEOLOGIZING

JASON HOLT

'Twas not by ideas, – by Heaven; his life was put in jeopardy by words.

Laurence Sterne, *Tristram Shandy*

Coming up with new words is rarely necessary, sometimes useful, and often fun. Few pleasures can rival that of minting new linguistic coin. Now you may be thinking, "Come on, '*neologizing*?' There's no call for that." Well, consider yourself lucky. I was tempted to go with "neologismry" or "neologistry," but a little googling revealed that I'd been beaten to both punches. Besides, "neologizing" is a well-established word, though not an often-used one. By contrast, when *The Simpsons*' schoolteacher Mrs. Krabapple asks her colleague whether "embiggens" is legitimate lingo, Miss Hoover replies, "It's a perfectly cromulent word."[1] I'm glad that better judgment prevailed when I titled this chapter, but I'm also glad – and you are too – that it often doesn't prevail when the *Daily Show* team writes their scripts, and this goes double for *The Colbert Report*, where the neologisms fly, sometimes crumbelievably. Although both shows are habitually wordplayful, both hosts punsters extraordinaire, there's no doubt who the master word coiner is – Stephen Colbert.

"Neologism" means *new word*, derived from the Greek *neo* (new) and *logos* (word). The term can also refer to new meanings that are given to old words (which we might call "paleologisms"), but it's neologisms in the first sense that concern us in this chapter. Philosophers of language often focus attention on features of natural languages (like English) that are already established, already in use. They also focus on idealized, "timeless" visions of what language is or might be. Even when the dynamic, evolving features of language are acknowledged, however, the prevailing view that a language is something "received" tends to marginalize the significance of such dynamic features of language as coining new words. This is a pity. On a practical level, neologisms run the gamut from the atrocious (think of the unknown coiner responsible for "irregardless") to the sublime (think of Milton coining "Pandemonium" in *Paradise Lost*), and it would be useful to know why this is. On a more theoretical plane, as every word was a neologism at some point, figuring out how words become words at all – how something becomes a meaningful word in a language – will enrich our understanding of language in general, of what it means to mean. It will also help us figure out what's going on in some of the best *Daily Show* and *Colbert Report* humor.

Humpty Dumpty and the French Academy

How do words get to have the meanings that they do, how do they become the words they are? A traditional answer to this question reflects a common view of how communication works. Say I'm dining with Jon Stewart, and I want him to pass the salt. I can express this desire in words: "Please pass the salt." I encode my thoughts in language, and he decodes the message to understand my thoughts. What seems to give meaning to the message is the mind behind it, because I succeed in being understood by Stewart when he comes to know my thoughts, my intentions. But the words I use to express my thoughts already have meanings which can be found in any dictionary. It's my knowledge of English that allows me to encode my thoughts in it, Stewart's that allows him to decode the message. I know the language to the extent that I can use it properly.

To help sort out what's going on, we'll consider the sometimes conflicting roles played by dictionaries, which on the one hand *regulate*, in certain ways, how words are used, and on the other merely *report* such use, informing people about the meanings of words that predate, and so don't depend on, their inclusion in the lexicon. We'll look at these roles to see where the tension comes from and how neologisms seem to get caught in the middle.

Dictionaries regulate word use in several different ways. They identify which words, usually slang (such as "ain't" which, contrary to schoolyard wisdom, *is* in the dictionary) and unfortunate word-manglings (such as "irregardless," a botched mix of "irrespective" and "regardless") are simply bad form. These words are meaningful, of course, but their use is almost never appropriate. Dictionaries also set standards, in the form of definitions, for correct and incorrect use of words. Correct use conforms to the definitions, incorrect use doesn't. An exchange between Alice and Humpty Dumpty in Lewis Carroll's *Through the Looking-Glass* is worth mentioning. At one point Humpty Dumpty's peculiar use of "glory" mystifies Alice. After a lot of truth-pulling, he reveals that by "glory" he means "a nice knock-down argument." "When *I* use a word," Humpty explains, "it means just what I choose it to mean – neither more nor less," to which Alice replies: "The questions is . . . whether you *can*. . . ."[2] The apparent absurdity of Humpty's position – that a word's meaning is determined by the speaker's intentions in using it – reflects how dictionaries govern proper and improper word use.[3] Humpty Dumpty *can't* make "glory" mean "a nice knock-down argument" just like that. (Anticipating Colbert here? Good.)

Another way dictionaries are used to regulate words is to set limits, not on good or bad form, not on proper or improper use, but on the scope of meaningful items in the language, on what counts as a word at all. Think of playing Scrabble. A challenged play in Scrabble is considered guilty until proven innocent. If the dictionary doesn't confirm that the offered word is acceptable, it's deemed unacceptable, *not* a legitimate word, and the play doesn't count. In an episode of *Seinfeld*, Kramer advises Jerry's mother to play "quone" in a game of Scrabble. When Jerry challenges the word (successfully), Kramer retorts, "Nah, we need a medical dictionary! If a patient gets difficult, you *quone* him."[4] Clearly not a legitimate word. Although Scrabble is a game, and an artificial context for deciding what does and doesn't count as a word, everyday word use is often put to the same kind of Scrabble-style test. If you claim that a certain alleged word is legitimate, many people will often cite its absence in a dictionary as reason to believe it isn't. An extreme example is the *Académie Française*, the French Academy, an elite group that –

believe it or not – presumes to *decide* what does or doesn't count as a word in French. If the French Academy says *Non* to something, even if commonly used by most French speakers, it's deemed to have no meaning in the language, to be, in other words, not a word at all. (Colbert, you can tell, is grinding his teeth by now.)

What's gone wrong here is that we've neglected the other important function of dictionaries, which is to report how words are commonly used, presenting their meaning after the fact. In an episode of the Brit-com *Blackadder*, Dr. Samuel Johnson boasts that his just-completed dictionary contains every single word in the English language, and in response Blackadder wishes Dr. Johnson his enthusiastic "contrafibularities." Johnson, clearly upset, scribbles the alleged word in his manuscript. To rub it in, Blackadder then claims to be "anaspeptic, frasmodic, even compunctuous to have caused [Johnson] such pericombobulations."[5] Clearly Blackadder's intent in using such word-like nonsense – which resembles real words plausibly enough – is to deflate the chuffed Johnson. But it also illustrates the important point that in reporting common usage, that is, the meaning of words as used, dictionaries must always play catch-up. That's why Johnson's boast is an empty one. Given the dynamic nature of language, word use always outstrips the best attempts to report it.

To capture the conflicting roles of dictionaries, and to throw neologisms into the mix, consider Colbert's discussion in *America (The Book)* of what it takes to set a legal precedent. First, he says, have something bad happen to you, but not any of those things the law already covers: "They've already been precedented. 'Is "precedented" even a word?' you may ask. Well, it is now, Noah-fucking-Webster. I just precedented it."[6] The humor here is multi-layered. First, there's no good reason to coin a new word, to prefer "They've already been precedented" to "They already have precedents." Second, there's the circularity of using the alleged word in arguing that it really *is* a word. Third, there's the sense that since "unprecedented" is a common word, "precedented" ought to be too, only it isn't – likewise "kempt" and "evitable" versus the more common "unkempt" and "inevitable." Fourth, "precedented" actually *is* a word, although, like "unprecedented," it's an adjective, not a verb as Colbert uses it. Fifth, the attempt to coin "precedented" is the linguistic equivalent of trying to set a legal precedent, one that, if successful, would include *itself* in the range of things it referred to. Colbert would be able to brag that he'd precedented "precedented." Sixth, this is a terse satire ("tersatire" maybe?) of not only unnecessary word coining, but also using dictionaries to regulate word use artificially, which in the extreme effectively closes the door on coining altogether. Colbert's rage is ridiculous, but it also gets at something.

So where does this leave us? Obviously the truth lies somewhere in between the extremes of Humpty Dumpty's anything-goes-ism and the French Academy's not-if-we-say-it-isn't-ism. Mere intent isn't enough to make meaning at all, much less a spanking new word, nor does meaning have to wait for some official seal of approval. Dictionaries tell us what terms *at last count* and sanctioned by common use are meaningful words in the language. So meaning must emerge at some point between the first use of a term and its eventual common use. But where? How, in the relevant sense, does a term become a word? This is a particularly difficult and pressing question nowadays. In our mass media culture, the timeline between initial and widespread use of a term can be next to nothing. Colbert introduced "truthiness" (and by implication "truthy") to the culture on October 17, 2005, and it was the subject of blogging almost immediately, not to mention more traditional watercooler chat the next day. "Metrosexual" similarly took the fast-track to common use. *When* did "truthiness" turn meaningful, and *where* did the meaning come from?

Wordplaying by the Rules

Many theories of language tie meaning to the language community and the conventions or rules which govern common use. Think of a language *as it is* at a given point in time. Although there's a crucial sense in which, for obvious reasons, one can't coin a term in a language unless the language is there to begin with – let the origins of language for now remain a mystery! – such perspectives tend to marginalize, if not outright negate, the part that individuals can play in creating new words. If the meaning source of language is the language community, then individuals are all but powerless to neologize solo. They can offer new terms as possible candidates for meaning, and they can certainly suggest what that meaning might be, but the language community, the source of meaning, ultimately decides. This is a matter of whether a proposed term achieves word status, whether the community adopts it for use, and how it uses it if so. One proposes, the group disposes. Sound familiar? Is this the French Academy democratized, the *wordinistas*, as Colbert would call them, all over again?

There are rules that allow individuals to use non-words meaningfully, *as if* they were words, in special situations. You can *stipulate* the meaning of an arbitrary symbol ("*x*," "*φ*," and so on) or other non-words as a kind of shorthand, for convenience's sake (for instance, "Let 'glurf' = philosopher who writes on pop culture" – That makes me a glurf). You can also do the same thing with already meaningful words. Humpty Dumpty wouldn't have confused Alice if he had stipulated from the get-go that, for the purposes of their discussion, "glory" meant "a nice knock-down argument." But I haven't added "glurf" to the language, and Humpty Dumpty, had he made himself understood from the get-go, wouldn't have given "glory" a new additional meaning in the language.

The very same principles would seem to apply to neologisms. To make himself understood in using "wikiality" and "truthiness," Colbert seemingly needs to define them or, failing that, informally explain what they mean.[7] In Oscar Wilde's *The Importance of Being Earnest*, Jack is thoroughly confused by Algernon's use of "Bunburyist" (coined by Algernon/Wilde himself) until, without actually defining the term, Algernon gives an informal explanation of its meaning:

> You have invented a very useful younger brother called Ernest, in order that you may be able to come up to town as often as you like. I have invented an invaluable permanent invalid called Bunbury, in order that I may be able to go down into the country whenever I choose. Bunbury is perfectly invaluable. If it wasn't for Bunbury's extraordinary bad health, for instance, I wouldn't be able to dine with you at Willis's to-night, for I have been really engaged to Aunt Augusta for more than a week.[8]

Though not a precise, explicit definition, this informal explanation is sufficient to make the meaning of "Bunburyist" clear – one who devises a made-up person as an excuse to get out of undesirable social commitments and free oneself up for more desirable ones. Such explanations, like stipulative definitions, are stipulative, and so seem insufficient, by themselves, to make the terms meaningful English words (although they are, in the mold of Blackadder, pretty Englishy). The same goes for Kramer's "quone," which he apparently confuses with, or takes to be a synonym for, "sedate."

Does this mean that the *wordinistas* (democratized or otherwise) have won? Is a term only meaningful in a language when the public, or some special group, adopts it as its own? Not by a long shot. Terms like "wikiality" and "truthiness" may need definition or explanation, as proxies for common use, to be understood. But here's the rub. This *isn't* typical of *Daily Show* or *Colbert Report* neologisms, which, without any explicit explanation of meaning, tend to be readily understood, and so to be meaningful, *at first use*. Presumably since "fashionista" became widely used (deriving with peculiar irony from the Italian *fascista*) we know that the suffix "-ista" is used in English to signify someone who's overbearing, authoritarian, about whatever subject precedes the suffix, especially the do's and don'ts, mostly other people's don'ts. The root may be shortened, or have a linking "-in-" between root and suffix, to bring the resulting word in line with "fashionista." We know, without explanation, that a factinista (as Colbert uses the term, and if there could be such a thing) is overly concerned with facts and takes others to task for ignoring them, or being underly concerned with them. Philosophistas, like me, might be seen as too enamored of arguments, concepts, and distinctions.

Along the same lines, take the regularly updated neoadjective that comes at the end of the list of words used to describe Colbert at the beginning of the *Report*: "grippy," "megamerican," "Lincolnish," and – the jewel among them – "superstantial." The irony here, of course, is that the prefix "super-" often indicates something positive, superior, whereas "sub-" indicates something negative, inferior. But to have substance is to have quality, depth, and these are good things. To have *superstance*, then, despite the prefix's positive connotations, is negative, to be shallow, lacking in quality (that is, superficial). "Superstantial" is yet another delightfully superfluous neologism (as "subficial" would be). The point, once more, is that we understand these new words at first laughing blush. They're meaningful at first use, instantly part of the language.

Instantly meaningful first uses aren't always based on rough-and-ready rules like "'x' + '-ista' = x-authoritarian." *The Daily Show* and *America (The Book)* provide many examples where analogies with preexisting words and/or linguistic context will do. The portmanteau "infotainment" obviously derives from "information" and "entertainment." Add "propaganda," and *America* gives us "propatainment" and the exquisite oxymoron "infoganda" (p. 139). For some time, Stewart regularly used "Jewy" without explaining it. He didn't have to. The context made it quite clear that "Jewish" wouldn't quite do, that "Jewy" meant, had to mean, *stereotypically* Jewish. Stewart's sublime "catastrophuck," used to describe the Iraq war, combines the tragedy of a catastrophe with the someone's-to-blame of a fuck-up. Likewise, you've probably got a good idea what "philpopsopher" means even before I remind you to revisit "glurf," mentioned earlier. Insisting that there *must* be strict rules operating here, and that since they're already part of the language, so too are the neologisms they allegedly generate, *even before being coined*, is apt to elicit, and rightly so, a Stewartly "Uh?"

In these cases meaning *doesn't* come from the language community, or from language as it is. The language as it is allows new words to come into being, but the knowledgeable, intrepid wordsmith, working alone, can often exploit the untapped meaning potential of a not-yet-made word without the assistance or approval of the language community. One can make meaning solo. Of course this doesn't mean that anything goes. Language as it is puts quite severe restrictions on exploitable meaning potential. We can't just put Humpty Dumpty together again. One can fail to create a meaningful word on one's own, but one can also succeed, as *The Daily Show* and *The Colbert Report* continually remind us.

There are other ways to coin new words besides those we've discussed. Think of onomatopoeia, words that sound like what they signify, or slang, which often catches on by cultural accident, subcultural lingo infiltrating the mainstream or being appropriated by it. "Ka-ching" and "bling" come to mind here, respectively. Neologistic slang is a bit of a mixed bag, tending to help define a subculture as distinct from the mainstream and other subcultures, but by excluding others in the process, which frustrates understanding rather than facilitating it. Of course, that's often the point, to communicate covertly – the use of slang as code. The discovery or invention of new things *demands* neologizing, as with "quark" or "internet." Philosophiles do this sort of thing all the time, often without good reason – Oops! Sometimes it's just more efficient, more artful, to neologize, and if fresh words really catch on in a culture, the language is that much richer for it. Hundreds if not thousands of words are credited to Shakespeare's coinage ("aggravate," "critical," "fragrant," "hurry," "majestic," and "obscene," for six). Yet many new words stem less from linguistic need or artfulness and more from ignorance of what's in the toolbox of language as is. In the final analysis, it's this, more than anything else perhaps, that *Daily Show* and *Colbert Report* neologisms do, lampooning the often senseless proliferation of new-fangled lingo – ridicule by example.

Your Moment of Zen

It's hard to overestimate the importance of wordplay to the arch wit and humor of both *The Daily Show* and *The Colbert Report*, and neologisms, in the *Report* especially, are arguably the keystone. These new words run from the merely cute to the hilarious, and they remind us of two important things: one, an individual's power to create words, to create meaning, is much greater than is often supposed, and two, because of this, it's essential to use that power wisely, sparingly, especially in today's mass media culture, where neologizing seems to have run amok, and beautifully minted linguistic coin gets lost in a sea of language with bureaucratese at one end and überslang at the other.[9]

Notes

1 "Lisa the Iconoclast," *The Simpsons*, Fox (February 18, 1996).
2 Lewis Carroll, *Through the Looking-Glass* (New York: Dover, 1994 [1872]), p. 57.
3 Although the Humpty Dumpty theory of meaning is often thought absurd, it does have its advocates. See, among others, Keith Donnellan, "Putting Humpty Dumpty Together Again," *Philosophical Review* 77 (1968), pp. 203–15.

4 "The Stakeout," *Seinfeld*, NBC (May 31, 1990). Compare with "appucious" in Woody Allen's *Husbands and Wives*, Orion (1992), where the would-be coiner doesn't even try to explain the alleged word's meaning, yet insists that the term is a descriptively apt one nonetheless.

5 "Ink and Incapability," *Blackadder III*, BBC (September 24, 1987). Transcripts of this episode give various different spellings for these non-words, some of which come close to being, not nonsense, but instantly coined words. Later Blackadder expresses the wish to facilitate Dr. Johnson's "velocitous extramuralization," which seems to convey, since "velocity" and "extramural" are perfectly good words, what "speedy departure from the premises" would – similar to, if more difficult than, most of the *Daily Show* and *Colbert Report* neologisms we'll discuss.

6 Stephen Colbert, "So You Want to Be a Precedent," in Jon Stewart, Ben Karlin, and David Javerbaum, *America (The Book): A Citizen's Guide to Democracy Inaction* (New York: Warner Books, 2004), p. 92. Subsequent references will be made parenthetically in-text.

7 "Wikiality" means "popular opinion as presumed to constitute reality," which reflects the appeal to popularity fallacy (inferring the truth of a belief from its mere popularity), and "truthiness" means "what one feels or wants to be true irrespective of the evidence." The implied adjective "truthy" also suggests what *resembles* truth, or is truth-*like*, and connotes, in contrast to truth and falsehood, gradations, vagueness (think shades of gray instead of black or white). For more on truthiness, see Amber Griffioen, "Truthiness, Self-Deception, and Intuitive Knowledge," up next.

8 Oscar Wilde, *The Importance of Being Earnest* (New York: Avon, 1965 [1899]), p. 35.

9 For helpful feedback and enjoyable discussion I thank Ami Harbin, Larry Holt, and Bill Irwin.

18

TRUTHINESS, SELF-DECEPTION, AND INTUITIVE KNOWLEDGE

AMBER L. GRIFFIOEN

I love the truth – it's facts I'm not a fan of.
Stephen Colbert of *The Colbert Report*

On the very first episode of *The Colbert Report* (October 17, 2005), Stephen Colbert boldly introduced the word "truthiness" into the American vocabulary:

> I will speak to you in plain, simple English. And that brings us to tonight's word [*clang!*]: "truthiness." Now I'm sure some of the "word police," the "wordinistas" over at Webster's, are gonna say, "Hey, that's not a word!" Well, anyone who knows me knows I'm no fan of dictionaries or reference books. They're elitist – constantly telling us what is or isn't true. . . .
>
> I don't trust books. They're all fact, no heart. And that's exactly what's pulling our country apart today. 'Cause face it, folks: we are a divided nation. Not between Democrats and Republicans, or conservatives and liberals, or tops and bottoms. No, we are divided between those who think with their head, and those who *know* with their *heart*.

Colbert went on to give the audience a few examples:

> If you *think* about Harriet Miers, of course her nomination is absurd. But the President didn't say he *thought* about her selection. He said this:
> [*Clip of President Bush*]: "I know her heart."

Notice how he said nothing about her brain? He didn't have to. He *feels* the truth about Harriet Miers.

And what about Iraq? If you *think* about it, maybe there are a few missing pieces to the rationale for war, but doesn't taking Saddam out *feel* like the right thing [*laughter*] . . . right here [*pointing to stomach*] – right here in the gut?

There seem to be two related notions of truthiness implied in this clip: (1) the sense in which one chooses to believe something based on what one *wants* to believe, as opposed to the supposed facts, and (2) the sense in which one appeals to an intuition (or a gut feeling) to provide justification for a belief.

The American Dialect Society, which named "truthiness" its 2005 Word of the Year, officially defines it as "the quality of preferring concepts or facts one wishes to be true, rather than concepts or facts known to be true."[1] The philosopher might recognize this definition – it looks an awful lot like many of the phenomena we classify under the category of irrationality. Indeed, truthiness seems to be able to stand in for most obvious kinds of irrationality. In such cases, a certain desire leads one to assert that something is or is not true, or that a certain course of action is to be taken, despite the fact that one recognizes (on some level) that the facts might not support, don't support, or even completely undermine this assertion or course of action.

However, the second sense in which Colbert uses the word "truthiness" is another matter altogether. When Merriam-Webster voted "truthiness" its 2006 Word of the Year, it defined the term as "truth that comes from the gut, not books."[2] In this sense, truthiness amounts to *intuiting* the truth via some so-called "gut" feeling: "Because that's where the truth comes from, ladies and gentlemen . . . the gut" (October 17, 2005). Indeed, people *do* frequently appeal to a feeling or an intuition to justify a certain claim, often in ways we take to be perfectly legitimate. "Something doesn't feel right," we say, or, "This action just seems like the wrong thing to do." Indeed, our frequent references to phenomena like "gut feelings," "women's intuition," "rubbing someone the wrong way," and so on seem to indicate that we sometimes appeal to this kind of truthiness for making certain truth claims or performing certain actions.

Truthiness and Problems of Irrationality

There are three basic cases that philosophers traditionally classify under the term "irrationality." In the first two cases, wishful thinking and self-deception, a person *wants* something to be true and therefore ignores certain relevant facts about the situation, making it appear to herself that it is, in fact, true. The third case, weakness of will, involves a person undertaking a certain action, despite taking herself to have an all-things-considered *better* reason not to do so.[3]

While I think that truthiness might be able to fit the mold of each of these three kinds of irrationality, it applies most directly to cases of wishful thinking and self-deception – and it's these two types of irrationality that I wish to discuss extensively in the next section. As we will see, there are some troubling philosophical problems that arise regarding irrational behavior (especially self-deception). But we can use the concept of truthiness to resolve these "paradoxes of irrationality" without denying the fundamental irrationality of truthiness itself.

Wishful Thinking and Self-Deception: What Are They?

Wishful thinking and self-deception are two very closely related kinds of irrational belief-forming processes. However, there is a slight difference between the two. Wishful thinking occurs when someone who has a strong desire to hold a certain belief (call it "X") comes to believe X primarily *because* of that strong desire, but not for any "good" reason that takes the facts of the situation into account. Thus, wishful thinking does not require that the person *knows* the relevant facts of the situation, but merely that she comes to believe X primarily because she *really wants to*. Self-deception, on the other hand, occurs when someone comes to hold a belief *in the face of evidence to the contrary*. This latter case, then, entails that the person *knows* (or believes she knows) the relevant facts (which presumably fly in the face of X), but refuses to acknowledge them because she so strongly desires to believe X.[4]

Therefore, wishful thinking might often lead to self-deception. A woman might want to believe so strongly that her husband is faithful to her that she forms this belief without looking at whether the facts support it. However, suppose the relevant facts available to her *do* indicate that he is cheating. Maybe he continually comes home late at night with lipstick on his collar, smelling of cheap perfume, and making lame excuses. Perhaps a good friend even tells the hopeful wife that her husband has been seen cavorting with a younger woman. If she *then* continues to believe in his fidelity, *despite* knowing these facts, she is likely no longer a victim of wishful thinking, but is actively engaged in self-deception.

It is not difficult to see how appeals to truthiness can underlie both of these types of irrationality. Remember Colbert's assertion that the President doesn't need to make reference to Harriet Miers' brain or qualifications because he just *"feels* the truth" about her? The wife engaged in wishful thinking may say similar things without even bothering to see if the facts line up with her belief: "I don't need to look at the facts," she might say. "I love my husband, and I just *know* he would never cheat on me," or, "I can *feel in my heart* that he is faithful." And if she stubbornly continues to affirm this belief (both to herself and to others) in the face of strong evidence to the contrary – relying only on her unshakable and unquestioned "gut feeling" that he is faithful – this "truthy" behavior would then count not as mere wishful thinking, but as self-deception. In both cases, however, the subject has a strong desire for a certain claim to be true – and it is this desire that leads to the affirmation of something not borne out by the facts.

The Paradoxes of Irrationality

Cases like these are all too common in our everyday lives. However, what most of us fail to realize is how difficult it is to provide a philosophical account of *how* we are able to engage in such irrational behavior. On the one hand, wishful thinking seems to involve mere "epistemic irresponsibility." *Rational* agents are those who attempt to take into account the relevant facts and make a decision on the basis of those facts. If we told a person engaged in wishful thinking that there were relevant facts pointing to his belief's being false, the rational agent would come to realize that his belief is probably false, given the existence of these facts. If, on the other hand, he persists in holding this false belief – if he continues to believe something he *knows* in some sense to be false – then he is self-deceived, and this is a little trickier to explain.

Let us look first at the name of this phenomenon. Surely we call it "self-*deception*" for a reason. The name implies that it has something in common with the normal, everyday concept of deception, namely the deception of other people. So how does such interpersonal deception work? It's fairly simple. In cases of interpersonal deception, a person (let's call her "A") holds a certain belief (let's call it "X") to be false. (In other words, A believes "not-X" to be true.) Person A then tries to make some person B come to believe X. If B, through A's efforts, *does* come to believe X, then A has successfully deceived B about X. Let's look at an example: Stephen Colbert (the deceiv*er* in this scenario) can tell Jon Stewart (the potential deceiv*ed*) that he, Stephen, is going to be on *The O'Reilly Factor*, again, knowing (say) that this is false. If Jon comes to believe Stephen's false testimony, then he has been successfully deceived.

However, in the case of self-deception, one and the same individual is supposed to play the role of both deceiv*er* and deceiv*ed*. The individual engaged in self-deception tries, through her *own* efforts, to become deceived about some fact she does not want to admit. But it is unclear how she can ever succeed because she has to be aware (in some sense) of her own deceptive intention. (Philosopher Alfred Mele calls this the "dynamic paradox" of self-deception.)[5] Furthermore, it seems that even if an agent *could* succeed in deceiving herself, then she must somehow hold both the belief that "not-X" (in her role as the deceiver) and the belief that "X" (in her role as the deceived) *at the same time*. (Mele calls this the "static paradox.") Hence, we seem to embroil ourselves in two paradoxes when we attempt to explain how self-deception works – and self-deceptive truthiness will be no different.

So how is self-deception even possible? How can Colbert's notion of self-deceptive truthiness even get off the ground? The above paradoxes are quite troubling, and for this reason some philosophers try to explain self-deception away entirely, and say that it's not at all like interpersonal deception. They say self-deception is really just a person's being either mistaken about the facts or controlled by some external force. But we regularly hold people accountable for what appears to be self-deception, and if we wish to continue to do so justifiably, we cannot allow these accounts to explain away the phenomenon altogether. We must face the paradoxes head-on, and attempt to construct a view of self-deception that will allow us to understand not only how self-deceptive truthiness is possible, but also keep the irrationality of truthiness intact.

The Freudian Solution

One way that philosophers have attempted to resolve these paradoxes is simply to divide up the mind into independent structures that can deceive each other. Perhaps, like famed psychologist Sigmund Freud (1856–1939), we can simply postulate that there is some sort of "subconscious" mind that acts to deceive my "conscious" mind.[6] (Imagine Stephen Colbert and Jon Stewart in our above example being just one person! Frightening, isn't it? Otherwise just think of Stephen Colbert versus Stephen Colbert in *The Colbert Report*'s regular "Formidable Opponent" segment.) Of course, on the Freudian picture, we have two independent structures (the id and the super-ego), who "team up," so to speak, to deceive a third (the ego). Let's look at an example of how this would work: Rob Corddry wants to have, or wants to believe that he has, a full head of hair. Perhaps he also believes, in some sense, that he *should* have a full head of hair (the role played by the super-ego). Now, "deep down" in his unconscious mind, he knows he is bald. However, Rob's id and super-ego act to deceive Rob's ego into thinking he actually has a full head of thick, luscious hair! And since he is unconscious of his belief that he is bald and also of his strong desire to believe he has hair, he is easily duped by his subconscious into believing he has hair. Thus, although "Rob" believes both X and not-X at the same time, we don't have to worry about the static paradox, since one belief is on the level of the conscious mind, the other on that of the unconscious. Likewise, since the ego, super-ego, and id act independently, we don't have to worry about the dynamic paradox either. So far, so good.

But there are some significant problems with this view. The first is that we suddenly have a problem locating the *agent* (Rob Corddry himself). It looks as if all three structures of the mind have agent-like qualities. Each part can weigh possibilities, have beliefs and desires, interact with and independently act *on* the other parts of the mind, and so on. If this is the case, and the interaction between the parts of the mind works like interpersonal interaction, it appears that we have three agents instead of one. Who is the adjudicator on this view? Where is *Rob the person*? If we want to be able to hold *Rob* responsible for his self-deception, who can we blame? Is it Rob's ego's fault that it got hoodwinked? (Think about the example of interpersonal deception: We wouldn't normally hold Jon responsible for believing Stephen's lie, would we?) But if we instead blame Rob's unconscious, are we really blaming *Rob*? What would it mean to blame just his unconscious? Could we even find it?

This leads to a related concern. If the *cause* of Rob's conscious belief that he has hair were really subconscious, he could only discover that subconscious cause by somehow "transforming" or "transporting" it *into* his consciousness, in which case he (and we) could never be entirely certain that the now-conscious mental phenomenon was ever unconscious in the first place. Indeed, when self-deceived persons "snap out" of their deception, they tend to say things like, "Ah yes, I knew that 'not-X' was true all along. I just couldn't admit it to myself." But unconscious states are supposed to be those of which the person is entirely unaware! Suddenly the unconscious mind looks like a very spooky and strange kind of thing. Where is it? As soon as you pay attention to its contents, they are no longer unconscious. So perhaps the Freudian account isn't really the way we want to explain the paradoxes of self-deception and truthiness.

An Alternative Account

There is another way we can account for self-deception that might be less problematic. Instead of viewing self-deception as a *state*, achieved when one somehow causes oneself to hold not only belief not-X but also belief X, we can approach it as a *process*, a sort of "project," in which an agent actively engages herself, motivated by her desire. Generally, when we hold a belief, if the evidence to the contrary outweighs the evidence in support of that belief, the rational person will revise her belief accordingly. However, in cases of self-deception, this does not occur because the agent's desire to retain her (false) belief is so strong. Instead, the agent *consciously* undertakes a project of self-deception, likely employing several techniques to maintain her false belief in the face of the evidence. Let's return to our example of Rob Corddry's attempt to deceive himself that he has hair. On my account of self-deception, Rob is *aware* that the facts support his being bald and is *aware* of his desire to believe he is not. But he averts his attention away from these two facts, and focuses on the belief he wishes to cultivate, namely that he has hair. Indeed, we redirect our attention all the time, without thereby becoming completely *unaware* of the former object of our attention. Surely Jon Stewart can turn to Camera 3 and yet still be aware of Camera 1 (in his peripheral vision, say). He is not *paying attention* to Camera 1, yet he is still *aware* of it.

But *how* can Rob Corddry redirect his attention away from the belief he suspects to be false? There are several techniques he can employ. When Jason Jones points out that Rob's belief is false, Rob might rationalize in order to keep his belief intact: "Jason's just jealous of my luscious brown locks." He can push all evidence against the belief that he has hair to the "margins" of his awareness by ignoring criticism, or even stubbornly repeating to himself "I have lots of hair" over and over again until he fails to be swayed by reasons to believe the contrary. At no time does Rob become unaware that his two beliefs clash, and his defensive behavior when challenged demonstrates this. However, he holds these contradictory beliefs to different *degrees*, depending on how well he focuses his attention on the belief he wants to have and away from the facts. This entire process is what I term "self-deception." On the other hand, if Rob finally convinces himself *completely* that he has hair (and the belief to the contrary has disappeared), then he is no longer self-deceived, but rather *delusional*. He has perfected his technique(s) of avoidance, such that the belief that he is bald has faded away completely.

On this account of self-deception, then, the entire process is dynamic, with the agent fluctuating back and forth between stubbornly affirming the desired belief and having to deal with evidence to the contrary. The dynamic paradox becomes a moot point, since we don't have to say that Rob succeeds in truly convincing himself. And the static paradox dissolves because the phenomenon is no longer understood as a state, but rather as a process of waffling between a belief supported by the facts and a belief supported solely by desire.[7]

Truthiness and Self-Deception

I think it is fairly obvious that the first definition we gave above of "truthiness" (in which one chooses to believe something based on what one *wants* to believe, as opposed to the supposed facts) fits this model of self-deception to a tee. We sometimes prefer concepts we wish to be true, instead of what the facts tell us, even when we're aware that these facts don't support our belief. But Colbert's introduction to truthiness does even more than this. In a way, it ups the ante on self-deception: Colbert attempts to use truth or truthiness to establish the truth of truthiness!

Let's see how this works. Someone may wish a certain fact were true (say, that the Panama Canal was built in 1941), but all the books tell us that this is false (since the Panama Canal was, in fact, built in 1914). Colbert maintains that it is his "right" to believe the former proposition. However, to do so would be to embark on a process of self-deception, resulting in the claim that believing what one wants trumps believing what one is rationally required to believe. Yet Colbert obviously still acknowledges the importance of reasoning (he is, after all, making an argument and appealing to reasons), so we can see that he hasn't abandoned his commitment to rationality. Yet he is struggling to use reason to make a case for irrationality. This is almost "meta-self-deception," in the sense that what Colbert *wants* to believe is that we can "know" the truth with our hearts or "feel" it with our guts, and that the standards of what normally counts as evidence for rational belief (namely, the *facts*) are not the correct standards of rationality. And how does he know? He checked his gut! What's especially funny about this move isn't just that it's circular (trying to use truthiness to validate itself). It's also that the proposition "The gut is a more accurate standard for truth than facts" is itself an empirical question, one which can be investigated by looking at the facts! So Colbert is implicitly appealing to the facts in order to establish that facts are less reliable than our guts. It's the irrationality of this (first circular, then self-defeating) argument that makes us laugh. But it also raises some very interesting and important questions about the connection between rationality and irrationality.

Feeling the Truth: Can Our Guts Get Us Justified Belief?

Leaving Colbert's circular/self-defeating move aside, the empirical question still remains: Can we legitimately appeal to our guts for justification? Indeed, we often refer to "bad feelings" when asked why we're afraid of a certain place; and sometimes when asked why we dislike someone, we respond that he or she just "rubs me the wrong way." "Women's intuition" is supposed to account for how some women seem to instinctively know, say, that a loved one is in trouble. Does this mean that reference to our gut feelings can provide us with good justification for truth claims?

Without going into this question in too much detail, I just wish to discuss briefly this second sense of "truthiness." While it seems that we often legitimately appeal to gut feelings to justify certain claims or beliefs, I would argue that what we are implicitly doing is referring to other, more objectively salient facts about the situation, about which we merely fail to be explicit.[8] Take the example of a young woman who is approached at a bar by "Killer" (an intimidating member of Colbert's staff), who has just arrived back from his unsuccessful mission to rescue Stephen, Jr. (the eaglet named after Colbert) from the San Francisco Zoo.[9] After about 20 minutes, she sneaks off with her girlfriends to another bar. "Why didn't you stay and talk to that nice gentleman?" they ask. "I got a bad feeling about him," she replies. "He just rubbed me the wrong way."

Normally, we would accept this justification and move on. However, if we *really* wanted to know why she left, we would press her for more information. "What rubbed you the wrong way about him?" we might ask. In response, she would likely say something about his intimidating appearance, his angry behavior, or his poor choice of pick-up lines. And now we have an appeal to facts about the situation itself, not just about the young woman's gut feeling! Indeed, "truthy" claims, like "taking Saddam out feels like the right thing to do," can serve as implicit references not just to the desire to depose Saddam Hussein, but also to facts about his character or past actions that make us feel okay about removing him from power. These facts may give rise to certain feelings in us, to which we appeal for justification, but we must be careful not to mistake the feeling for what makes our belief justified (that is, the facts). We must definitely avoid saying that such feelings, by themselves, *make* a belief true or false.

Taken in this second sense, truthiness remains suspect, unless it's clear that we have good reasons for our gut feelings (in other words, that we have legitimate reasons which appeal to the facts of the situation). Indigestion ought not serve as rational justification for why I didn't vote for a certain politician, but perhaps a bad feeling grounded in certain "shady" behavioral cues given off by the politician in question, can.[10] However, in the latter circumstance it is not the feeling that justifies my action; rather, it is the fact that such behavioral cues have, in the past, been exhibited by persons of less than reputable moral character. And this is an important distinction to make, since, in such cases as these, feelings don't seem to be able to make a certain claim true or false, whereas facts about the world *do* appear to accomplish this task.

Conclusion: A Tip of the Hat

In conclusion, I would like to commend Stephen Colbert for coining a word that captures both the essence of irrationality and the difficulty we have in trying to overcome it by rational means. Although it may be the case that some instances of irrationality may not necessarily be morally suspect, Colbert shows us the amusing – and potentially dangerous – consequences of forming opinions and making decisions by going "straight from the gut." In fact, I propose that from now on we call claims that appeal solely to the gut instances of "the fallacy of *argumentum Colberti ad ventrem*."[11] The inclusion of this fallacy among other, more well-known informal fallacies (like the *argumentum ad hominem* and the straw man fallacy) would be a welcome addition to logic textbooks everywhere, which often ignore the kind of fallacious reasoning involved in appealing to one's gut when attempting to make cogent arguments. To further ignore a phenomenon that both reflects what human beings often do and exposes certain irrational tendencies in human reasoning would be to do a disservice to philosophy.

And that's the truthiness.

Notes

1 "Truthiness Voted 2005 Word of the Year," *American Dialect Society* (January 6, 2006); www.americandialect.org/Words_of_the_Year_2005.pdf.

2 " 'Truthiness' is the word of the year" (December 9, 2006); www.cnn.com/2006/SHOWBIZ/TV/12/09/word.year.ap/index.html.

3 There are surely other important kinds of irrational reasoning and behavior, but these three kinds of cases tend to be the ones most focused on by philosophers. I think the reason for this is that these phenomena occur very frequently in human beings, and yet it is very difficult to explain philosophically (or psychologically) how they are even possible in the first place!

4 Philosopher Béla Szabados makes this distinction in his article "Wishful Thinking and Self-Deception," *Analysis* 33 (6) (1973), pp. 201–5.

5 See, for example, Alfred Mele, *Self-Deception Unmasked* (Princeton: Princeton University Press, 2001).

6 Philosopher Donald Davidson (1917–2003) was also a proponent of the divided-mind view, although he resisted using Freudian terms to talk about partitions in the mind. See Donald Davidson, "Paradoxes of Irrationality," in *Philosophical Essays on Freud*, ed. R. Wohlheim and J. Hopkins (Cambridge: Cambridge University Press, 1982), pp. 289–305.

7 Of course, if the contrary belief is completely eradicated, and the person thereby becomes delusional (not self-deceived), we could say the person was in a *state* of delusion.

8 It's also possible that we might be *incapable* of being explicit about these facts. However, in my experience, this is not usually the case. Most

people, when pushed on why they have a certain gut feeling, can (and will) explicitly elaborate on particular, relevant features of the situation that give rise to that feeling.

9 Stephen, Jr. has since "defected" to Canada.

10 In fact, it has recently been suggested that certain snap-fire decisions (called "rapid cognition") are often more accurate that deliberative, explicitly reasoned-out decisions. This doesn't undermine the claim that when one makes such snap-fire decisions, one is completely unaware of the relevant facts at hand. However, it does imply that one isn't taking the time to explicitly reflect on those facts, which seems to be exactly what's at work when we legitimately appeal to our guts for justification. For more on this, see Malcolm Gladwell, *Blink: The Power of Thinking Without Thinking* (New York: Little, Brown, 2005).

11 Or, "the Colbertian appeal to the stomach."

19

STEPHEN COLBERT, IRONY, AND SPEAKING TRUTHINESS TO POWER

KEVIN S. DECKER

Though fancy journalism schools will tell you otherwise, all you need to be successful in the world of television news is a rudimentary understanding of fashion and six different facial expressions. Oh, and a crippling need to be liked.

Stephen Colbert, *America (The Book)*

According to Roger Rosenblatt of *Time* magazine, perhaps the only good thing that might have come from the domestic cultural reaction to the 9/11 attacks on the United States in which 3,000 lost their lives would be the "end of irony."[1] No longer would culture be dominated by the cynical attitudes of Generation X'ers and the narrative absurdities and moral nihilism of wildly popular television shows such as *The Simpsons* and *Seinfeld*. But many, including myself, found the rumors of irony's demise greatly exaggerated. We found irony abundant in the weeks and months after 9/11: in the revelation that national security agencies had information about the possibility of a major attack but did nothing about it; in the facts that none of the 9/11 bombers were from invaded Iraq (all were legal visitors to the US); and that Osama bin-Laden had escaped from invaded Afghanistan. Finally, more and more Americans have found a tragic irony in the internal attack on civil liberties, rationalized by the external attack on our lives and freedoms.

No, post-9/11 America is still full of irony, and given that, we're lucky to have *The Daily Show* and *The Colbert Report*. On a "somewhat" daily basis, viewers tune in for Comedy Central's sarcastic strand of irony, the kind that *Webster's* defines as "the use of words to express something other than and especially the opposite of the literal meaning."[2] But *Webster's* identifies another, more philosophically significant sense of irony, that of an "incongruity between the actual result of a sequence of events and the normal or expected result." This sense of irony is important for our purposes because it links irony with "contingency," the fact that the way things are isn't necessarily the way they had to be, and thus that things *could have been different*.

In this chapter we'll examine *this* sense of irony along with the parallels between the persona of "Stephen Colbert of *The Colbert Report*" and the "ironist" called for by contemporary philosopher Richard Rorty. For both Colbert and Rorty, irony can be funny and refreshing, and yet at the same time disturbing. Who is Rorty's "ironist," and to what extent does Colbert fit this profile? More importantly, does embracing irony have serious implications for how we deal with our political responsibilities in the new and more precarious post-9/11 world?

Truth Compass vs. *Daily Show* Stooge

Ironic humor invites us to guffaw if we are willing and able to suspend belief about what is being *explicitly* said or done and instead *interpret* the situation at hand to see what's *implicitly* going on.[3] This fits in nicely with the sense of irony that emphasizes the contingencies of life, the sense in which we remark on "incongruity between the actual result of a sequence of events and the normal or expected result." Ironic humor defeats our expectations by showing us that what we took for reality was more elusive than we thought. In addition, irony, like its cousin satire, often plays cultural tropes off against each other. Irony's appreciative audience, therefore, needs to be not only self-reflective but also culturally literate. This fact has led to criticisms of preponderant irony in the media as leading to a wry inwardness, a cultural contemplation of our own navels that shows how narcissistic and self-obsessed the citizens of the Western world have really become.[4]

Stephen Colbert consistently defeats our expectations in ironic and memorable ways. One of the most memorable was Colbert putting

Jon Stewart "on notice" during the August 10, 2006 installment of *The Daily Show*. Grimly, Colbert accused Stewart of taking cheap shots at Fox News' Geraldo Rivera, who, to be fair, will probably be best remembered for discovering a few old bottles in Al Capone's vault in 1986.[5] Why did Colbert "turn" on Stewart? It's no secret that Colbert, just like his old *Daily Show* cohorts Rob Corddry and Ed Helms, adopts an on-air persona to conspicuously mock the amiable, depth-free lack of authenticity of most of today's "real" news anchors. Yet Colbert's arrogant and condescending persona has developed since his transition from the *Daily Show* to the *Report*. This was put into stark relief as Colbert put Stewart "on notice." After showing a clip or two of Stewart taking cheap shots at Rivera, Colbert rolls tape of *himself* tracing in the sand various strategic movements through Iraq, which famously ends up with Geraldo's "head up his own ass."[6] Surely there's something wrong here? Colbert has made a mistake, and needs to apologize for his apparent hypocrisy in accusing Stewart. But, as our omni-reliable "truth compass" explains, he hasn't shown us Stephen Colbert of *The Colbert Report*, but "Stephen Colbert, *Daily Show* stooge, a tool forced by his corporate overlords to turn on the very heroes of the news business!"

What exactly is Colbert up to in all this? It's no secret that the format, stage design, and even the graphics of the *Report* are not-so-gentle mockeries of the Fox shows of conservative ideologues Sean Hannity and Bill O'Reilly. So, on a first pass, Colbert is gleefully glossing over the noticeable differences between his old left-leaning persona on the *Daily Show* and his "genuine" conservative sensibilities, which have been "liberated" by having his own show. But Hannity, O'Reilly, and Colbert are *so* over-the-top that the discerning viewer simply *must* ask the question, "Are these guys for real?"[7] While the success of these first two pundits depends entirely upon our belief that behind their appearance of bluster, there beats the red heart of a true-blue all-American, Colbert, by spotlighting his own inconsistency on *The Daily Show* (and in other venues), encourages us to suspend belief in what he *really* stands for as long as possible. Colbert engages in what Rorty calls "redescription" to blur the distinction between how he appears and what he really is, what he actually stands for.

While Colbert ridicules conservative pundits like Hannity and O'Reilly simply by acting like them, he also claims (during in-character interviews) *not* to be satirizing them, because he *agrees* with them! And, he continues, how could these pundits muster any evidence that would refute his testimony in this respect? Even the seemingly damning "Geraldo's head up his own ass" incident can be redescribed by Colbert, tongue firmly in cheek, as an instance of coercion, not choice. When not truth but "truthiness" (see below) is the standard for what "evidence" is, and when what matters is how loud and sincere our own personal self-redescriptions sound, there's not much room left for ideas like "self" and "character."

Colbert has seized upon and made fully his own an aspect of our experience of ironic humor, the dizzying and discomforting *centerlessness* that we feel in extended situations of irony. These situations, by using humor to force us to reflect continuously on incongruities between actual results of events and the defeat of their expected results, drag us toward a new understanding of the world around us as marked by *contingency* rather than necessity. Indeed, "contingent" simply *means* "not necessary." Is there a *necessary* connection between hypocrisy and feeling shameful, as the Geraldo incident might indicate? Does one *have* to behave respectfully in front of the President, as the setting of the 2006 White House Correspondents' Association Dinner would demand? Is it *necessary* for a news anchor to believe in the truthfulness of what he or she reports? Colbert gleefully answers "no" to each of these questions and many others. By watching him, we acknowledge that, in return for enjoying ironic humor that consistently defeats our expectations, we begin to think in different ways, and we accept that the lines between reality and appearance are very easy to efface. Perhaps the lines weren't even there to begin with. We seem to see irony everywhere in social performances. Self-centeredness and apparent hypocrisy glossed over by radical self-redescription may convince us that there isn't a stable core of self or character around which the public faces of famous individuals orbit. The persona is, as Friedrich Nietzsche (1844–1900) held, simply a mask concealing a regress of masks, with no face beneath. And if this is true of talking heads, why shouldn't it also be true of us? At this realization, we may experience anxiety at the *centerlessness*. But as philosophers from Socrates to the present never tire of reminding us, feeling discomfort about a realization is no evidence against its truth.

Irony vs. Common Sense

Richard Rorty sees our willingness to accept centerlessness, or what he calls the "contingency of selfhood," as a mark of maturity in the educated, secular, liberal culture of the Western world. Accepting contingency over necessity as a fact of life, Rorty says, has wide-ranging implications for our whole worldview: "The drama of an individual human life, or of the history of humanity as a whole, is not one in which a preexistent goal is triumphantly reached or tragically not reached."[8] Stephen Colbert of *The Colbert Report* would disagree, steeped as his persona is in the rhetoric of the ringing necessity of truth and über-patriotic nationalism. Colbert's persona is supposed to be a journalistic hero, and the heroic individual is a familiar trope within American mythology, standing for "pull-yourself-up-by-your-bootstraps" success by following a principled, moral compass.

Richard Rorty's hero is the "ironist," an ideal that emerges from Rorty's own subversion of the anxiety we might feel about our own centerlessness. The ironist fundamentally gives up the serious search for ultimate, unifying principles to make sense of ironic contradictions and embraces a Nietzschean sense of philosophy as play or art. Rorty's ironists are "never quite able to take themselves seriously because [they're] always aware that the terms in which they describe themselves are subject to change, always aware of the contingency and fragility . . . of their selves" (pp. 73–4).

The image of the ironist emerges from Rorty's attempt to synthesize strands from three very different schools of contemporary philosophy. From European philosophies influenced by Nietzsche, Rorty takes the idea that philosophy is a kind of literature or poetry, the point of which is to provide alternate narratives about the meaning of "life, the universe and everything" for the use of individuals in the process of "self-creation." Secondly, Rorty interprets American pragmatist John Dewey (1859–1952) as offering "a picture of human beings as children of their time and place, without any significant metaphysical or biological limits on their plasticity."[9] Finally, Rorty understands both the process of Nietzschean self-creation and the Deweyan capacity for plasticity through our capacity for language. From mainstream philosophy of language in the twentieth century, Rorty adopts the notion that philosophy must shift its attention to language-use as the special way in which human beings construct their world.

All three of these central ideas – self-creation, the "plasticity" of human nature, and the idea that reality is constructed through language – come together in Rorty's idea of a "final vocabulary." "All human beings," Rorty tells us, "carry about a set of words which they employ to justify their actions, their beliefs, and their lives" (p. 73). Examples of such central words, invoked to *justify* and *make sense of* what we do on a daily basis, are "true," "good," and "right," as well as "Christ," "progressive," "America," and "professional standards."[10] Rorty calls the set of words that characterizes our deepest commitments our "final vocabulary." We can use these words to try to justify our actions and beliefs, but we can't ultimately justify our acceptance of the final vocabulary *itself*. Rorty's ironist, though, is someone who has a special kind of relationship to her final vocabulary:

> I shall define an "ironist" as someone who fulfills three conditions: (1) she has radical and continuing doubts about the final vocabulary she currently uses, because she has been impressed by other vocabularies, vocabularies taken as final by people or books she has encountered; (2) she realizes that argument phrased in her present vocabulary can neither underwrite nor dissolve these doubts, (3) insofar as she philosophizes about her situation, she does not think that her vocabulary is closer to reality than others, that it is in touch with a power not herself. (p. 73)

In other words, we should accept our basic centerlessness and attempt to make the best of it. The ironist withholds "devotion" to the terms of her final vocabulary because, after all, the world's contingency teaches us that what works in terms of belief today may not be so good tomorrow, next week, or next year.

Rorty clarifies this idea by noting that irony is the *opposite of common sense*. The follower of common sense takes for granted the notion that everyone shares their final vocabulary, and more importantly, that the obvious, self-evident meaning of "America" or "goodness" is *necessarily* obvious and self-evident to everyone. Perhaps Rorty ignores the idea that common sense might be a kind of "default" vocabulary for many of us, used to coordinate our actions without justifying anything.[11] But since Rorty claims to be a pragmatist in the mold of John Dewey, we should see the ironist's "final vocabulary" as only coordinating, not justifying. For most people, things are reversed: a vocabulary is "final" because it's the "final word" on how things stand, and necessarily so. But the ironist would, according to Rorty, refuse to take a part in the widely accepted self-deception that vocabularies aren't contingent, or, to put it another way, she doesn't accept that there are some words in a final vocabulary that it is absolutely necessary to stand behind.

Truthiness vs. Truth

Now we can ask the question, is Colbert a "Rortian ironist"? Is he, in entertaining us, also showing us how to hold our deepest commitments at arm's length?

On the one hand, he's clearly not. Contrary to his over-the-top conservative, patriotic persona, it's clear that Colbert's real sympathies lie with liberals. Colbert satirizes his opponents by amplifying the right-wing noise machine to the point of arrogant, blustering absurdity. Nowhere is this more obvious than in the 2006 White House Correspondents' Association Dinner and Colbert's "homage" to Bush. Ironically defeating our expectations of how a featured entertainer would balance humor with respect for the highest elected position in the nation, Colbert made himself a hero to liberals and progressives by showcasing the weaknesses of the administration's ideology and record. Colbert's stinging performance was ignored by the media but embraced by liberal and progressives, especially bloggers, as "speaking truth to power."

Just to appreciate *The Colbert Report* and *The Daily Show*, liberals and progressives have to value irony, but the vast majority of liberals and progressives *aren't* Rortian ironists. They don't view their final vocabularies as "no closer to reality" than the vocabularies of their political opponents. If Colbert ultimately takes their side, then he isn't a Rortian ironist.

But on the other hand, there's "truthiness," a concept made for ironists if ever there was one. "I don't trust books," Colbert announced early on in the October 17, 2005 premiere episode of *The Colbert Report*. He continued:

> They're all fact, no heart. And that's exactly what's pulling our country apart today. 'Cause face it folks; we are a divided nation. Not between Democrats and Republicans, or conservatives and liberals, or tops and bottoms. No, we are divided between those who think with their head, and those who *know* with their *heart*.

Colbert didn't invent truthiness. He merely coined the term to spear President Bush's folksy, "from the heart" attempts to "justify" questionable decisions in a manner more at home in the *Andy Griffith Show* than in a liberal democracy. Some immediately saw the cultural significance of "truthiness" beyond the humor. In a *New York Times* piece almost as well known as the segment on the *Colbert* premiere, Frank Rich pointed to Republicans for elevating "truthiness"-telling to an art form, claiming that "it's the power of the story that always counts first, and the selling of it that comes second."[12] Colbert himself targeted the open-ended, user-maintained Web encyclopedia Wikipedia, "challeng[ing] facts with a heavy dose of 'truthiness'" by urging viewers to edit entries about elephant populations in Africa to reflect a non-existent rise over the last ten years.[13]

Colbert identifies "truth" with "facts" in opposition to "truthiness," which is what his gut tells him. At its worst, truthiness is a form of what philosophers call *subjectivism*, or acting as if what is true or right for me is true or right for everyone *simply because* it's true or right for me. At its best, the fact that there are those who find Bush's "truthiness" appealing is evidence that it is no longer politically necessary to separate policy reality from the emotive or spiritual package appearance through which it's sold to the public: eventually, all we are left with is the packaging.[14] Once again, media theorist Marshall McLuhan proves prescient, as the medium *really is* the message.

Rorty's ironist ought to make use of "truthiness," since it protects us from feeling we have to justify our final vocabularies by necessities or absolutes. An ironist who embraces truthiness doesn't need to make sense of her preferences as demanded by "the American Dream" or as evidence of "God's grace." Instead, she declares, "Hey! This news reporting/this book by Nabokov/this documentary about the Sudan/this person's life has provided me with an alternative, refreshing way of looking at my life! You ought to check it out!" "From the gut" truthiness doesn't, admittedly, release us from the "tyranny of facts," but it does release us from the tyranny of facts *taken as necessary and sacred*. Final vocabularies can only be loosened and made more flexible by *open conversations* in which alternate visions of the good life can be shared freely, without cruelty, humiliation, or coercion. To make this happen, Rorty enjoins us to "take care of political freedom, and truth and goodness will take care of themselves" (p. 84).

But of course what the ironist has in mind here is precisely *not* what Colbert discloses in his parody of Bush's "from the heart" truthiness. The ironist, contrary to her name, takes truthiness *quite seriously*. She uses the idea to remind herself that while *her* final vocabulary may be filled with resonant terms like "workplace democracy" and "world peace" and while the President's final vocabulary is filled with terms denying the significance of her final vocabulary, neither person's sets of final words better represents what's good and true, in the end. By contrast, an interview with an out-of-character Colbert clues us in to why we need to be suspicious of truthiness:

> It used to be, everyone was entitled to their own opinion, but not their own facts. But that's not the case anymore. Facts matter not at all. Perception is everything. It's certainty. People love the President because he's certain of his choices as a leader, even if the facts that back him up don't seem to exist. . . . Truthiness is "What I say is right, and [nothing] anyone else says could possibly be true." It's not only that I *feel* it to be true, but that *I* feel it to be true. There's not only an emotional quality, but there's a selfish quality.[15]

This sense of "truthiness" hides an implicit subjectivism about the facts that is unequivocally dangerous in leaders who are supposed to be accountable to the public good. Truthiness is a bill of goods sold to our citizen-audience, as a bold method for decision-making that appears to be more in touch with reality than the facts actually admit.

But Bush isn't a subjectivist – he is clearly working to a plan – and there *are* obvious and understandable political justifications for the decisions made by his administration. The justifications are understandable in the same way that political bribery is: we can see how they come about, but that doesn't make them good for equality or democracy. Bush's policy decisions reflect the mundane fact that most public policies are sponsored by and carried out for the benefit of special interests. Beyond this fact, one clear rule for determining whether public policies that serve special interests are *just or not* is to judge on a case-by-case basis whether or not the policies unfairly place burdens on or selectively grant benefits to those affected by them.

What Do You Stand For?

Maybe "truthiness" is appealing – at least to Bush's supporters – because it seems to preserve the sense of individuality key to the American ideal of the hero. It also makes for good conversation when everyone is, like the Rortian ironist, equally involved in flexible and honest experiments in what their own "good life" might consist in. But if we have learned nothing more by this point, we should acknowledge that appearances can be deceptive, and our expectations of the charms of truthiness are likely to be defeated if we don't see how these charms can be abused by those who use truthiness to mask their true intentions. This masking is a fact of life identified by some of Rorty's own philosophical heroes. Nietzsche, for example, calls our attention to how the "will to power" crafts what we take as true and what we condemn as lies. Dewey, in a more positive vein, observes that the institutions of liberal democracies need to be constructed so as to dissolve concentrations of power by giving individual citizens control over the conditions that affect their lives. And in a much less abstract context, *New York Times* columnist Frank Rich points out:

> [The] genius of the right is its ability to dissemble with a straight face while simultaneously mustering the slick media machinery and expertise to push the goods. It not only has the White House propaganda operation at its disposal, but also an intricate network of P.R. outfits and fake-news outlets that are far more effective than their often hapless liberal counterparts. (p. 16)

At different levels of abstraction, all three perspectives underwrite the idea that the Rortian ironist may be selling herself short in attempting to speak "truth to power" with critical tools no sharper than a constantly shifting final vocabulary and a weak, vaguely subjectivist sense of the truth.

Colbert recognizes this. While acknowledging, sometimes in a painfully ironic way, the fact that most public policies are sponsored by and carried out for the benefit of special interests, Colbert's irony illuminates the points at which those interests are especially narrow, unrepresentative of the common good, reflecting blatant *quid pro quos*. Colbert's absurd truthiness attacks the very idea that we ought to be satisfied when, in a liberal democracy, no justification at all is offered for such public policies. Even if we are really "centerless," Colbert's irony challenges Rorty's ironist by noting that while we all may be in this struggle for self-creation called "life" together, not all of us are playing by the same rules.

Notes

1 Roger Rosenblatt, "The Age of Irony Comes to an End," *Time* 158 (13) (September 24, 2001), p. 79.
2 *Webster's Ninth New Collegiate Dictionary* (Springfield, MA: Merriam-Webster, 1983).
3 At this point I want to offer a warning, and in doing so to join dozens of philosophers, comedians, and cultural critics. Not only will this explanation itself not be funny, but it's a truism that when we try to describe *why* something is funny, we make that thing a *lot less funny* in hindsight. This is why, when someone asks us to explain a joke, we often reply with, "Forget it. It's not worth it." If reading this section ultimately makes you see Colbert as less funny in the future, I can only apologize and, of course, note the irony.
4 This is the basis for the untimely rumors of the "end of irony" cited earlier. It also grounds the criticisms made by "real" political pundits who find themselves aped by Colbert, Jon Stewart, and their writers.
5 Did you watch it? I did – and now I've given away how old I am. See "A Century of News Milestones," in Jon Stewart, Ben Karlin, and David Javerbaum, *America (The Book): A Citizen's Guide to Democracy Inaction* (New York: Warner Books, 2004), p. 135, where the Capone incident is offered as evidence that Geraldo is "an incredible asshole."
6 The further satire here is that Colbert was making fun of Geraldo's magnificent gaffe in Iraq of tracing infantry movements in the sand for

all to see. I want to thank Terrance MacMullan, who ironically is Geraldo's biggest fan, for filling me in on the background of this joke-upon-a-joke.

7 One could ask a similar question of guests on, and viewers of these shows: why subject yourselves to this farce-played-straight? *America (The Book)* gives one possible answer: "The political arena can confuse the ethics and morality of even the most self-assured. If you have forgotten if you are a good guy or a bad buy, why not go on a show [like O'Reilly's] that will tell you!" (p. 163).

8 Richard Rorty, *Contingency, Irony and Solidarity* (New York: Cambridge University Press, 1989), p. 29. Subsequent references will be made parenthetically in-text.

9 Rorty, "Trotsky and the Wild Orchids," in his *Philosophy and Social Hope* (New York: Penguin, 1999), p. 15. While Rorty relies heavily on Dewey for what some might call his "neopragmatism," his interpretation of Dewey is very controversial among most Dewey scholars.

10 Of the examples given, the first three are examples of words that represent "thin" ideals that are "flexible" and universally acknowledged as important. The last four represent "thick" ideals, the meanings of which are "more rigid" because they're less subject to interpretation. Also, these terms – like "America" – aren't acknowledged by *everyone* to have moral force, a fact apparently missed by those whom Colbert spoofs who can't see why the entire world fails to see America for the "City on a Hill" it is.

11 I want to thank Jason Holt for pointing out this possible notion of "common sense."

12 Frank Rich, "Truthiness 101: From Frey to Alito," *New York Times* (January 22, 2006), Section 4, p. 16. Subsequent reference will be made parenthetically in-text.

13 Jake Coyle, "Colbert Works to Become Online Phenom," *Spokane Spokesman-Review* (September 1, 2006), D1.

14 Cognitive scientist George Lakoff has addressed this question by talking about the manipulation of "conceptual frames" that can be used to convince a subject of something when hard evidence can't or won't be assessed. See his *Moral Politics* (Chicago: University of Chicago Press, 2002) and *Don't Think of an Elephant!* (White River Junction, VT: Chelsea Green Publishing, 2004).

15 An interview with Stephen Colbert in "The A.V. Club," *The Onion*, quoted in the Wikipedia entry for "Truthiness;" www.en.wikipedia.org/wiki/Truthiness, accessed August 29, 2006.

SENIOR PHILOSOPHICAL CORRESPONDENTS

Judith Barad is Professor of Philosophy and Women's Studies at Indiana State University. She received her PhD in philosophy from Northwestern in 1984. In 1985 she accepted a position in Philosophy at Indiana State, where she eventually served as the chairperson for nine years. She is the author of three books and numerous articles on ethics, including such topics as feminist ethics, the role of emotion in moral judgments, the treatment of animals, the philosophy of Thomas Aquinas, and the *Ethics of Star Trek*. She has given dozens of national and international scholarly presentations, and has been an ethics consultant for Boeing, Corp. Due to her obsession with ethics, she deeply appreciates the ironic aspects of life.

Alejandro Bárcenas is a PhD candidate in philosophy at the University of Hawaii at Mānoa, and did his undergraduate studies at the Central University of Venezuela. His research focuses primarily on political theory and history of philosophy. He translated Machiavelli's *The Prince* (with J. R. Herrera), and his essays have been published in Colombia, Spain, and Venezuela. Growing up in South America taught him how to understand monkeys in a philosophical way.

Kimberly A. Blessing is Assistant Professor of Philosophy at Buffalo State College. She publishes on Descartes' ethics (or lack thereof) and has edited *Movies and the Meaning of Life*: *Philosophers Take on Hollywood*. One day she hopes to find the meaning of life on *The Daily Show*, but she's not optimistic. In the meantime she'll keep searching in more conventional places.

252

Kevin S. Decker is Assistant Professor and Coordinator of Philosophy at Eastern Washington University. He is co-editor of *Star Wars and Philosophy* and the forthcoming *Star Trek and Philosophy*, and has published in the areas of American and Continental philosophy. He's proud that Stephen Colbert modeled the Tek Jansen character on him (with his permission), and he has the skin-tight coverall to prove it.

Liam P. Dempsey teaches philosophy at Dalhousie University. He received his PhD in philosophy from the University of Western Ontario in 2003. His research areas include philosophy of mind and consciousness, cognitive science, history of philosophy of mind, personal identity theory, and British empiricism. He has published articles in *Studies in History and Philosophy of Science*, *Philosophical Psychology*, and *Southwest Philosophy Review*. Fallacious reasoning is dead to him.

Gerald J. Erion is Assistant Professor of Philosophy at Medaille College. His current research includes work in ethics, philosophy of mind, and the teaching of philosophy. He has long yearned for his own guest appearance on *The Daily Show*, and he prepares for it by reviewing video of Harry Frankfurt's appearances and rehearsing with a God-Machine that he built for himself in his garage.

Brad Frazier is Assistant Professor of Philosophy at Lee University. He is the author of *Rorty and Kierkegaard on Irony and Moral Commitment*, and he has published articles in *Philosophy and Social Criticism*, *International Philosophical Quarterly*, *Journal of Religious Ethics*, and *History of Philosophy Quarterly*. Most importantly, he is Defender of the God-Machine and Humble and Faithful Servant of Starlamb, at least until the Rapture.

Michael Gettings is Associate Professor of Philosophy at Hollins University. He has published papers on topics ranging from ontological arguments for God's existence to the HBO series *The Sopranos*. His future path to infamy includes Obscene Television Coverage of his trial as a disgruntled loner accused of kidnapping Leonardo DiCaprio's baby. That's 120 Buttafuocos of newsworthiness by our count.

Amber L. Griffioen is a PhD candidate at the University of Iowa. Her areas of interest include ethics (specifically issues dealing with rational agency and problems of irrationality), medieval philosophy, and philosophy of religion. She has both engaged in and written several papers on self-deception, which is partly what makes her such an "expert" on truthiness. And despite her deep mistrust of books and journals, she has an article forthcoming in *American Catholic Philosophical Quarterly*. Like Stephen Colbert, she can recite the Nicene Creed from memory and is of the opinion that bears are "giant marauding godless killing machines." She promises not to write philosophy *to* you, but to feel philosophy *at* you.

Jason Holt is Assistant Professor in the School of Recreation Management and Kinesiology at Acadia University, where he teaches courses in philosophy and communication. He is the author of several books, including *Blindsight and the Nature of Consciousness*, which was shortlisted for the 2005 Canadian Philosophical Association Book Prize. His work in philosophy and pop culture includes essays on Woody Allen, film noir, Alfred Hitchcock, Stanley Kubrick, *The Matrix*, *Seinfeld*, *The Simpsons*, *The Terminator*, and *Twin Peaks*. Some of these essays have been translated into Hebrew, Hungarian, Italian, Japanese, Korean, Portuguese, Russian, and Turkish. He's proud to be one of those Canadian gringos.

Matthew S. Lopresti teaches humanities at Hawaii Pacific University. He doesn't have cable, and hopes that this will help facilitate completing his dissertation on Whiteheadian religious pluralism at the University of Hawaii at Mānoa. His research interests include South Asian philosophy, process philosophy, and phenomenology of the body. Since beginning his essay, *The Daily Show* seems to have lost interest in producing "This Week in God." This has forced Matthew to return to the Catholic Church just to get his weekly fix of God Stuff.

Terrance MacMullan is Assistant Professor of Philosophy and Honors at Eastern Washington University. He has published in American philosophy, philosophy of race, and feminist philosophy. Terry lives with his partner Rebecca and daughter Sylvia in Spokane, Washington where he spends his free time cooking, walking his dog Caleb, and thinking about how to use his position as a liberal academic to destroy America. He is currently ranked 1,342,582 in Richard Posner's most recent list of the most influential public intellectuals in America.

Joseph J. Marren is Assistant Professor of Communication at Buffalo State College. In another life he was a newspaper reporter and editor for various community dailies (think papers with small circulations). He began his journalism career when newspapers still used typewriters. He thought computers were a passing fad, but they never went away, and he now teaches online journalism, as well as old-fashioned courses in editing, media history, and media ethics (yeah, as if). His areas of research include the above, and how to better teach communication and journalism courses. He'll keep researching until he finds a theory that espouses watching sports while grading, and he's praying for the day when Don Cherry appears on *The Daily Show*.

Steven Michels is Assistant Professor of Political Science at Sacred Heart University. He has written on political theory (including Plato, Tocqueville, and Nietzsche), but wishes that more of his research could be conducted while eating pizza, drinking beer, and watching television. His ultimate Moment of Zen would include seeing his beloved Cubs win the World Series.

Massimo Pigliucci is Professor of Ecology and Evolution and of Philosophy at Stony Brook University. His research in biology focuses on nature-nurture problems. As a philosopher, he is interested in what philosophers have to say, if anything, about the fundamental concepts underlying scientific theories. He has been at the forefront of the so-called creationism-evolution controversy, writing several articles and giving public talks on the topic. He has published four technical books, including *Making Sense of Evolution* (with Jonathan Kaplan), and two books for the general public, including *Denying Evolution: Creationism, Scientism, and the Nature of Science*. He writes regular columns for *Skeptical Inquirer* and *Philosophy Now*, and attends Jon Stewart's shows live in New York City, hoping to convince him to run with Colbert for the Presidential ticket.

Andrew Sneddon is Associate Professor of Philosophy at the University of Ottawa. His research specializations are moral philosophy and philosophical psychology. He did his PhD at Queen's University. He is the author of *Action and Responsibility*, and of articles which have appeared in numerous scholarly journals. He thinks lots of world leaders deserve to be greeted with fewer than five fingers, not just George W. Bush.

Rachael Sotos is Adjunct Professor of Humanities at the New School for General Studies. She received her PhD in philosophy in 2005 from the New School for Social Research, and she is pursuing a second PhD in classics at Fordham University. Her dissertation, *Arendtian Freedom in Greek Antiquity*, is a sympathetic critique of the political theorist Hannah Arendt, and will be published as a book. As soon as she figures out this "internets thing" she's going to sign up as one of Steven Colbert's "heroes."

Roben Torosyan is Associate Director of the Center for Academic Excellence and Adjunct Assistant Professor of Education at Fairfield University. He leads innovation in teaching and learning through leadership initiatives and faculty development workshops and consultations, and has been a featured presenter at numerous teaching conferences on topics such as moving from controversy to cooperation. He holds a PhD in cultural studies, philosophy, and education from Teachers College, Columbia University and his scholarship on communication in the classroom and teaching for transformation has appeared in scholarly and lay publications. An amateur triathlete, he dreams of finding a gear as big as Stephen Colbert's cojones.

Steve Vanderheiden is Assistant Professor of Philosophy and Political Science at the University of Minnesota Duluth, where he specializes in environmental politics and normative political theory. He is the author of numerous scholarly articles on issues of justice, democracy, and the environment, and recently completed *Atmospheric Justice*, a book-length manuscript on political theory and climate change. A longtime fan of *The Daily Show*, he claims to have learned more about American politics from Jon Stewart than from his several professional political science journal subscriptions. Insomnia is his greatest inspiration.

Michael Ventimiglia is Assistant Professor of Philosophy at Sacred Heart University. His favorite prior publication is "Seven Lessons in Philosophy You Already Learned Playing Texas Hold 'Em," in *Poker and Philosophy*. He thought *The Daily Show* would flop when Craig Kilborn left.

Jason Zinser is currently finishing his PhD in philosophy at Florida State University. His dissertation, on metaphysical issues in evolutionary biology, should have already been completed. He has presented papers at numerous conferences and has several entries in the *Harvard Companion to Evolution*. He's originally from Wisconsin, where the effects of global warming are eagerly awaited.

INDEX

authority, challenging 87
"axis of evil" 129

bad faith 119
banking information, government
surveillance of 147, 148
Barad, Judith 69–80
Barber, Benjamin 210
Bárcenas, Alejandro 93–103
Baum, Matthew 46, 50, 87
Baumgartner, Jody 89–90
Baym, Geoffrey 206, 207
Bee, Samantha 21, 32, 36, 107–8,
124
Begala, Paul 11, 35, 62, 71, 98
begging the question 125
Benedict XVI, Pope 177
Bennett, William 111–13, 118
Berg, Eron 90
Berger, Peter 177–8
Bertelsmann 34
"Better Know a District" 124
Bin Laden, Osama 129, 240
Black, Lewis 130, 191, 193
Black Sox scandal 139
Blackadder 220, 226n 5
blame game 123, 181–3
Blessing, Kimberly A. 133–45
blogs 30, 42, 45, 49, 65–6, 246
Bourdieu, Pierre 61
Brave New World (Huxley) 7–8
"breaking news" 10
Brokaw, Tom 17–18
Brooks, David 149
Brown, Mike 64
Brownback, Sam 125
Bryan, William Jennings 194
Buckley, William F. 12, 14n 14,
61
Buddhism 165, 170, 171
Bullen, Katherine 76
bullshit 133–57
academic bullshit 150–2, 153,
155

attitude towards the truth 142,
143
bullshit/lie distinction 135–8,
146–7, 149
Daily Show bullshit 148, 155–6
defense of 153
essence of 134–6
inevitability of 139
media bullshit 148, 154
origin of 137–9
political bullshit 140–5, 147–50,
152–4, 156
Bunburyist 222–3
Burke, Edmund 113
Burns, Eric 31
Bush, George W. 19–20, 22, 78,
119, 124, 126, 127, 144
and creationism 194–5
and democracy 83
policy decisions 249
and political spin 129, 141
Presidential elections 17, 59, 63
and the Press Corps Dinner 14n
5, 35–6, 86–7, 165, 243, 246
"the decider" 35, 97
truthiness 227–8, 230, 247, 248
and the White House Press Corps
Dinner 40n 13
Bush administration 24, 26, 63, 64,
127, 156
"Bush v Bush" 149

Camus, Albert 119, 176
Carell, Steve 97
Carlson, Tucker 11, 35, 40n 12,
71, 78, 86, 88, 98, 111
Carroll, Lewis 219
Carson, Rachel 48
Carson, Tom 207
Carter, Jimmy 122
CBS 17
centerlessness 243, 244, 245, 250
Cheney, Dick 25, 71, 123, 141,
148

Freud, Sigmund   176, 232
fundamentalism   177, 178, 183, 195

Gadamer, Hans-Georg   113
gay marriage   112–14, 124, 178
Geist, Willie   88
General Electric   34
genetic engineering   200
genetic fallacy   198
Gettings, Michael   16–27
Giuliani, Rudy   90
global warming   199
God-Machine   161, 162, 164, 167
Goldblum, Bernard   67
Gonzales, Alberto   147
good faith   119
Good Morning America   24, 25
Gore, Al   17
Gorgias   95
Goss, Porter   21
Gould, Stephen J.   192
government
    demographic profile   211–12
    media as propaganda arm   214
    two-party system   212–13
    see also Bush administration;
        elections
graphics and photos   9, 23, 62
"Great Moments in Punditry as Read
    by Children"   11
"Green Screen Challenge"   38
Griffin, David Ray   169
Griffioen, Amber L.   227–39
gut feeling   7, 14n 5, 228, 235–8,
    247, 248

Habermas, Jürgen   61
Hannity, Sean   242
Hardball   11, 132n 3
"Hearing Impaired"   109
Helms, Ed   22, 71, 84, 89, 115,
    116, 127, 162, 192, 194, 242
Heston, Charlton   178
Hilton, Paris   57

Hinduism   162, 163, 166, 169, 171
Hippias   95
Holt, Jason   217–26
homophobia   168, 183–4
Hume, David   176, 195
humor, philosophy of   205, 206–7
Hurricane Katrina   64, 123, 181
Hussein, Saddam   129, 130
Huxley, Aldous   7–8
hyperbole   19, 20, 23
hypocrisy   243

ignorance
    elite   89
    exposing   73, 75, 85
    feigned   22
    ironic claim to   32–3
    mass   89
The Importance of Being Earnest
    (Wilde)   222
"Indecision 2004"   88, 121, 130,
    143
individualism   89
infotainment   41, 224
intellectual imperialism   166
intellectuals
    anti-intellectualism   58–9, 61,
        194
    isolation of   61
    public intellectuals   57, 59–62
    replaced by media pundits   61–2
    university intellectuals   61
intelligent design (ID) theory   190,
    191, 196, 197, 199, 200n 1
    see also creation-evolution
        controversy
"International Pamphlet"   9
internet   38, 45, 85
intuitive knowledge   236
    see also gut feeling
Iran   41
Iraq   41, 64–5, 79, 109, 122, 126,
    129, 130, 141, 144, 149, 193,
    228